CIVIL WAR LADIES:

Fashions and Needle-Arts of the Early 1860's

PRIMARY SOURCE MATERIAL from

Peterson's Magazine 1861 and 1864

Additional Hair Styles and Hair Jewelry from

Campbell's *Self-Instructor in the Art of Hair Work*

R.L. Shep
Mendocino

c.1 Copyright©1987 by R.L. Shep
This work contains excerpts and illustrations from *Peterson's Magazine 1861 and 1864*; and from Campbell's *Self-Instructor in the Art of Hair Work 1867*
ISBN 0-914046-09-8
Library of Congress #89-091791
Printed in the United States of America
Published by:
    R.L. Shep
    Box 668
    Mendocino, CA 95460

Library of Congress Cataloging-in-Publication Data

Civil War ladies : fashions and needle-arts of the early 1860's.
    p.   cm.
   "Primary source material from Peterson's magazine, 1861-1864;
additional hairstyles and hair jewelry from Campbell's Self
instructor in the art of hair work."
   ISBN 0-914046-09-8 : $24.95
   1. Needlework--United States--Patterns. 2. Fashion--United
States. 3. Hair-work, Ornamental--United States. 4. Needlework-
-United States--History--19th century. 5. Fashion--United States-
-History--19th century. I. Shep, R. L., 1933- . II. Peterson's
magazine. III. Campbell, Mark. Self-instructor in the art of hair
work, dressing hair, making curls, switches, braids, and hair
jewelry of every description.
TT753.C58 1989
391'.2'09730934--dc20   89-91791
                                             CIP

CONTENTS

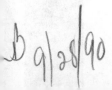

NOTES

This is not a costume book in as much as it does not just look back on a period and discuss what was worn at that time with some illustrations. This is primary source material in the form of excerpts from *Peterson's Magazine* of 1861, which was just into the Civil War, and *Peterson's Magazine* of 1864, which was just before it ended.

Peterson's was a combination style magazine, workbook, and literary publication; sort of a cross between *Vogue*, *Cosmopolitan*, *Sew News*, and *Family Circle*. What we have done, essentially is to take out the fiction and poetry, and leave the parts relating to fashion and needle-arts. By this means you can see hundreds of articles of clothing and accessories that were in common use at that time. We have also left in a selected number of songs and dances of the period for the benefit of those who might find them useful.

In looking at the practical aspects of *Peterson's Magazine*, whether it comes to making a garment or knitting a work-bag, etc., the instructions will probably not be as complete as those you would find in a modern book or magazine. Women were brought up to sew, knit, embroider, etc., and elaborate instructions were never given. And so one might say that these instructions are 'as good as it gets'. The pattern drafts given were common for that day. The first full size pattern was said to have been published by Butterick in 1860, although Mme. Demorest claims to have originated them. You will find a couple of articles by Mme. Demorest in the 1861 Peterson's in which she offers a number of full size patterns that can be obtained directly from her. We did not find any of these articles in the 1864 issues. She did have her own quarterly magazine during this time, *Mme. Demorest's Mirror of Fashions*, which was started in the autumn of 1860.

Campbell's *Self-Instructor in the Art of Hair Work* is one of the very few sources of hair jewelry illustrations that we have. He also gives illustrations of hair styles and instructions for achieving them which will prove useful to both re-enactors and actors. We have reprinted only a few of the illustrations of hair jewelry, however all of these (without the hair styles) and instructions on how to make them have been reprinted recently by LACIS.

Women's Dress of this period is best characterized by the crinoline, or hoop skirt. When it first came into fashion in the 1850's it was very circular, but by 1860 it had flattened out in front and the bulk of the skirt had moved to the back. This general line is repeated in the chignon, or bun at the back of the head, and in the jackets and over-garments or outerwear.

The crinoline was said to give a woman freedom. It might have been freedom in terms of what went before it, but certainly not in terms of present day dress.

A woman of this period on leaving the house might typically wear:

drawers, or underpants — of cotton or linen and trimmed with lace,
a chemise — usually linen, covering the top part of the body,
a boned corset or stays,
a petticoat bodice, corset cover, or camisole — worn over the stays,
the crinoline, or hoop skirt,
stockings — held up with garters,
petticoats — 1 or 2,
the skirt — which was very full and had a definite hem,
the bodice — which was boned and fastened in front,
a belt — often of the same fabric as the skirt and bodice,
an outergarment — jacket, mantle, shawl, etc.,
gloves, or mitts,
boots — which buttoned,
a parasol,
a bonnet — for formal occasions, or a hat,
a bag or purse,
a handkerchief,
and often a fan.

Aside from this there were any number of specialized garments worn for special occasions such as mourning gowns, ball gowns, riding habits, garments worn only in the house, etc.

Make-up, referred to as 'paint', was considered very vulgar.

Children were treated as 'little people' and were elaborately dressed. It is well to note that many of those children you will see illustrated in cute little dresses are in fact little boys. There was little difference between a dress worn by a girl and one worn by a boy under the age of 5, with the exception that boys did not wear crinolines even though they wore petticoats. Boys, after about the age of 5, wore either short or long trousers, or knickerbockers.

For a better understanding of the uses of the garments of this period we would suggest that you read one of the books listed in the Bibliography.

Hair Jewelry is a fascinating subject. There is no doubt that it was very popular in its time, being used in rings, bracelets, watch chains, earrings, necklaces, brooches, etc. In fact you can still find examples of it for sale, as I did recently in a little shop in New York. But you won't find it mentioned in most costume dictionaries, costume histories, or encyclopedias. Modern writers often seem to find it morbid, 'grisly', and perhaps unclean.

Apparently hair work of this type started in Norway and Sweden, but it really came into its own in France. Napoleon mentioned various pieces of it in his will and left instructions as to whom they should be given. He also instructed that his own hair should be conserved and that it should be made into small bracelets with gold clasps and given to various people. Marie Louise, ex-Empress of France, had a bracelet made of hair of her son, the King of Rome; his hair being interwoven with gold threads.

This type of jewelry was sometimes known as 'sentimental' jewelry and was often given as a token of love or friendship. However, with the Victorian pre-occupation with death (strengthened by the death of Prince Albert in England and the Civil War in the United States), it really came into its own as mourning jewelry. There is an often quoted story about a man's funeral in Boston where more than 200 mourning rings, made from the hair of the deceased and bearing inscriptions like "Prepare to follow me," were given to his friends.

Wendy Cooper points out that in this era when even a piano leg had to have ruffles on it to disguise it, hair became a sexual fetish and held a certain fascination for people. She relates a story about Lord Byron, who apparently was pestered by a woman he did not like to give her a hair ring as a keepsake, so finally he had one prepared from the braided pubic hair of his mistress and presented that to her as if the hair were his own.

Hair jewelry was popular from 1820 to the 1880's after which its popularity declined rapidly. In the E.V. Rodin & Co. catalog of "Jewelry, Watches, & Silverware" dated 1895 there are only two items of findings for hair jewelry shown out of the thousands of jewelry items that they offered. They state "Fine Rolled Gold Hair Chain Mountings. Price per set complete, including braiding the hair." There are no examples of hair jewelry or findings for hair jewelry shown in any of the following catalogs: Bloomingdale's, 1886; Lord & Taylor, 1881; Marshall Field's Jewelry and European Fashion, 1896.

Bibliography

Costume
Buck, Anne. *Victorian Costume*, 1984. UK
Burgess, Janet. *Clothing Guidelines for the Civil War Era*. 1985. IA
Calasibetta, Charlotte. *Fairchild's Dictionary of Fashion*, 1975. NY
Collard, Eileen. *Cut of Women's 19th Century Dress: Victorian Gothic*. 1978. Ont.
De Courtais, Georgine. *Women's Headdress and Hairstyles*. 1988. UK
Winter, J. & Shultz, C. *Victorian Costuming: 1860-65*. 1980. CA

Hair Jewelry
Cooper, Wendy. *Hair: Sex, Society, Symbolism*. 1971. NY
Eichler, Lillian. *The Customs of Mankind*, 1937. NY
Martin, Mary. *Glooms and "Hair-Looms"*. House & Garden. Dec. 1928.
Parsons, Frank Alva. *The Psychology of Dress*. 1923. NY

ALPHABET FOR MARKING.

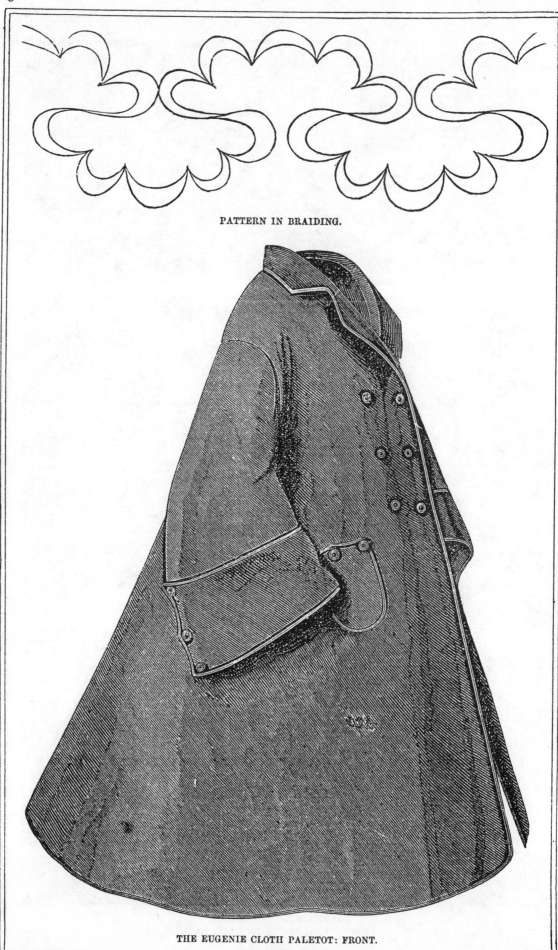

PATTERN IN BRAIDING.

THE EUGENIE CLOTH PALETOT: FRONT.

PATTERN IN EMBROIDERY.

BUTTON-HOLE.

THE EUGENIE CLOTH PALETOT: BACK.

THE VICTORIA PALETOT: FRONT.

THE VICTORIA PALETOT: BACK.

12

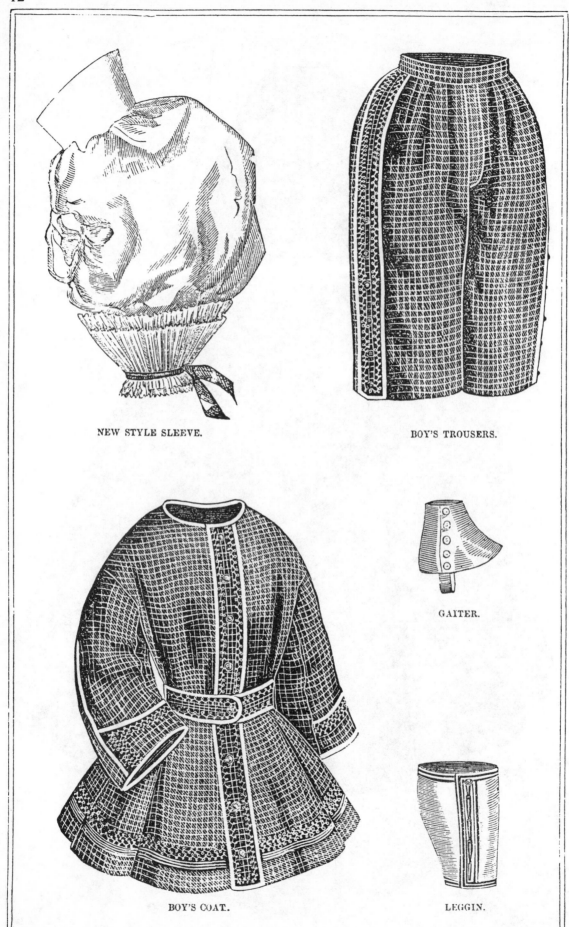

NEW STYLE SLEEVE.

BOY'S TROUSERS.

GAITER.

BOY'S COAT.

LEGGIN.

CHILD'S SACQUE.

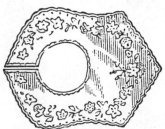

BABY'S BIB.

CHILD'S UNDER SKIRT.

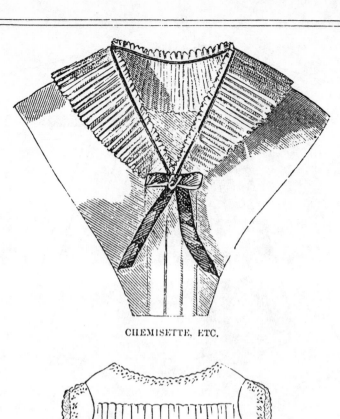

CHEMISETTE, ETC.

HOUSE SACQUE FOR INFANT.

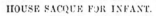

CHEMISE.

CHILD'S DRAWERS.

NEW STYLE MUSLIN BODY.

"I'm Waiting, Love, I'm Waiting."

ARRANGED FOR THE GUITAR.

WORDS BY MRS. L. L. DEMING, MUSIC BY W. J. DAVIS.

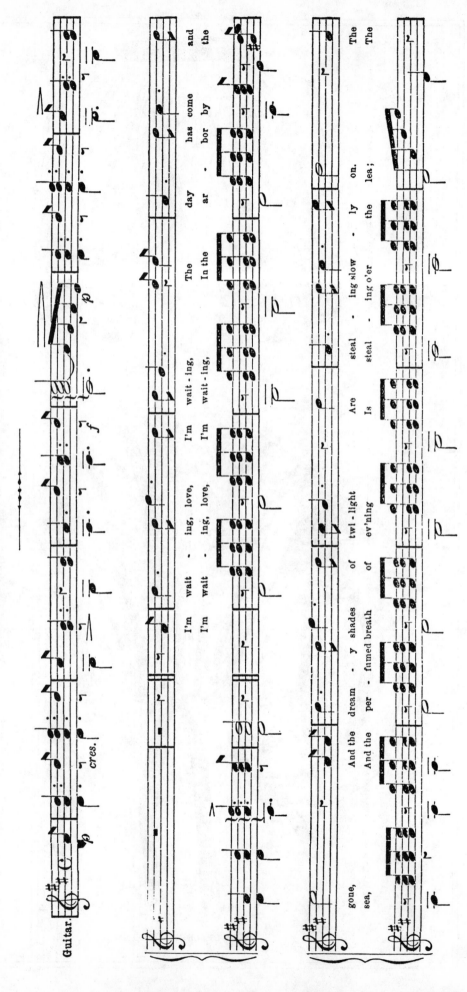

17

PALM LEAF IN BRAIDING: FOR SCARF.

CHILDREN'S FASHIONS FOR FEBRUARY.

A NORWEGIAN MORNING OR BONNET CAP,
IN SHETLAND WOOL.

BY MRS. WARREN.

MATERIALS.—Half an ounce each of Cerise and white Shetland wool; two steel knitting pins, No. 12; crochet hook, No. 2.

Cast on 240 stitches. K (or knit) two plain rows *; now knit one stitch; take two together; knit 115 stitches; take two together, and take two together again; now K the remainder, taking two together before the last stitch. The next row back is plain; now repeat from * till there are 18 ribs of knitting in which there are 36 rows alternately decreased and plain. Take the white wool—knit three rows in the same way, which is one rib and one row, decreasing as before; K one stitch; take two together; wind the wool twice over the pins; take two together, wind twice over the pin again till there are 41 holes; then take two together twice; make 41 holes again; take two together; K 1; now knit 3 rows plain, again decreasing as before.

Now, with Cerise wool, knit six ribs or twelve rows, decreasing as before. Then with white the same as the first white stripe. Then continue with white and Cerise alternately till there are four white and four Cerise stripes irrespective of the first deep border. Now, with Cerise, knit 16 rows, decreasing as before. This finishes with one stitch. For the border along the front, with Cerise, make 2 L stitches, with 1 ch between each L; in one loop of the knitting 3 ch; 2 more L as before in an equal space to the 3 ch; this is along the front only. 2nd row, 9 L with 1 ch between each u the 1 ch; 1 ch dc between next 2 L; 1 ch 9 L with 1 ch between each u next; 1 ch repeat. This last row is worked with the knitting at the back within the row of L stitches. Run Cerise ribbon in the alternate holes of the white rows, and the same in the alternate L stitches of the border.

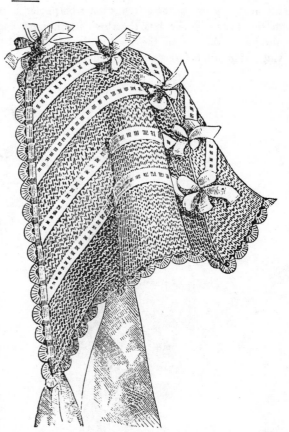

THIBET KNITTING.

BY MADEMOISELLE ROCHE.

THIS knitting, which has been lately introduced, is likewise sometimes called the Railway Knitting, from the extreme quickness which it allows in the execution. As it forms a pleasant occupation and produces extremely comfortable articles for winter wear, it is sure to receive favor. We therefore think instructions for working it may be acceptable to those of our subscribers who may not know it. Very large wooden pins and the twelve-thread fleecy are required, as a fine material is quite unsuitable for it. Cast on two stitches, place the right-hand needle in the left-hand, and put the wool over it twice; then insert the needle through the two stitches at the back, purling them. There will then be three stitches on the needle; the next row two of the stitches must be purled in the same manner, but the third stitch must always be thrown off the needle without knitting; this stitch forms the open edge. When a sufficient number of strips are knitted they are joined together, but this is done in a particular manner. The two edges of each strip are placed together, and united with a row of herringbone-stitch in black wool, of the same kind as the knitting, taking care that the stitch of herringbone comes between each stitch of the knitting. A little observation will show how much the regularity of this part of the work affects the appearance of the whole. Very handsome comforters are formed of colored strips, which contrast well with each other, the black row between greatly adding to the effect.

A CREPED NECK-TIE.

BY MRS. WARREN.

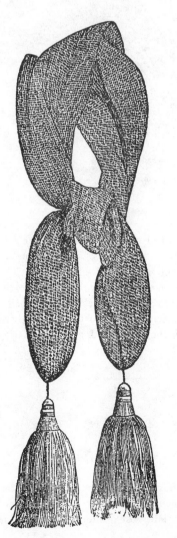

MATERIALS.—Cotton, No. 60; a pair of Bone Knitting Pins, No. 12; two lumps of sugar dissolved in half a pint of hot water, and let remain till cold; two Chenille Tassels.

This is one of the prettiest articles for a neck-tie that can be made; having, when finished, all the appearance of soft white crape, and may be adopted either in mourning or out, by adding either black, colored, or white tassels. Cast on the pin for hundred and fifty stitches, and knit in plain garter-stitch till it is five nails wide; then cast off, but not too tight; then sew a strip of calico on to each side, but only so that it can be easily untacked. If the work is at all soiled, wash it with white curd soap and water; then rinse it perfectly, and squeeze it in a cloth very dry; after that dip it in the sugar and water, squeeze it slightly, and lay it out on a doubled sheet, to dry; afterward take off the calico, sew it up, and add the tassels. The washing and rinsing in sugar and water will always give it the appearance of being new.

BABY'S KNITTED SHOE AND SOCK.

BY MRS. JANE WEAVER.

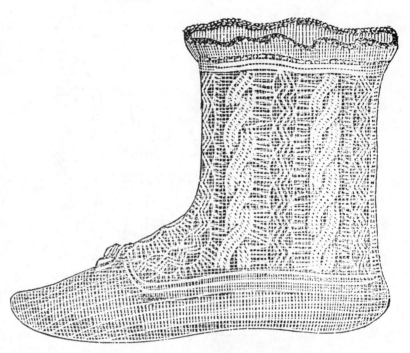

THESE are knitted on steel needles, in Berlin wool of two colors. The shoe in one color, and the sock in white, form the prettiest contrast; pink and white, maize and white, or blue and white, are all suitable. The shoe is in plain knitting, and ought to be worked tight and even; the sock is in the cable and hemstitch pattern, the top being completed by two rows of netting, the first row being on a larger mesh than the second, one stitch of the netting in every stitch of the knitting. A narrow ribbon, the color of the shoe, is interlaced round the ancle, which ties in the front with a bow, and keeps it from slipping off the foot. The row of netting on the fine mesh ought to be in the colored wool.

BONNETS AND CAP.

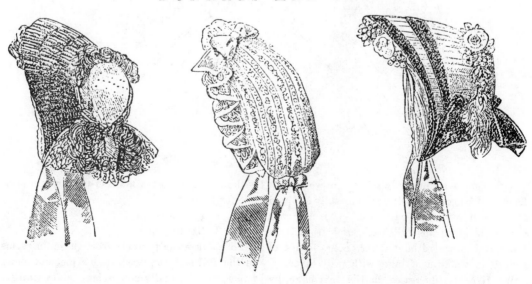

GREEN SILK BONNET.   CAP.   WHITE SILK BONNET.

PRINCESS ROYAL BODY.

BY EMILY H. MAY.

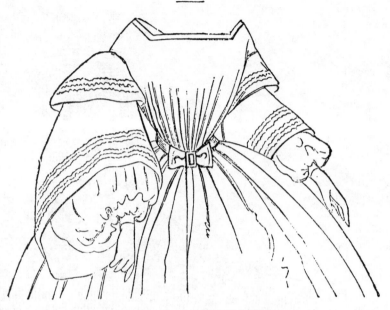

FRONT OF PRINCESS ROYAL BODY.

BACK OF PRINCESS ROYAL BODY.

THE very elegant Body of which we give a front and back view, will be universally adopted for muslin robes for balls, &c. It is a square baby's body, made full back and front. In Paris it is worn without a *chemisette*. This, of course, is a matter of taste with the wearer.

We give also diagrams, on the next page, by which to cut out the body, so that any lady, without the aid of a mantua-maker, can make one for herself.

No. 1. FRONT.
No. 2. BACK.

To enlarge the pattern, from these diagrams, to the full size required, take a piece of newspaper, or, if equally convenient, plain white or brown paper, of the size you suppose to be

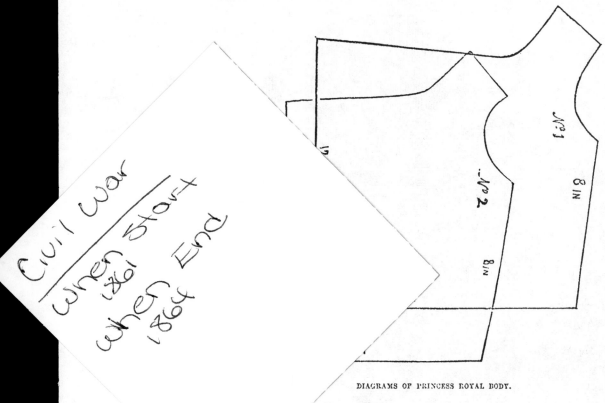

DIAGRAMS OF PRINCESS ROYAL BODY.

that it shall be large ... the bottom line of No. 1, ... ches long, as marked in the ... draw, at right angles, the left side, ... ches high. Next, the right side, at a slightly obtuse angle (the exact angle can be transferred from the diagram) eight inches long. And so on till the whole is finished. Afterward enlarge No. 2 in the same way: then cut out by the enlarged pattern.

BRIDAL PINCUSHION.

BY MADEMOISELLE ROCHE.

The materials of which this beautiful Pincushion is formed must be either white satin or white watered silk, and two sorts of small beads. Commence by cutting a strip of cardboard two inches wide and fifteen inches long; form this into a ring, and cover it with the satin well stretched. Then take some of the fine wire used for making artificial flowers, and some small beads, and thread a sufficient length to form a loop or leaf. Fasten this down at its stalk end with a few stitches, and thread a second loop of the different beads as much smaller as will allow of its being placed within the first, so as to form a double loop. Continue this in the way shown in the engraving, until a sufficient length is done for one-quarter of the circle, which must have had a mark placed on each of its quarters before commencing the beadwork. Having completed the four divisions of the wreath, make the four flowers, and attach them in their respective places. A row of larger beads may or may not be carried through the centre of this leaf-work, according to taste; but if the stitches which fasten down the wire should happen to show, it will be an advantage to insert them. This being done, a round cushion of white calico or linen must be made to fit the interior of the circle, and raised up in the inside, and a round of cardboard sewn in for the bottom. All this being done, another round of cardboard must be taken for the stand, sufficiently large for the pincushion to be placed in the centre, and leave two inches clear, all round, on which a similar row of leaves and

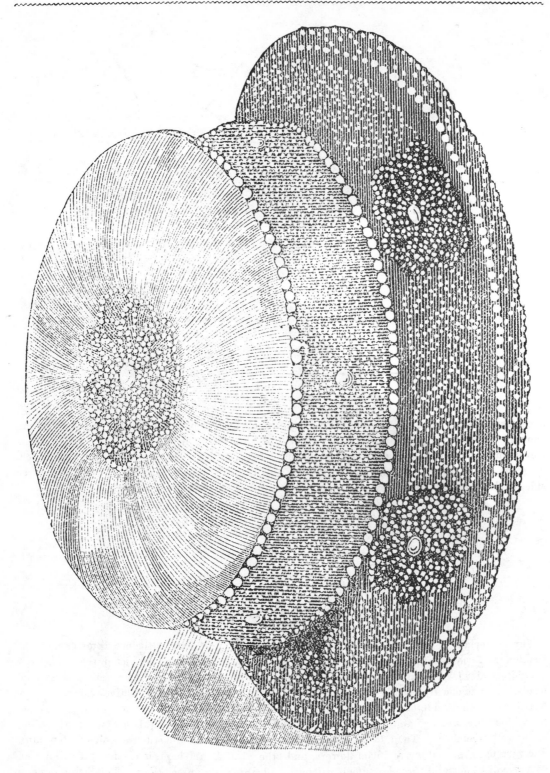

flowers is to be worked; after which it is to be
lined and have short loops of beads carried all
round its edge, as a border, one over-wrapping
the other.   The cushion must then be placed in
the exact middle of the mat, and strongly tied
down by means of a mattress-needle brought
through from underneath, looped through a
bead-flower previously prepared, returned down
again through the cushion, and the two ends
finally tied together.   The beads employed may
be white, both opaque and transparent, pearl,
gold, silver, or steel; and with any combination
of these a most elegant article may be produced,
well worthy of its name of the "Bridal Pin-
cushion."

PURSE IN CROCHET.

BY MRS. JANE WEAVER.

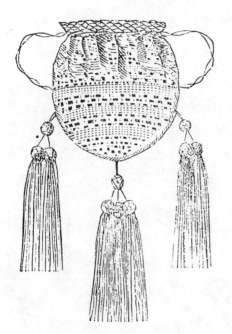

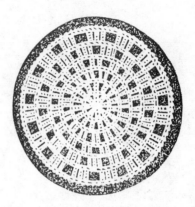

WE give an engraving of a new and pretty purse, to be crocheted with gold thread. Annexed is the pattern for the bottom. Below is the side. They are to be crocheted together, and the purse finished with tassels. These purses, made in gold, are all the **rage** this winter.

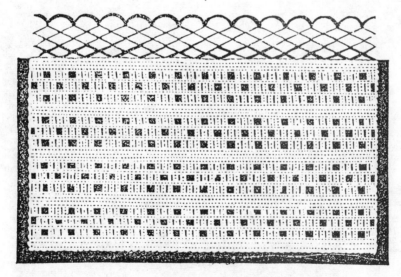

THE BERLIN WOOL-WORK PATTERN.

BY MRS. JANE WEAVER.

THIS pattern, so elegant in design and color, and altogether the most costly affair of the kind ever got up in America, is intended for a bag, which should be mounted with a broad steel clasp and steel chain. It should be worked in very bright wools, and, in selecting the shades, care must be taken that they are all very distinct, and the colors dissimilar. It may be grounded in any color that the worker may prefer; for instance, maize, white, or even a beautiful light-blue, would have a very good effect.   Worked on coarse canvas, in double wool, it would answer for the bottom of a chair, by extending the grounding on the four sides to the size required.

ALPHABET FOR MARKING.

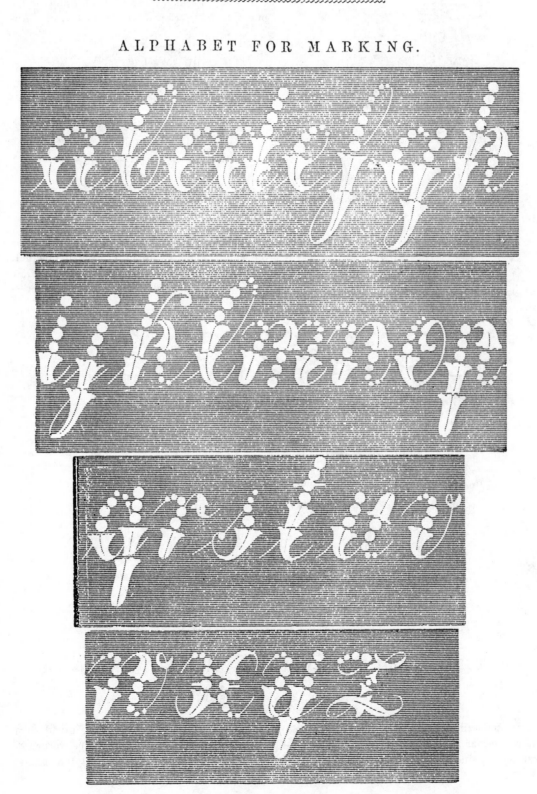

VELVET PORTMONNAIE.

BY MRS. JANE WEAVER.

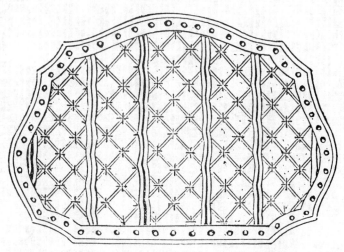

WE give, above, an engraving of a new portmonnaie, full-size, to be done in green velvet and gold braid. Lay the gold braid in diamonds, as seen in the engraving, sewing a small jet bead at the points of the diamonds. The horizontal stripes are made by sewing gold braid over the diamonds. Many might prefer the portmonnaie without these horizontal lines. Send it to a portmonnaie manufacturer to make up.

LADY'S WORK-BAG.

BY MRS. JANE WEAVER.

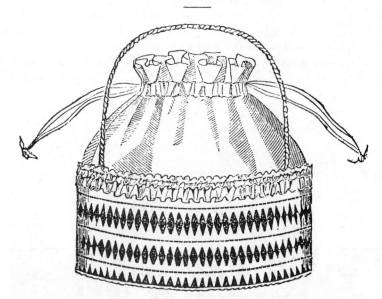

WE give, above, an engraving of a new style of Work-Bag, to be done in Berlin wool, in light-blue, dark-blue, and yellow floss silk. The ground-work is light-blue, the diamonds

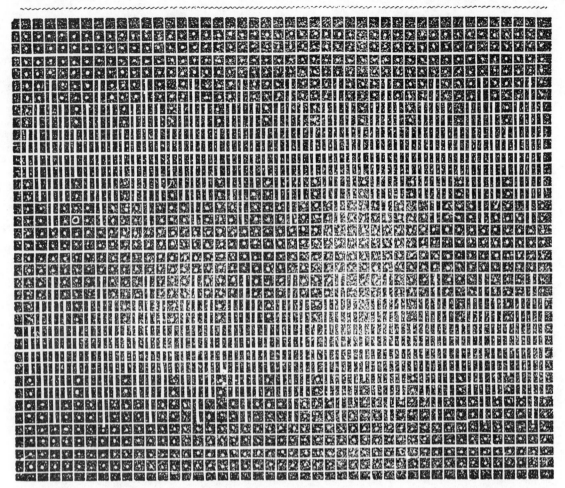

PATTERN FOR PART OF SIDE OF LADY'S WORK-BAG: FULL-SIZE.

are in dark-blue, and the lines are in floss silk: as seen in the pattern above, which is of the full-size.

The bottom, which is circular, should be twelve inches in diameter, and covered with light-blue silk. The side should be five inches high. It will be seen that we give only a por-tion of the pattern of this side; but this is all that is necessary. This side is to be sewed to pasteboard, and lined with silk. The bag is to be made of light-blue silk; the handles to be made of cord.

Where the bag is sewed on to the side there should be a quilling of blue ribbon.

COMBINATION DESIGNS IN PATCHWORK.

BY MRS. JANE WEAVER.

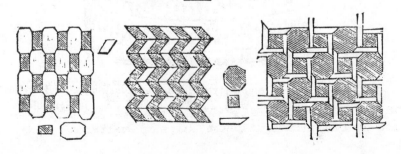

THE GIRDLE POCKET.

BY MRS. JANE WEAVER.

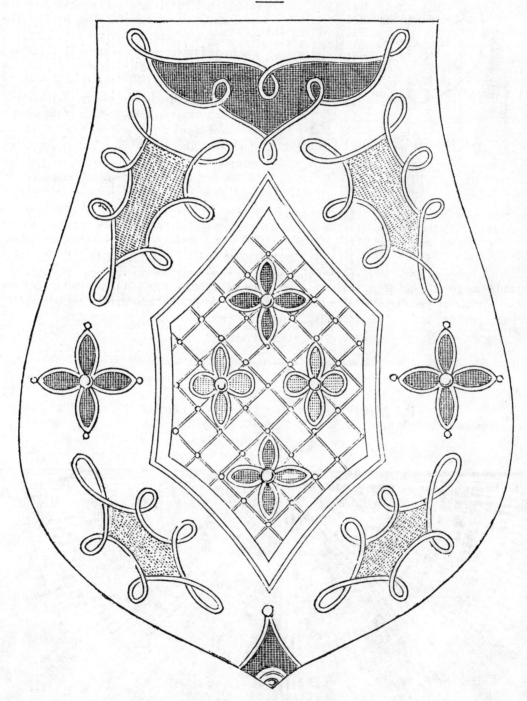

PATTERN FOR GIRDLE-POCKET: FULL-SIZE.

THIS beautiful affair has just appeared in Paris, where it is all the rage. It is used to carry a handkerchief and portmonnaie. We give, on the next page, an engraving of it, as it appears when made up; and above a pattern of one side, full-size.

MATERIALS.—Quarter of a yard of sky-blue silk; some small pieces of black, red, and green

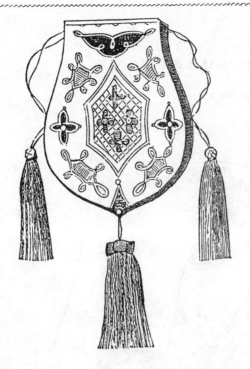

larger so as to allow for the seams; cut the centre-piece of green velvet, and lay it on the blue silk, as in the design, covering the edges with the gold braids. The four stars, in this centre-piece, are to be as follows: the top and bottom ones of black velvet, and the two side ones of red velvet: and they are put on in the same manner as the centre-piece itself. The gold thread is now to be laid across, in diamonds, and fastened on the under side: and the smaller sized jet beads are to be sewn on, at the points of the diamonds: the larger sized jet beads to be sewn in the centre of the stars. The four corner patterns, outside of the centre-piece, are of red velvet, and are braided, on the edges, with the gold braid. The two stars on the outside of the centre-piece, and the patterns at the top and bottom, are of black velvet, braided like the corner-pieces, and finished with beads. The whole is now to be sewed on the pasteboard. Make two sides in this manner. Put them together with a piece of velvet ribbon, bonnet width; line the bag with silk; and finish with cord and tassels. This pocket is worn at the waist, being attached to the belt, as seen in one of the full-page fashion figures (the sitting one) given in the front of the number.

velvet; a spool of gold braid; a spool of gold thread; and two sizes of black beads.

Cut a piece of pasteboard of the size of the full-size pattern; and the sky-blue silk a little

---

PINCUSHION IN CROCHET.

BY MRS. JANE WEAVER.

THIS is to be worked in different shades of pink, as seen by the marks, interspersed with white. We give part of the top. It is easy enough even for beginners.

THE SHANGHAI CLOAK.

BY EMILY H. MAY.

THIS garment is made of cloth, silk, or velvet.

No. 1. FRONT; this part must be cut 13 inches longer than our pattern; it is rounded in front and is 26 inches wide at bottom.

No. 2. GORE, added to the front and back to give fullness to the garment. This gore is sewed to the front from C to C; and to the back from D to D.

No. 3. SLEEVE; this sleeve is divided into three parts. The seam which begins at the

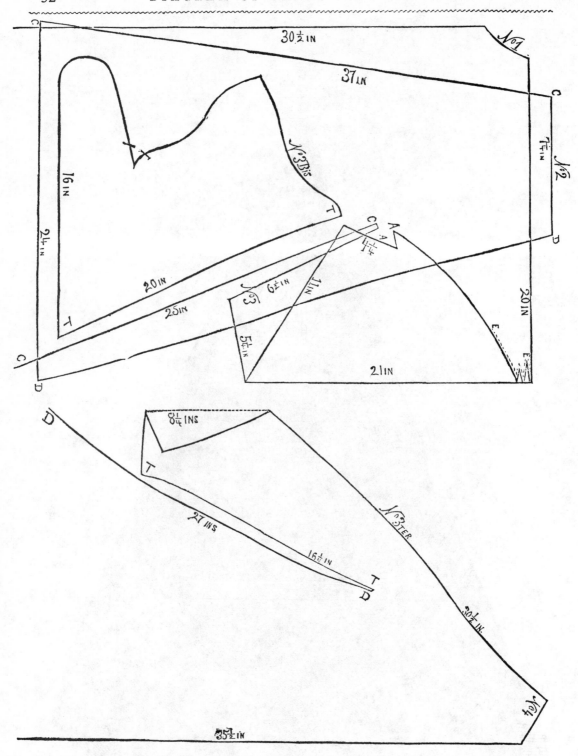

neck, and joins the back to the front, continues along the sleeve, and makes it form an elbow.

No. 3 *bis.* SECOND PART OF SLEEVE. This part is joined to No. 3 *ter* by a seam running from T to T, it then returns on the front of the sleeve and forms a tab fastened by a button.

No. 3 *ter.* THIRD PART OF SLEEVE. This part is joined to the back.

No. 4. BACK; this must be cut 15 inches lon- ger than the pattern, and is, at bottom, 15 inches wide.

The trimming of the cloak consists of two rows of braid placed three-quarters of an inch apart. It laps over in front, and has three buttons to fasten it. Two small pockets are cut slanting in front. There is no seam at the sleeve-hole. It is another seam which forms the elbow.

WATCH-POCKET IN BRAIDING.

BY MRS. JANE WEAVER.

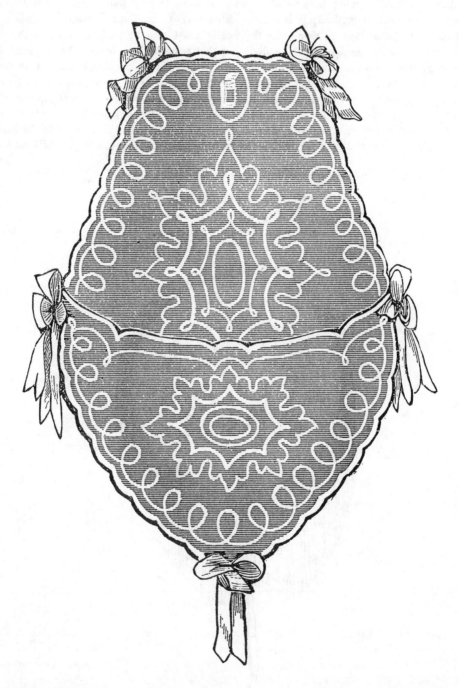

Thᴉs Watch-Pocket is to be made in white marcella, braided with scarlet, white, star, or variegated braid. It is finished at the corners and bottom by bows of narrow ribbon, matching the braid in color. As will be seen by the engraving, the hook is placed quite at the top.

HOW TO TRANSFER PATTERNS.

BY MRS. JANE WEAVER.

As many new subscribers have asked how to transfer patterns, we take an early occasion to answer them. Transfer paper is certainly the most easy and convenient method; if it cannot be purchased: it can always be made in a few minutes in the following manner. Take a sheet of thin writing-paper, and with a piece of wadding or flannel rub it all over with a little sweet oil, carefully removing any superfluity on the surface of the paper; then rub on to this oiled paper a little color, either light or dark, according to the color of the material on which the work is to be executed; if a dark cloth, for instance, a little chrome yellow is the best; if a light drab or any pale color, a little common blue makes the lines perfectly visible. This color must also be well rubbed into the paper, so that none shall be left on the surface. When the paper is thus prepared, place it on the material and lay over it the pattern to be transferred, and with an ivory knitting-needle or a stiletto trace the outline of the pattern, which will be found to be transferred to the material with perfect distinctness, if properly managed.

HAND SCREEN.

BY MRS. JANE WEAVER.

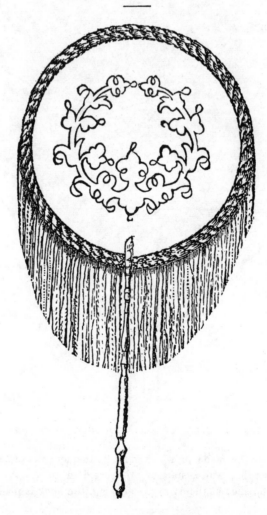

THIS is a new and beautiful Hand Screen, of which we give, on the preceding page, an engraving as it looks when made up; while, on this page, we give an engraving of one half of the braiding pattern, of the full-size of the screen.

To make the circle of this pattern complete, it is only necessary to trace the part given on transferring paper, and then, by taking the other side, the pattern will be had in reverse. Place this reversed pattern against the one here given and the circle will be complete. If transferring paper is not at hand, lay the pattern against a window-pane, and so trace it on writing paper.

The screen is to be worked, with gold braid, on crimson, green, or black silk, as the taste of the person making it, or the person for whom it is intended, may prefer.

After the screen is thus braided, it should be neatly sewn on stiff cardboard, covered, on the back, with any colored silk that will harmonize with the front.

The edges should then be trimmed with a row of gold-colored cord. A fringe should then be added of the color of the silk interspersed with gold.

A neat, carved handle should be sewn on before the back is covered, so as to hide the spot where it is sewn on. This handle may be of dark wood.

DESIGN FOR BREAD-CLOTH IN TAPE-WORK.

BY MRS. WARREN.

MATERIALS.—Cottons, Nos. 20 and 30; a piece of tape the width as in engraving; and a fine sewing-needle.

In the ordinary way of sewing tape into points, make 16 of the latter (that is, on *both* edges, there are together 32), but 16 points on each edge; then join these together in a circle evenly, so that the join shall scarcely be perceived; slip the needle to the point nearest the join, and make a tight stitch *; now through the next point, and through the next; draw up these together, and fasten them with a tight

stitch; now slip the needle up the tape to the next point on the outside edge; make a tight stitch; pass the needle to the next point, draw it up close to the former point; make a tight stitch; pass the needle downward again to the next point below; make a tight stitch; now repeat from *. When finished, make another square, and sew them together as in engraving. Then with 30 cotton fill in the centres with crossed bars, diamonds, and wheels; the latter is simply loose button-hole stitch worked round; then sew round a stitch loosely the reverse way to which the button-hole stitch was worked. The bars are merely two threads taken across. Then work button-hole stitch to the centre; now take the threads across the reverse way; work button-hole over them to the centre; pass the thread across to the other threads; work button-hole stitch over again to the centre; fasten the threads together well, and finish working over. The diamonds are two threads taken from point to point; then button-hole stitch worked over. Make of a sufficient size, as a border will not be required.

CROCHET ANTIMACASSAR.

BY MRS. JANE WEAVER.

MAKE a chain of 12 stitches, unite into a ring, on which work 36 stitches in single crochet. Work 1 double and 3 chain into every other loop (making 18 double stitches); work 2 double and 5 chain on to each of the 3 chain in last row. On these 5 chain work 2 double, 3 chain, 2 double (these 4 double are all worked into the centre stitch of the 5 chain of last row), 3 chain, loop in to the 2 double of last row, and continue 3 chain, 2 double, 3 chain, 2 double, 3 chain all round, chain 9 (looping in to the 3 chain between the 2 double of last row); continue all round. On this row work 4 chain, 1 double, 1 chain, 1 double, 1 chain, 1 double (these 3 double must be all worked into the centre stitch of the 9 chain of last row), 4 chain, looped in over the centre of the previous 3 chain

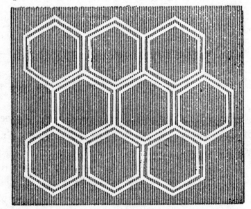

between the 4 double. This completes the star of 18 points. For the outer line, chain 7 between each point, looping into the centre stitch of each; there are three points to each of the six sides; at the six points of the hexagon there must be three stitches in one stitch to form the shape when the next row is worked. This row, which is the last, is 1 long 1 chain missing one stitch of last row. These hexagons are sewn together as given in the small diagram annexed.

PATTERNS IN SILK EMBROIDERY.

BY MRS. JANE WEAVER.

CARRIAGE DRESS.

WALKING DRESS.

HEAD-DRESS: SIDE AND BACK VIEWS.

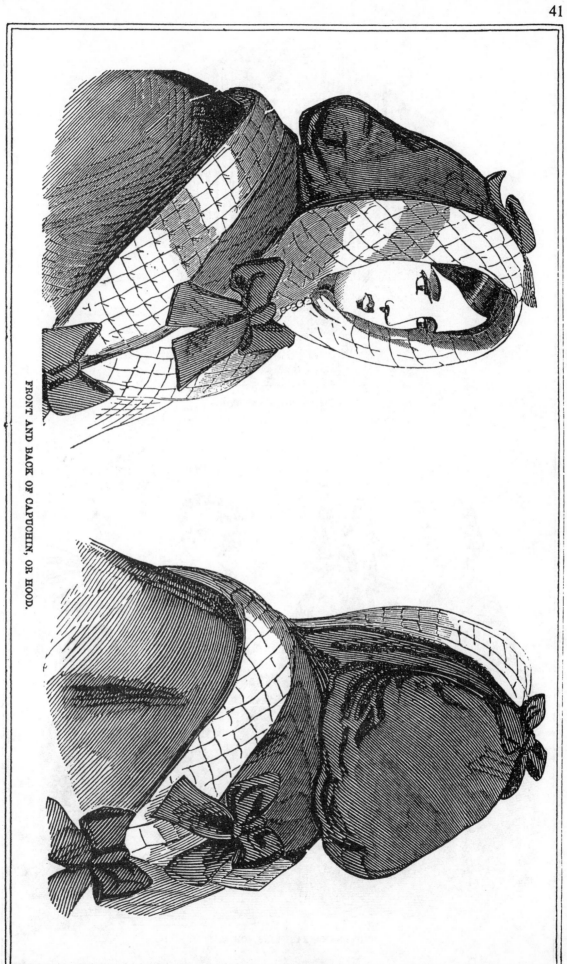

FRONT AND BACK OF CAPUCHIN, OR HOOD.

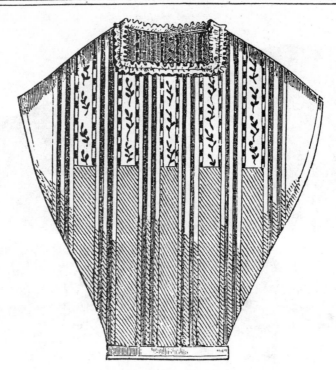

SWISS CHEMISETTE.

CHILDREN'S FASHIONS FOR MARCH.

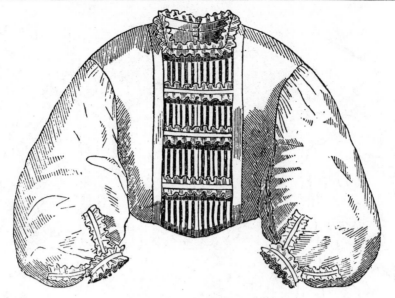

CHEMISETTE FOR ZOUAVE JACKET.

NAME FOR HANDKERCHIEF.

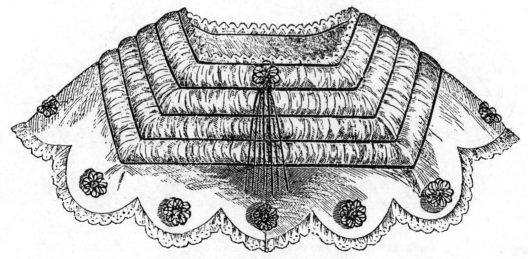

ITALIAN FICHU.

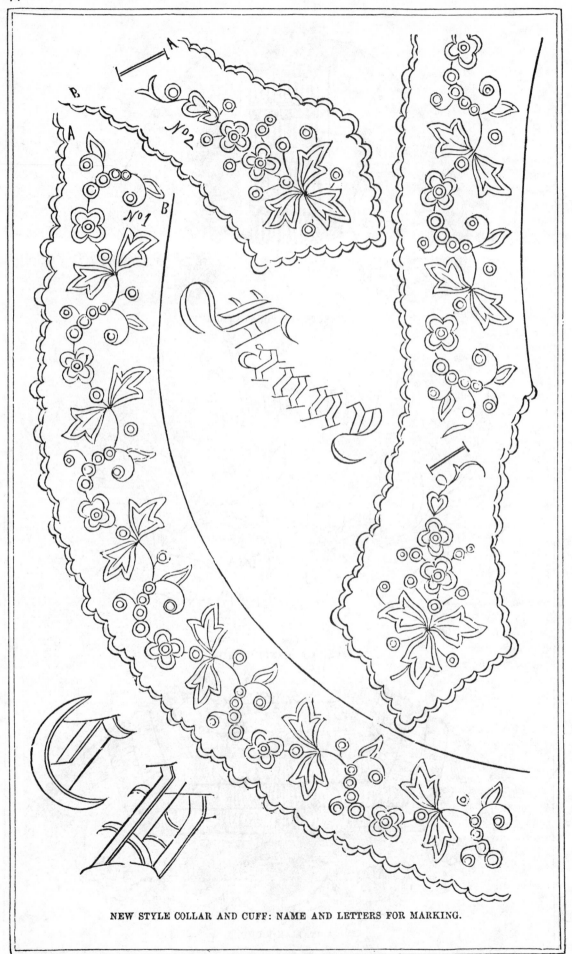

NEW STYLE COLLAR AND CUFF: NAME AND LETTERS FOR MARKING.

KNITTING BASKET.

BY MRS. JANE WEAVER.

PERHAPS there are few kinds of work which require a basket expressly arranged for their own reception so much as knitting, on account of the almost fatal injury which it sustains when needles are drawn out and loops are dropped. Accordingly we give a pattern for a knitting basket, which has just come out in England. The large engraving represents one half, being of full size. By reversing it, the other half can be had. It is to be worked on fine canvas, as, if a coarse one should be unwarily taken, the basket will exceed in size the useful purpose for which it is intended. The outlines of the waving or serpentine lines of our design are in steel beads, filled up with clear white, those of the diamonds of gold filled with chalk-white. The ground of the central opening is in bright blue Berlin wool, as well as the small part within the loop at each end. The

ground within the diamonds is in maize-color. Both of these are much improved by being worked in floss silk. The ground on the exterior of the design is shaded crimsons, dark, medium, and light. It requires three pieces of this form (each twice the size of our large engraving, which is but half a piece) to make the basket; the two sides must be worked alike, but the third, which is the bottom of the basket, only requires to be worked in the stripes of the shaded ground. All three must be stitched on cardboard of the same shape and size, neatly lined with silk or German velvet, and sewn together on the outside, the stitches being concealed by a row of beads. After this the handle must be attached, which may be of double wire, twisted round with a little cotton wool, and then with ribbon and beads. All this being done, a silk cord must be taken, the end fastened down close to the handle, and the cord wound round and round, each twist touching, but not over-wrapping the last, until about an inch and a half of the end of the basket is enclosed, this being an important point for the safety of the needles.

In addition to the full-size design for working, we also give, below, an engraving of the basket as made up.

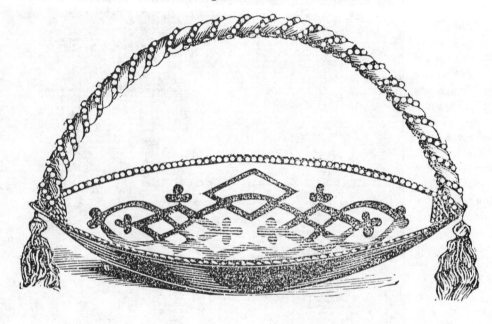

PATTERNS FOR SILK EMBROIDERY.

BY MRS. JANE WEAVER.

NETTED CURTAIN.

BY MADEMOISELLE ROCHE.

WINDOW-CURTAINS netted after the above pattern look very well over a color. They are very suitable also for a French bedstead lined with pink, and for a baby's *berceaunette* and its coverlet, also for the drapery of a toilet-table lined to match the other articles. Speaking of these various applications, we must beg our readers not to be alarmed at the amount of work which they appear to involve, since it is so extremely easy of execution, that great quantities can very soon be completed. The cotton should be coarse and the mesh rather under three-quarters of an inch wide. For a window-curtain of moderate length a hundred loops may be cast on and four rows netted. The fancy row is done by twisting the cotton three times round the fingers in the same manner as the single one in simple netting, and then putting the needle through them in the common way. The next row is done on a mesh half an inch wide, which forms what may be called the stalk of the pattern, but in this the treble loop made in the last row must be taken up as one. After this the former fancy row must be repeated, and then four plain rows, which form the whole of the pattern.

IMITATION STAINED GLASS.

BY MRS. JANE WEAVER.

MATERIALS.—Some fine Swiss muslin, and the finest French glaced furniture chintz.

From the chintz cut out all the flowers, leaves, etc., very neatly; lay them aside. Prepare the window by having it thoroughly cleaned. Cut the muslin exactly the size of the panes of glass, and with some arrow-root starch, paste it upon the inside of the glass. Be careful to smooth out all the creases. When dry, arrange the flowers, etc., in bouquets, or wreaths, as the fancy may suggest, pasting them upon the muslin.

By this simple process an excellent imitation of painted glass may be made.

48

INFANT'S HOOD IN CROCHET.

BY MRS. JANE WEAVER.

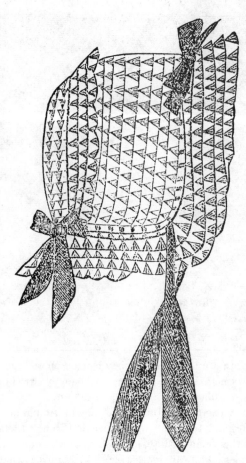

MATERIALS.—½ oz. white split zephyr; ½ oz. colored split zephyr; 2½ yards of narrow ribbon.

FOR THE HEAD-PIECE.—With the white wool make a chain three-eighths of a yard in length. On it work 27 shells, 4 dc stitches to each shell, 1 chain stitch between the shells. Work 15 rows in this manner.

FOR THE CROWN.—Make a chain of 40 stitches, on it work 5 shells as in the head-piece. Work 4 rows. 5th row, widen 1 shell between the first and second, and fourth and fifth shells of 4th row. Work 9 rows. 10th and 11th rows, narrow by dropping 1 shell at each end of the row. This completes the crown. Sew the crown and head-piece together. Where they join, tie the colored wool and work four rows of shells, making 44 shell stitches around the crown. The last row, work 1 sc stitch between the shells.

FOR THE BORDER.—With the colored wool, work all around the hood in shell stitch as before, observing to work 1 shell in every shell of head-piece, and 1 shell between every shell. Work 6 rows, finishing the last row with 1 sc stitch between every shell.

FOR THE FRILL OR CAP.—With the white wool make a chain three-eighths of a yard long. On it work 1 row in dc stitch, 1 ch between every 2nd row, 1 dc, 1 ch, 1 dc, 1 ch into every stitch.

3rd Row.—Same as 2nd row.

4th Row.—Same as 3rd row.

This piece of work will be very full, and must be laid upon a table and fluted. Sew the frill in the face of the hood, at the point where the colored wool is joined.

Run the ribbon just above the border all around the hood, tying in a bow on top and at the back. Strings of the ribbon, and the hood is complete. If preferred, the hood may have a quilted lining of silk.

SWISS STRIPED CUSHION.

BY MADEMOISELLE ROCHE.

MANY ladies have by them more or less of remainders of Berlin wool, for which they would be pleased to find a pretty and useful application. These have accumulated from former finished labors, and must rest as neglected stores, unless some desirable appropriation can be suggested. It is for this express purpose that we are now introducing the Swiss Striped Cushion, which can be executed with great ease and quickness, and yet has a pleasing and even rich effect. The mode of working the stitch is as follows: Bring out the needle from the back toward the left-hand, count six threads upward, and insert the needle four threads toward the right, bringing it out in a line with the first stitch; then return to the line of the first stitch,

SWISS STRIPED CUSHION.

insert the needle four threads from it on the right hand side, and bring it out two threads above the first stitch, but in the same line. There will now be a long cross of the wools, with the wool brought out at the left side ready for repetition. This forms the whole of the stitch, being repeated to the end of the row, the pretty effect being obtained by the over-wrappings of the wool, which as the line progresses assumes the form of a plait. Between each stripe there is a row of stitching in either white or black wool, which both conceals the threads of the canvas, and much improves the appearance of the work. The colors of the stripes should be a little studied, so that their successions may be harmonious. As this Swiss stripe is so easy of execution, and produces most agreeable results, ladies who wish to undertake work that will not give them any trouble of thought, cannot do better than commence it, even if they purchase the wools expressly for the purpose, and in this case stripes of three colors look remarkably well, separated by stitched rows either of black or white. If, however, one of these three stripes should be black, with two other colors, then the stitched rows should be either white or gold-color. Although we have spoken first of the cushion, yet the Swiss stripe is equally applicable for various other articles. Mats of all sorts, the fender-stool, and slippers, being among the number. For the last, the precaution should be used of working one stripe down the center of the slipper, and then repeating the colors of the stripes on each side, so that each half of the slipper may correspond.

SIMPLE DESIGN IN BERLIN WOOL-WORK,
FOR MATS, SLIPPERS, CUSHIONS, ETC.

SIMPLE patterns in Berlin wool-work, producing lively and pleasing effects, are amongst those supplies for the Work-Table which every lady finds most useful for various purposes, enabling her with perfect ease to make many pretty articles, which, if great arrangement were necessary, would never be undertaken. The little design which we have now given is one of these, being perfectly easy of execution, and especially pretty when completed. Wools of three different colors are all that are required, worked in the following manner: The lines which form the sides of the diamonds are in a brilliant green, inclining to a blue; when they appear to cross, the small square becomes a very dark green, approaching to a black, the ground or under diamonds being white. Another pretty arrangement of colors is to take a ruby for the sides of the diamonds, a black for the crossings, and a white for the ground; or a blue may be substituted for the ruby with equally good effect. This little design will be found well-suited for cushions, mats, slippers, and many other articles, and it may be worked on either fine or coarse canvas, according to the article for which it may be required.

SPECTACLE-CASE.

BY MADEMOISELLE ROCHE.

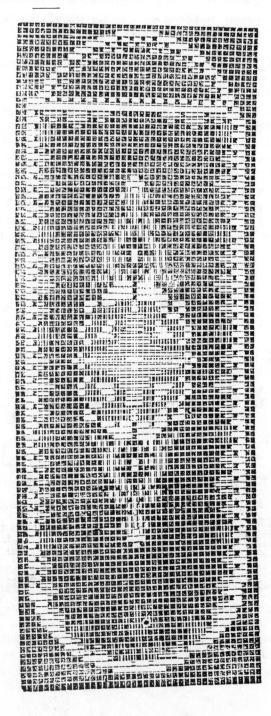

This little article is to be worked on fine silk canvas with floss silks in tent-stitch. This will prevent the necessity of filling in the ground, and it also leaves the design more distinct when it is worked.

The center cross is in three colors, the little star in the middle is four white stitches with one gray in the center.

Round it there are eight stitches in rich dark crimson; the four straight lines in the middle of the cross are in lighter crimson; round these four lines the cross is enlarged by two rows of bright blue stitches, in two shades.

The six little stars around are in two shades of crimson. The remainder of the scroll pattern round the cross is in grays, shaded with black, the lightest parts being worked in white.

The little pattern which is carried round the edge is in alternate blue and scarlet, with the rows nearest the edge in black.

This will be found, when worked, a pretty effective arrangement of colors. When the two sides are completed, they must be lined with crimson silk, and joined together afterward.

The stitches are to be hid with a row of small beads, either white, steel, or gold. The case is closed at the bottom and left open at the top.

NEW STYLE ZOUAVE JACKET.

BY EMILY H. MAY.

We this month give a diagram of a *Zouave* jacket, differing from any we have before given. At the back the figure is well defined; the front is not closed except at the throat, but the *contour* of the figure is given by the seam of the front which goes from the shoulder to the bottom. The pattern consists of five pieces, viz: the back, having seam down the middle, the side-piece of back, the two pieces forming the front, and the sleeve: the small notch in the side-piece, and the side of front at the seam under the arm, indicate how far this seam is to be stitched, it being open below the waist, and the corners rounded to correspond with

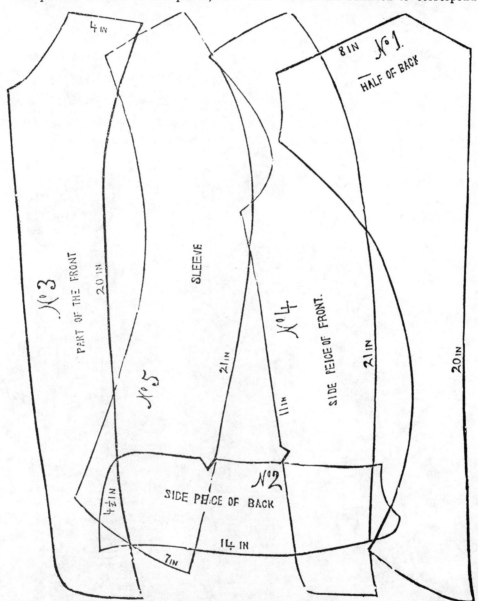

those of the front. The sleeve is shaped at the elbow; a loose sleeve may be substituted if preferred. This jacket is to be made in velvet or cashmere; if in velvet, whether black, dark green, or violet, the seams should all be covered by a thick gold cord, and either embroidered round with gold thread, or braided with a narrow gold cord. Either a silk waistcoat or chemisette of full muslin may be worn with it.

No. 1. HALF THE BACK.
No. 2. SIDE-PIECE OF THE BACK.
No. 3. PART OF FRONT.
No. 4. SIDE-PIECE OF FRONT.
No. 5. SLEEVE.

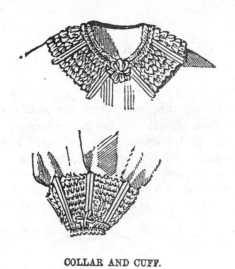

COLLAR AND CUFF.

EMBROIDERY IN SILK.

CHILDREN'S FASHIONS FOR APRIL.

NEW STYLES OF CAPS.

THE PRINCESS ALICE.

THE QUEEN CAROLINE.

NAME FOR MARKING.

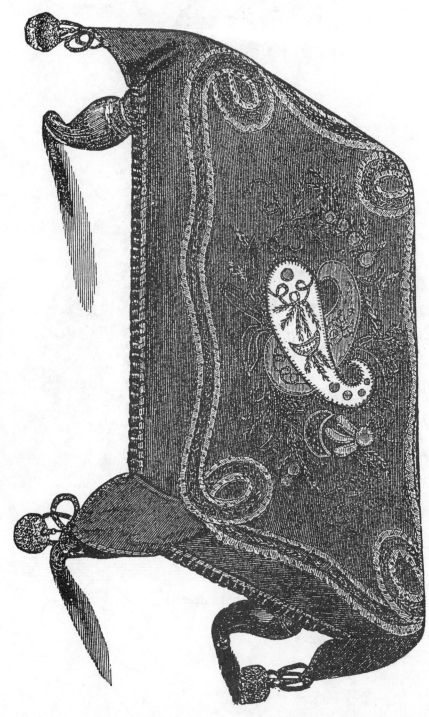

OTTOMAN AND COVER.

HALF THE CROWN OF INFANT'S HOOD.

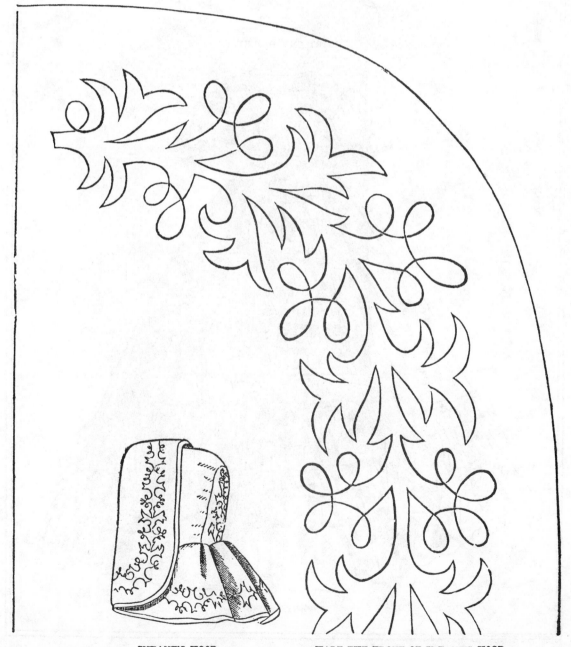

INFANT'S HOOD.   HALF THE FRONT OF INFANT'S HOOD.

SKIRT EMBROIDERY.

INFANT'S ROBE.

POLONAISE TRAVELING-DRESS.

BY EMILY H. MAY.

WE give, this month, a pattern of a beautiful Polonaise Traveling-Dress, accompanied by diagrams by which it may be cut out. The diagrams of the fronts and backs are not given the full length; but we give all that is necessary; and they may be extended according to the size of the wearer. Of course the gores also are to be extended.

No. 1. FRONT, a.
No. 2. FRONT, b.
No. 3. BACK, a.
No. 4. BACK, b.
No. 5. SLEEVE.
No. 6. CUFF.

To make the front, join A A, and B B. For under the arm, join C C and D D; and join E E and F F on the skirt. Make one large box plait of the fullness, coming under the arm. Join H H and I I to make the side-body, of the back, as far as the waist. Join K K and L L on the skirt, plaiting in the fullness. Make a seam from P to M on the sleeve. Join the cuff at M M and O O.

This makes a very stylish traveling-dress. We give it thus, in advance of the season, in order that our fair friends may have time to make their traveling-dresses before summer comes in.

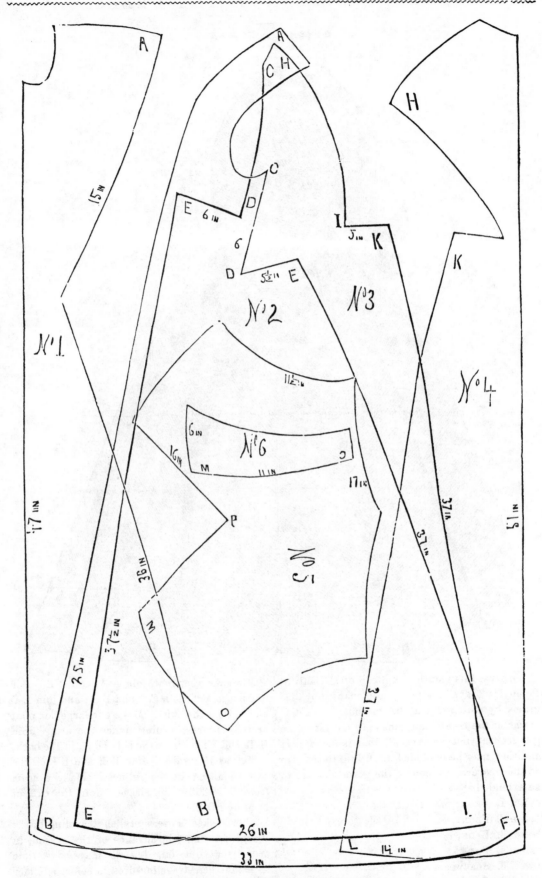

DIAGRAM OF POLONAISE TRAVELING-DRESS.

WATCH-POCKET.

BY MRS. WARREN.

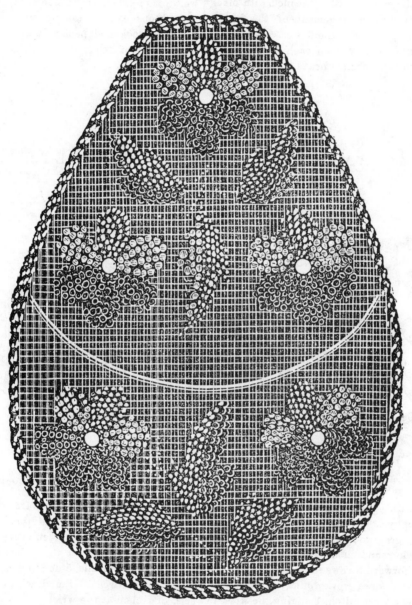

MATERIALS.—Cotton, No. 20. Quarter of a yard of Penelope canvas, that which has 12 double threads to the inch; 6 skeins of magenta-colored Berlin wool, and one skein of black; half an oz. each of opaque white, crystal, and chalk-beads, sufficiently large to cover the threads of canvas; a bunch of No. 10 steel beads, and five good-sized pearl beads, to fill in the center of each flower. Use ink, in which put a little loaf sugar and a camel's hair brush, and a piece of tissue paper.

First, place the tissue paper over the engraving, and with brush and ink trace off the entire outline, but only the upper or pointed part of the design; then on another part of the paper trace off the pocket part of outline and design; this pocket part must be cut a trifle larger in the canvas than the outline taken off in paper, and another ink tracing made outside. This will allow of the pocket hanging fuller than the back, for the reception of the watch. Now work the outline in black wool, then fill in all but the design with magenta-colored wool. The stems and veins of leaves are all of steel beads. There are six divisions, or leaves, of flower; one leaf must have all chalk beads; the two leaves on each side of it be opaque white; the two next of crystal, and the lowest, opposite to the chalk. The crystal beads must be threaded with black cotton. By this arrangement of the beads, shade of tint is given to the flower. The leaves on stem must be sewed on each stitch of the corners, the vein of steel beads, the upper part of the leaf in chalk, the lower of crystal beads; the edge has four or five chalk beads, crossed slantways over. Previously to putting the beads on edge, or sewing on the pearls, slightly tack with tin tacks the work on to a board, the right side downward; then with gum water brush it well over; when dry remove it, cut off the superfluous canvas, tack down the edge, line both the back and pocket with silk, then sew on the edge of beads.

BABY'S MITTEN IN CROCHET.

BY MRS. JANE WEAVER.

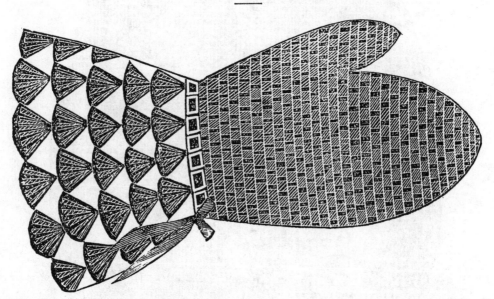

MATERIALS.—½ oz. gray single zephyr; ½ oz. crimson zephyr.

With the gray wool make a ch of 40 stitches, join. Work round in sc 4 rows; work backward and forward 8 rows to make the place for the thumb; 5 rows work round; 3 rows narrowing every other stitch, bringing the work to a point. Take up the stitches for the thumb, work 8 rows plain, 2 rows narrowing off to a point. Work in dc around the hand 1 row; 2nd, 3rd, and 4th rows widen every 10th stitch; 6 rows plain. Tie on the colored wool, and work 4 rows of shells, 5 dc stitches to the shell, 1 ch stitch between. Finish with cord and tassels, or ribbon at the wrist.

CLOVER-LEAF: IN TATTING.

MAKE four pearl stitches and loop, until you have five loops; draw up; then make five scallops, and join each one in the loops made at first. A subscriber sends this pattern, which will be new to many.

LADY'S NETTED WORK-BAG.

BY MRS. JANE WEAVER.

This is a very beautiful affair, which can be easily and economically made. The foundation of the bag is netted, in diamond netting, with black purse-twist. All of the solid squares, seen in the full-sized pattern below, are to be darned in with white floss silk; and the dotted squares in yellow floss silk. Both sides of the bag are to be made after this pattern. When the netting is finished, cut a piece of thin cardboard of the size of netting, and cover, on both sides, with crimson silk. Next stretch the netting over this. Finish the bag with tassels of the color of the lining, with a little gold thread intermixed. For strings use crimson and gold cord.

FANCY BASKET IN CROCHET.

BY MRS. JANE WEAVER.

FOR the engraving, see front of the number, where the basket is printed in colors.

MATERIALS.—1 spool white crochet cotton, No. 14; 1 spool pink crochet cotton, No. 14; finest steel hoops.

With the white cotton make a ch of 8. Join, into that work 18 dc stitches, join.

1st Row.—Work all round in sc.

2nd, 3rd and 4th Rows.—Work in dc, widening enough to keep the work flat.

5th Row.—Work in sc, making the stitches in the upper edge of the chain made by the last row.

6th Row.—Turn the work from right to left, working backward in dc, making the stitches in the under edge of the chain made by 4th row. This row forms the foundation for the sides of the basket.

7th Row.—3 ch, 8 dc, * 2 ch, 9 dc, 2 ch, 9 dc, *. Repeat all around the row, joining the last stitch to the first stitch, which was made by the 3 ch stitches at the beginning of the row.

8th Row.—3 ch, 6 dc over the 9 dc of last row, * 2 ch, 1 dc stitch into the center of the two ch stitches made in 7th row, 2 ch, 7 dc over the 9 dc as before, *. Repeat, joining as in the 7th row.

9th Row.—3 ch, 4 dc over the 7 dc of 7th row, * 2 ch; miss 1, 1 dc, 2 ch; miss 1, 1 dc, 2 ch; miss 1, 5 dc over the 7 dc as before, *. Repeat all around, join.

10th Row.—3 ch, 2 dc over the 5 dc of last row, * 2 ch; miss 1, 1 dc, 2 ch; miss 1, 1 dc, 2 ch; miss 1, 1 dc, 2 ch, 3 dc over the 5 dc as before, *. Repeat.

11th Row.—3 ch, *; miss 1, 1 dc, 2 ch, 1 dc; miss 1, 2 ch, *. Repeat.

FOR THE EDGE.—Tie in the pink cotton.

1st Row.—Work in sc.

2nd Row.—4 dc, * 2 ch, 4 dc, 2 ch, 4 dc, *. Repeat all around the row.

3rd Row.—3 ch, 2 dc over the 4 dc of 2nd row, * 3 ch, 1 dc in the loop made by the 2 ch stitches of the 2nd row; 3 ch, 2 dc over the next 4 dc, *. Repeat. This completes the sides of the basket.

THE BASE.—Tie the pink cotton to the 5th row, 4 dc, with 3 ch between all round the row; then 1 row of sc. Finish off with 1 row of ch, taking up 1 stitch at the points, making 3 ch between every point.

HANDLE.—With the white cotton make a ch of 70 stitches. On it work 3 dc, * 1 ch; miss 1, 3 dc, *. Repeat to the end. Join the pink cotton, 5 ch, 1 sc between the 3 dc stitches of white. Repeat all round 2 rows of pink. Sew on the handle, starch and shape until dry.

CROCHET SLIPPER.

BY MRS. JANE WEAVER.

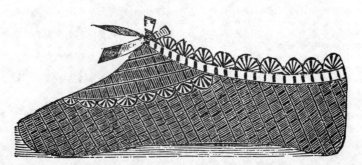

MATERIALS.—1½ oz. blue single zephyr; ½ oz. Chinchilla.

With the blue wool make a ch of 11 stitches.

1st Row.—Work in sc, widening 3 stitches in the 6th, or middle stitch.

2nd Row.—Work in the same way, making 3

stitches in the middle stitch of 1st row; but observe to work always into the under loop of ch stitch made by the previous row, otherwise the work will not be ridged. Repeat the blue 4 rows, Chinchilla 4 rows, and in this manner alternate the colors, until you have 30 rows of work, or 15 rows of ridge work. This is for the toe of the slipper; 12 stitches for the sides; work 12 rows plain. Sew the side to the toe, and edge all round with 1 row of shells worked with blue. Turn over the point on the top of the slipper. Sew the slipper to a cork-sole, and run an elastic in the top of slipper.

NETTED BED FRINGE.

BY MRS. WARREN.

MATERIALS.—Cotton, No. 6, and cotton for darning the pattern. Two meshes, one round, which should measure in the string which should be placed round it half an inch; and one flat mesh, a full half inch in width; a long netting needle.

FOUNDATION.—Net on a string four diamonds, and continue netting for as long as may be required these four diamonds; then gather one edge of this length of netting into a string; on the other edge net two rows of netting to form one diamond.

BORDER, WITH WIDE MESH.—Net 7 stitches into a loop, 1 stitch into next loop, and continue.

2nd and 3rd rows with round mesh; two rows, or one diamond.

4th row, wide mesh—one row.

Outside row, wide mesh—one row, taking the seven loops into one.

In the center of foundation draw a row of diamonds, and along the edge work with needle and some cotton a single stitch in each diamond, turning back at the end of length of netting, the reverse way.

AN INFANT'S HOOD.

BY MRS. JANE WEAVER.

IN the front of the number we give an engraving of an infant's hood, to be made of white merino, and braided with narrow silk braid. We give, also, half the crown and part of the front, full size, to show the pattern for the braid. The cape is to be braided to match the rest. The hood should have a quilted silk lining, to make it soft to the head.

KNITTED LEGGIN.

BY MRS. JANE WEAVER.

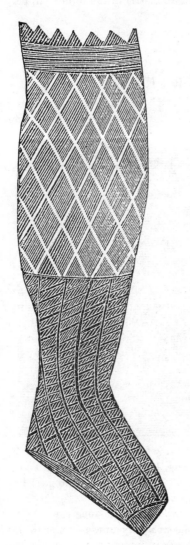

MATERIALS.—1 oz. colored single zephyr; 1 oz. white single zephyr; small bone needles.

With the white wool cast on 51 stitches.

Knit 2 rows plain.

3rd Row.—Knit 2 stitches plain, * throw the thread forward, knit 1, slip and bind, knit 1, *. Repeat to the end of the row.

4th Row.—Purl.

This pattern to be repeated 6 times.

2 rows plain, 1 row widen and narrow. 50 rows plain, or in block of 4 stitches plain and 4 purled, knitting 4 rows to form the block. The next row of blocks, reverse; knitting the plain stitches over the purled ones of last row, and the reverse.

51st Row.—Narrow 1 stitch at the beginning of the row.

6 rows plain.

58th Row.—Narrow same as 51st.

Tie on the colored wool, and knit either plain or ribbed as in a stocking, narrowing every 6 rows, until the leggin is long enough for the ankle. Knit 18 rows for the ankle; then for the foot, knit only the 12 center stitches, working 24 rows; after which take up all the stitches around the foot, and knit 10 rows plain. Bind off. Finish with a strap of leather under the foot, and cord and tassels at the top of the leggin.

CROCHETED BASKET.

BY MRS. JANE WEAVER.

FOR the engraving, see front of the number, where the basket is printed in colors.

MATERIALS.—8 doz. smallest size curtain rings; 2 spools colored crochet cotton, No. 14; fine steel hook.

Cover the rings, by working in sc, with the cotton (or zephyr may be substituted in its place); then arrange them, beginning at the center of the base of basket; place one ring in the center, and six around it; sew fast at the points where the rings touch, keeping them perfectly flat; twelve for the second row. This completes the base.

For the sides, two rows of rings, arranging them to stand upright; sewing as before. Little direction can be given for the sides, as the shape depends upon the inclination given to the two rows of rings forming the sides. One row, laid flat, for the edge, and one row at the base, as seen in the design. Cover two larger rings for the handles; either sew them on, or tie with a piece of narrow ribbon, same color.

This basket may be made with two colors, if preferred: blue and brown, or pink and white; making the sides of one color entirely, and edging with the other at the top and base.

PURSE IN CROCHET.

BY MRS. JANE WEAVER.

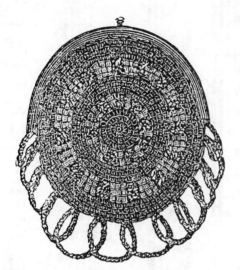

MATERIALS.—1 skein white purse twist; 1 skein emerald green; bunch gold beads, No. 6; fine steel crochet hook; gilt clasp.

With the green silk make a ch of 3 stitches, join. Work 4 or 6 rows in sc, widening enough to keep the work flat; join the white silk (having previously threaded the beads upon it); work 4 stitches in sc, putting a bead at every stitch, * 4 stitches without beads, 4 stitches with beads, *; repeat all round the row; work 4 rows in this manner, widening on the blocks where there are no beads; 4 rows of green, still widening only enough to keep the work flat; 4 rows of white, with beads, as before; finish with 3 rows green. The number of rows to be worked depends upon the size of the hook, also upon the manner of working. Some persons working much closer than others, several rows more or less will not affect the design of the purse. This completes one side of the purse. The other work in the same way. Join the two sides about half way, leaving space enough for the clasp; finish with a fringe of beads, as seen in the design.

INSERTION: IN TATTING.

MAKE a scallop; turn it over; make one **pearl** stitch, join it, proceed as before. A very simple pattern, yet a very pretty one, as the engraving shows. This insertion has been furnished by a subscriber.

COMBINATION DESIGN IN PATCHWORK.

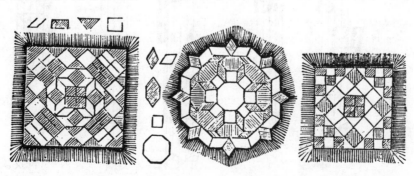

68

ROCHESTER SCHOTTISCHE.

COMPOSED BY W. H. KULISON,

ARRANGED BY SEP. WINNER.

69

BELTS AND SASHES.

CHILDREN'S FASHIONS FOR MAY.

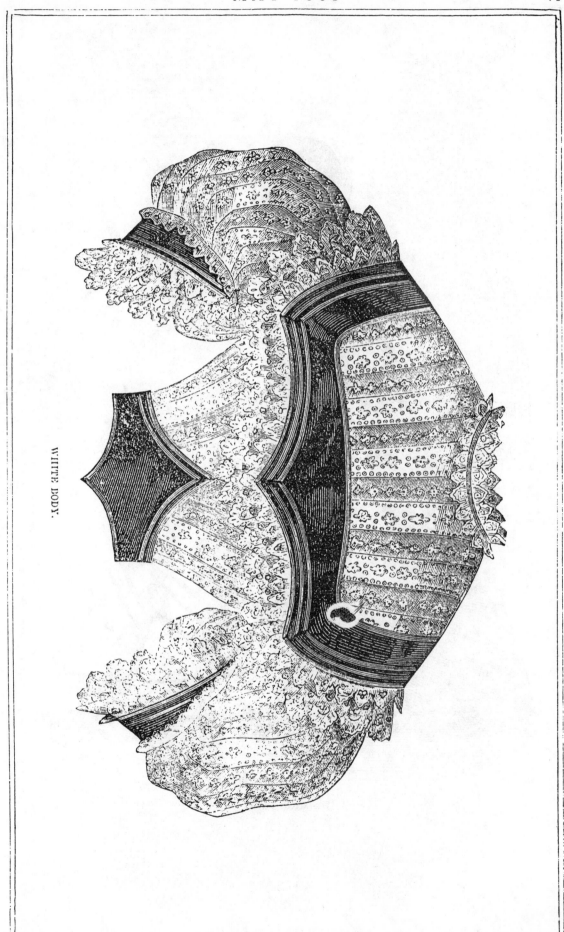

WHITE BODY.

WALKING DRESS.

MORNING DRESS.

74

FULL SIZE PATTERN FOR DRAWING-ROOM CARD-BASKET.

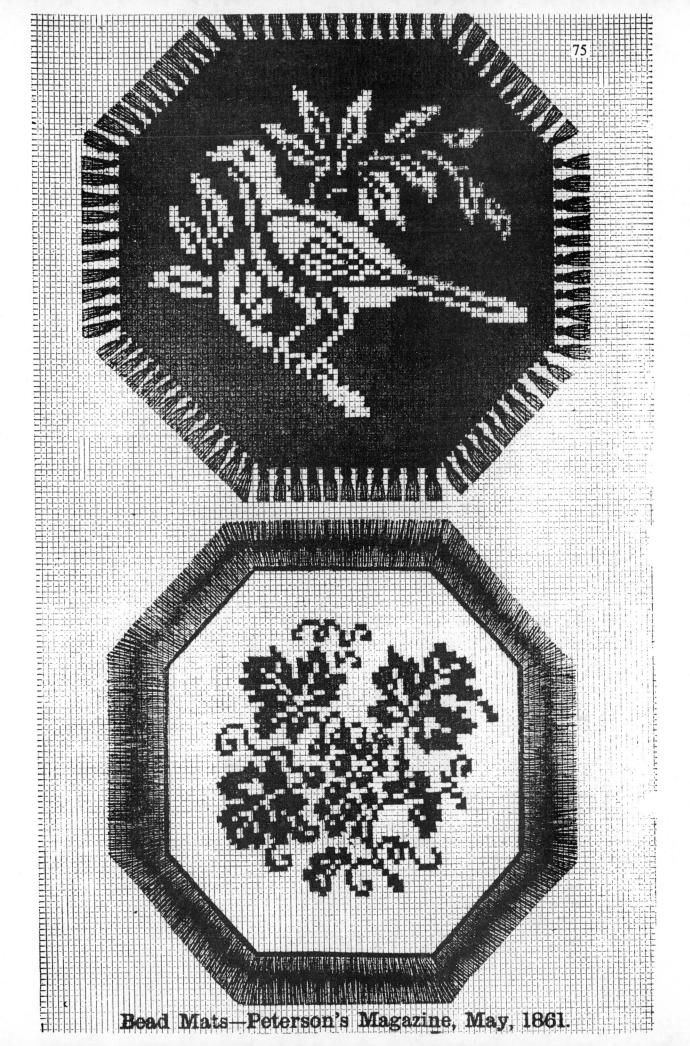

Bead Mats—Peterson's Magazine, May, 1861.

DRAWING-ROOM CARD-BASKET.

BY MADEMOISELLE ROCHE.

In the front of the number, we give a design for the half of this beautiful Drawing-Room Card-Basket, which is made in the new application of straw-work which has been lately introduced. From this half it is easy to complete the whole, by merely repeating the three outside bouquets, and finishing the center one.

The first inspection conveys a strong impression that we are looking at some handsome Indian article of native manufacture, and when we come to a closer examination, we are surprised to find that the chief material is simply a few of the shining straws gathered from our happy harvest-fields. In commencing to make the Drawing-Room Card-Basket given in our illustration, the first measure will be to cut the entire shape in one piece of pasteboard, giving the six-sided shape which forms the bottom its exact form by a fold of each part all round. This being done, take as many pieces of fine cloth, or good French merino, cut them to their required shapes, one for the bottom of the basket and six others to form the sides. These may be scarlet, blue, and a deep maize-color, with a black for the bottom of the basket; or they may be all of different colors. On these

embroider the flowers given in the slightest possible way. For the center the flower leaves may be put in merely with a double stitch, the spots being only a little *point d'or*—that is, a sort of irregular stitching worked very close. The other flowers may be done with as little labor. Contrast of colors must, however, be considered. On the red work a white flower, on the black a red, on the blue a maize-color, on the maize a purple, and vary the greens of the leaves as much as possible.

The embroidery being done, lay the six-sided piece on the bottom of the basket, fasten it carefully in its place, on this lay one of the side-pieces, face to face, stitch through the two edges and the pasteboard, turn the side up and tuck it firmly all round the edge of its own piece of cardboard, and so repeat until the whole six are done; then commence the straw-work by laying on first all the fine lines, which are nothing more than finely-split straws, such as are used for bonnet-making, fastening them down with little cross-stitches of blue and scarlet silk. When all the fine lines have been put on, add the wide ones, which are the whole coarse straws flattened down, crossing them also with the silk, leaving only for the present the outer line of the six pieces which form the sides. Then take some crimson German velvet for the under side of the basket, and cut each part so much larger as will just pass over the edge, coming exactly under the line of the wide straw which is next to be added, thus completing the pattern of the straw-work. In this way a very neat edge is secured. The last line of stitches, which may show at the under side of the basket, may be covered with a line of the wide straw. Each point is to be fastened to the next with a pretty bow of ribbon. The handle may be cardboard covered with red cloth and crossed with straw, or it may be a broad plait of straw, or a straw cord, which must be purchased, being one of those used for trimming bonnets. A little practice may be necessary to execute the straw-work with the dexterity and neatness necessary for its elegance; but when proficiency has been obtained, many beautiful articles can be easily produced worthy of any drawing-room.

LADY'S WORK-BAG.

BY MADEMOISELLE ROCHE.

In Paris, a "Work-Bag" is now the indispensable morning companion of every lady. One of the most fashionable is that which we give above. The material may be dark-blue or green cashmere, and the ornaments are executed in silk braid and embroidery. The bag consists of four distinct pieces, identical in shape, and equal in size. The illustration in the front of the number shows one of these pieces in its proper size, together with the design which ornaments it. The serpentine pattern, forming the border of the piece, is to be executed in flat silk braid, of a color harmonizing with the cashmere. It is stitched on with sewing silk of any hue presenting a broad contrast to that of the braid. In the middle of the braid a row of herringbone-stitch is worked with the same silk as that used for the stitching. The flowers in the inner pattern are formed of pieces of white and red cashmere neatly cut out and stitched down. These two colors may be tastefully varied on the four sides of the bag. The branches are worked in silk of different shades of green, brown, etc. The ornamental patterns being finished, the four pieces must be sewed together, and the stitches covered by a thin silk cord of the same color as that of the bag itself. The tassels may be either of one color, or a mixture of various hues. The bag is drawn at the top by a cord, finished with tassels.

COLLAR IN IRISH TATTING.

BY MRS. JANE WEAVER.

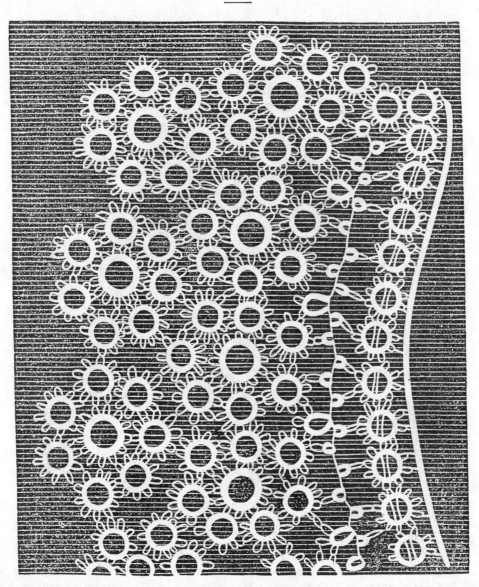

This Collar is worked in the usual way of tatting, which involves the necessity of being completed with the needle. The stars are worked separately, and sewn together at the different points. Each star is composed of a center circle, with seven loops round. The collar may be formed of either one or two of these rows. One row of single loops, worked at a little distance from each other, and fast-ened together one over the other at each end, makes the line of the collar round the neck to which the large stars are attached.

SEGAR-CASE IN BRAIDING.

BY MRS. JANE WEAVER.

THIS may be braided on morocco, cloth, or velvet, though the first is preferable; and any colors may be chosen. Gold braid on black is very pretty. After the sides are worked, they should be taken to a pocket-book maker. in order to be made up. This is an exceedingly easy kind of work, and is, at the same time, lady-like.

NEW STYLE OF OPEN BODY.

BY EMILY H. MAY.

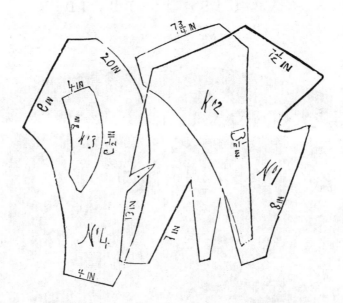

OUR pattern, this month, is that of a high dress body, opening to the waist in front, with *revers* turned back; the pattern consists of four pieces, viz: front, back, side-body, and sleeve. The *revers* is marked by a pricked line, and that it should sit perfectly flat when turned back, a small puff is taken out at the edge of front, the joining together of which is hidden by the trimming of *revers*. Some ladies are having a small collar at the back to meet the *revers*, leaving an opening between them, the collar of course being trimmed to correspond. The wide sleeve is shaped at the elbow, and has a deep *revers*, the position of which is marked on the pattern; at the bottom of sleeve a corner piece must be added at the seam at the back of the arm.

No. 1. ONE FRONT.
No. 2. HALF OF BACK.
No. 3. ONE SIDE-BODY.
No. 4. SLEEVE.

FOR A SOFA-PILLOW IN MUSLIN AND TAPE.

BY MRS. WARREN.

MATERIALS.—Some pieces of tape same size as pattern engraved, and of the soft kind which does not curl. Sufficient book muslin, of good quality, for the size of pillow. No. 24 cotton, and embroidery cotton, No. 8.

First make with a pencil spaces along each edge of muslin an inch and a half square; crease some lines from point to point, and run a white thread in these creases; now tack on the tape at each intersection, and stitch it in a small square; then with pencil trace out the patterns one at a time, leaving a square of muslin in the center of each pattern. (This is where the cross-bars of cotton are.) Run the pattern round twice, widening the running at the point of each leaf; then overcast this very thickly with close button-hole stitch; now cut out the small square of muslin in the center, turn in the edges close to the running, and sew in sewing-stitch thickly over. The cross-bars in the center of these are worked with 24 cotton. The book muslin is now to be cut away.

The cushion should be covered in colored material to suit the hangings of the room, and this work made up as a simple pillow-covering, to which a border may be added of the pattern engraved for bread-cloth, only that the tape must be that used for the sofa-pillow.

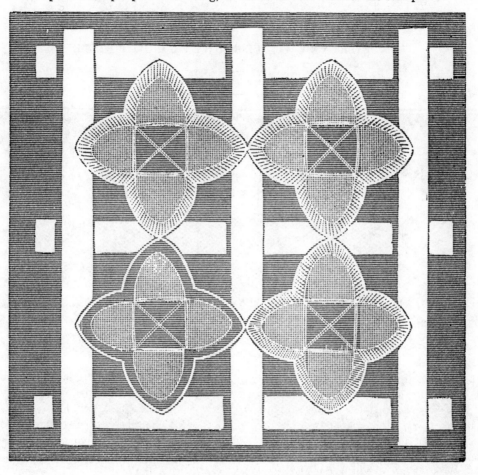

BEAD MATS IN COLORS.

BY MRS. JANE WEAVER.

For these patterns see front of number.

No. 1.

The pattern is worked in small white beads, the ground work in Berlin wool.

No. 2.

The pattern is for colored beads, either pearly or Torquoise, on a white ground of Berlin wool; or it may be worked in white beads, or small white bugles, on a colored ground, bordered with a fringe of beads, or of the wool as shown in the design. Make up on a piece of stiff pasteboard, covered with silk.

COMBINATION DESIGNS IN PATCHWORK.

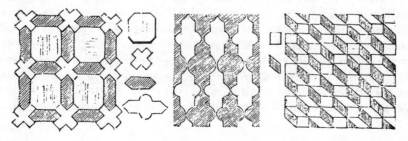

NETTED D'OYLEY FOR TARTLET

OR FOR ANY OTHER USEFUL PURPOSE.

BY MRS. WARREN.

MATERIALS.—Cotton, No. 10, and Trafalgar cotton. Bone mesh three-eighths of an inch wide; another a quarter of an inch. A long netting-needle, and a long rug or darning-needle.

On a foundation, with small mesh, net fifty-five stitches; then net twelve diamonds or twenty-four rows; then * decrease by netting two loops together every third row, at the beginning of the row only, till there are eighteen rows or nine diamonds; then decrease at the beginning of every row till there are twenty stitches. Now cut off from the foundation, turn ends with the netting, and net the other side, only commencing at *; now gather the netting through the center on to a string, net two rows all round, netting at the corners four stitches into one loop. There should be twenty-five loops at each end, and sixty-four down each side. Count the number of stitches, and mark with colored cotton each corner. With wide mesh net ten loops into the stitch next the colored mark at the end, but not at the side, miss seven loops, net ten into the eighth loop, *; then miss three loops; net ten into the fourth, repeat from * again, then miss seven loops; net ten into the eighth; (this will be the loop immediately before the colored mark;) net ten into next loop, which will be immediately after the colored mark; miss seven loops, net ten into the eighth, †; miss three loops, net ten into the fourth, repeat from † three times more, then miss four loops, net ten into the fifth, repeat from † twice more ⸮; miss three loops, net ten into the fourth, continue to repeat from ⸮ till the corner, where net as at the other corner; then continue along the end and side the same as the one just netted. With narrow mesh net four rows all round. This will make two diamonds. Cut off the cotton, tie it into the loop directly over the colored mark, net nine stitches,

T (or turn on reverse side), net eight stitches, thus missing one, and continue turning and decreasing a stitch at the end of every row till the netting is reduced to a point. Continue this all round. Darn as in engraving with the Trafalgar cotton and long needle.

A HYACINTH GLASS-STAND.

BY MRS. WARREN.

MATERIALS.—A skein each of three very distinct shades of magenta, violet, and maize-colored wool; four distinct shades of green, and one of light-brown. A wooden mesh, half an inch wide, two nails of green cambric, some stiff paper and gum, a circle of stiff cardboard, and a crochet hook.

Cut the circle of cardboard a little larger than the hyacinth glass; lay it down on the cambric, and cut the latter half an inch larger; then snip this half-inch all round, so as to admit of its being turned over the edge of the cardboard; now gum this snipped part and carefully turn it over the edge of the cardboard; now cut a circle the exact size, and gum it over. In stiff paper measure the size round of this circle, having the paper one inch and a half in depth, and cut the length a little longer than will go round the circle; lay this also on a strip of the cambric, and cut it half an inch also beyond the paper; then, without snipping, gum the cambric on to the paper, then gum a piece the exact width on to this again; when this is dry, sew the strip round the circle and up at the side.

FOR THE FLOWERS.—Take the lightest shade of maize or any other color, tie a loop over the mesh, insert the hook under this loop and make 1 ch; still keep the wool on the hook, wind the wool over the hook, make another tight chain. Continue this till there are fifteen loops, then tie on the next shade and make thirty loops, then the darkest and make fifty loops; draw the wool through and cut it off. Cut some circles of the cambric about an inch in diameter; carefully slip the wool off the mesh, then sew round the cambric in the form of a small rosette. In the next flower begin with the darkest shade, make fifteen loops; next shade thirty, and lightest fifty loops. Thus there will be one flower with a dark center, and one with a light; and they must be so arranged that the dark outside shall come against the light edge of next flower. When all the flowers are made, sew them round the cup as closely together as possible.

TO MAKE THE MOSS.—With No. 10 steel knitting-pins knit each single skein of the green and brown wool in common garter stitch; then, when completed, throw it into a basin of boiling water for a minute, take it up, wring it dry in a cloth, and press it with a hot iron; when cold, ravel it out and put three shades together, and sew it in bunches top and bottom of the cup, afterward pulling it out of any stiffness which the sewing on may have given it.

BORDER FOR A KNITTED COUNTERPANE.

BY MADEMOISELLE ROCHE.

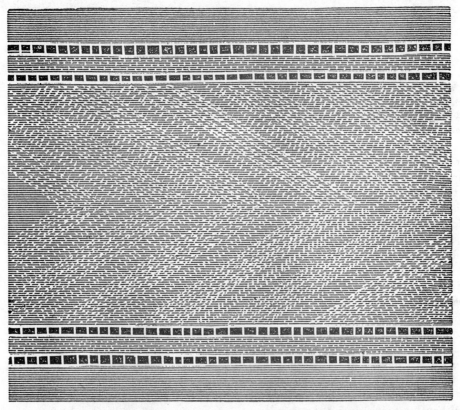

BEING intended to accompany a counterpane of solid knitting, we have given this border in raised slanting stripes, meeting down the center, as being the most suitable. Commence in the following way: Cast on 47 stitches. For the first row of the pattern—Knit 3, bring the thread forward, knit 4, purl 4, knit 4, purl 4, knit 3, slip, narrow and bind (these are the three central loops), knit 3, purl 4, knit 4, purl 4, knit 4, thread forward, knit 3. The first and last 3 of the row form the edge, and are always knitted in every row, both in the front and back rows.

Return Row.—Knit 3, purl 5, knit 4, purl 4, knit 4, purl 7, knit 4, purl 4, knit 4, purl 5, knit 3. In all the back rows it will be an easy rule to remember that all the knitted stripes are to be purled, and all the purled stripes are to be knitted, the 3 at each edge being always knitted, as we said before.

Second Front Row.—Knit 3, thread forward, purl 1 (this one is the commencement of a new stripe), knit 4, purl 4, knit 4, purl 4, knit 2, slip, narrow and bind, knit 2, purl 4, knit 4, purl 4, knit 4, purl 1, thread forward, knit 3.

It will be unnecessary for us to go through all the rows, as they are merely repetitions, if the following rule is carefully observed: In every front row a new loop is made by bringing the thread forward and forming the hole, after knitting the three at the edge, and this additional loop is always taken up by the narrowing in the center, so that new stripes are continually being formed in the exact degree that they are being lost in the center when they meet. As there may be some little danger in taking up and laying down the work, if not distinguishing the front and back rows at a glance, we recommend that a little knot of red wool should be tied to the end of the cotton left after casting on; when, simply noticing whether this mark is on the right hand or the left, will show at once which is the front or the back row. This border may be made of any width by casting on as many more loops as will make fresh stripes, in fours, on each side of the central line.

TIC-TAC POLKA.

ARRANGED BY ALICE HAWTHORNE.

SLIPPER IN COLORED BERLIN WORK.

BY MRS. JANE WEAVER.

VARIOUS ladies having asked for a slipper, which may be easily worked, we give, above, a pattern for the front of one; and below, a portion of the side and back. It is worked in five colors, and has a very pretty effect indeed. The white squares are to be done in white; the black parts in black; the next darkest in green; the next darkest in red; the next darkest in blue; and the next darkest in yellow.

Or, if you begin at the toe of the slipper, on the left, and work toward the right, the first bit (a triangle) is black; the next is green; the next (the lines of which run upward) is red; the next is black; the next is yellow; the next (the lines of which run upward) is blue; and the next black, which finishes the first row.

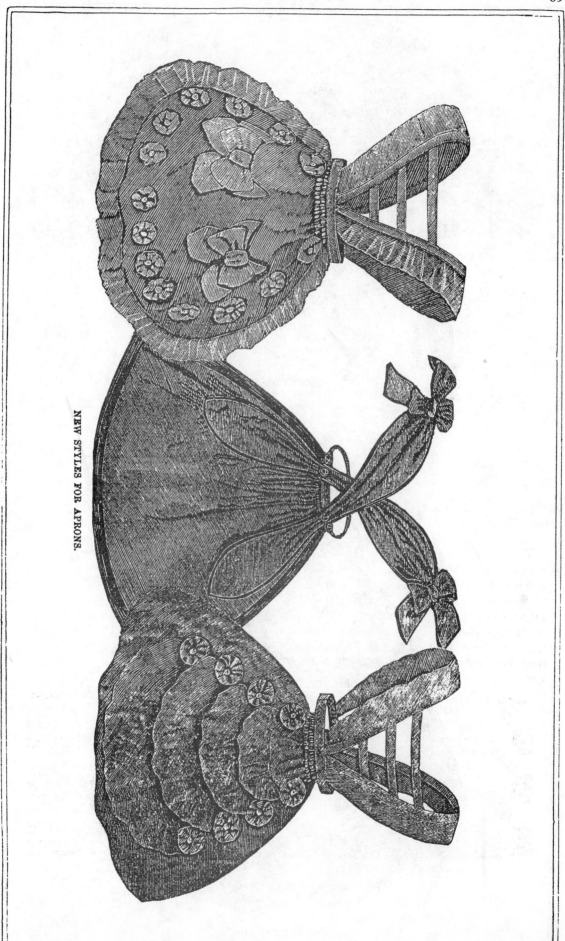

NEW STYLES FOR APRONS.

90

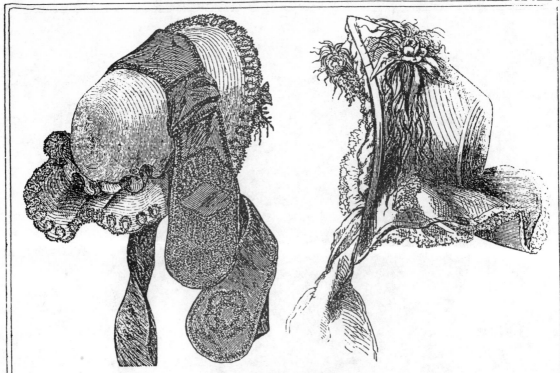

SUMMER BONNETS.

SILK MANTILLA.

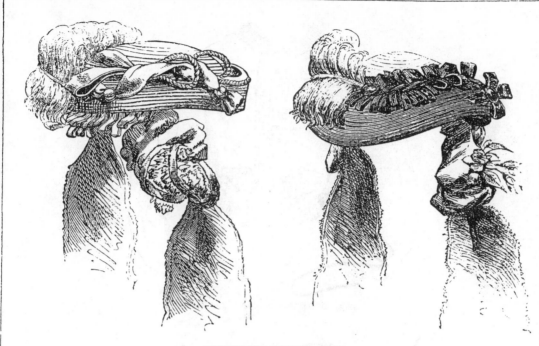

CHILDREN'S SUMMER HATS.

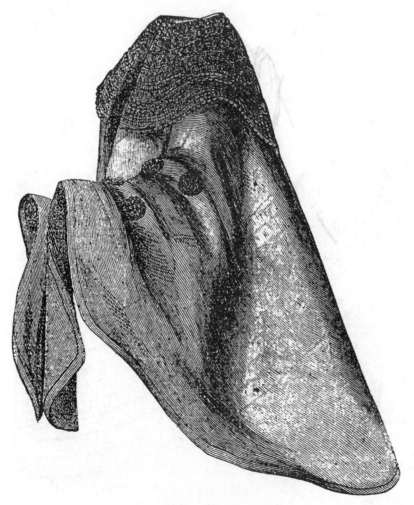

SHAWL MANTILLA.

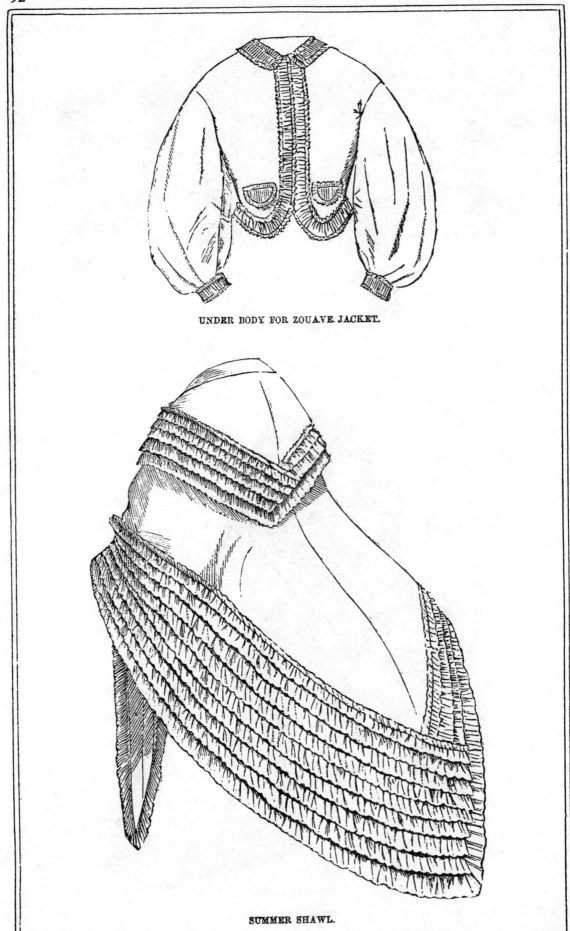

UNDER BODY FOR ZOUAVE JACKET.

SUMMER SHAWL.

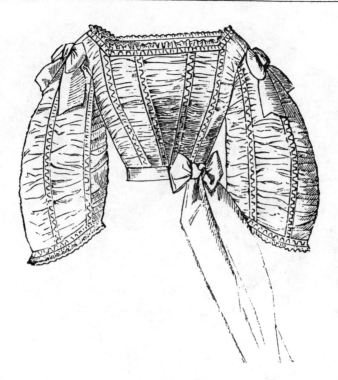

RUSSIAN BODY.

MUSLIN MANTLE.

THE ITALIAN: BACK AND FRONT.

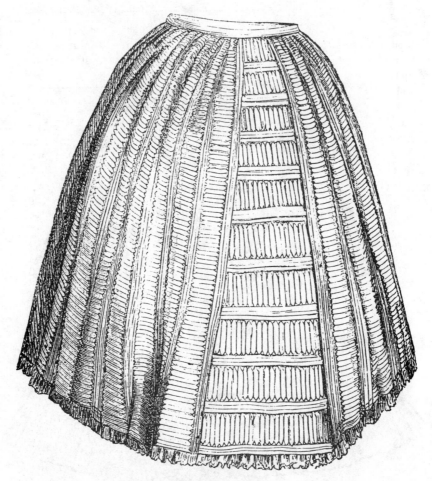

NEW STYLE SKIRT.

COTTAGE IN THE RURAL GOTHIC STYLE.

BY R. A. WILLIAMS.

It is our purpose to present to our readers, occasionally, original designs for suburban residences and cottages, prepared by eminent architects, expressly for "Peterson." The cottages will be so designed that they may be constructed at a price, placing an ornamental and convenient homestead within the power of any one designing to build. In a country like ours, where the means of building are so general among the people, it is surprising that there is no more attempt made at ornament, both in the dwelling and grounds of the middle classes. The plans we shall give, monthly, will be intended to improve taste in this matter.

We here present our readers with a perspective view of a small cottage in the rural Gothic style, from a design by R. A. Williams, Esq. Its general effect is pleasing, and it will furnish accommodations for a small family—the sizes of the rooms are given. The second story would contain three bed-rooms with stairs and store room. Built of wood and plainly finished inside, it would cost about $7.50. If unplaned boards, it should be yellow-washed, which, with white window-frames, etc., and the rustic pillars of cedar or other wood, would give a very picturesque appearance. The plans below make the interior arrangement sufficiently plain.

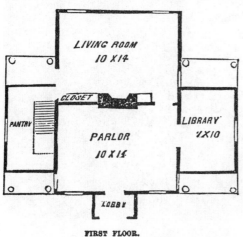

FIRST FLOOR.

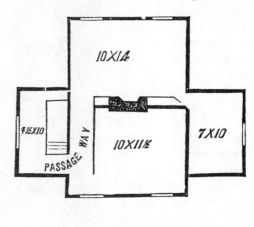

SECOND STORY.

CROCHET PINCUSHION.

BY MRS. JANE WEAVER.

This is formed of two rows of stars similar to the one given on the next page. There are nine in the upper row, which forms the top of the cushion, and twelve in the lower row, which lies as a frill all round.

The two rows are joined together with chains of crochet; the top edge is carried over within the circle, which is left open for either a scent-bottle or vase of flowers.

A ribbon is laced in and out between the two rows of stars, and serves to draw the crochet tight over the cushion, and finishes with a bow.

The following are the instructions for forming the stars, a pattern of one of which, of the full size, is given on the next page.

Make a ring of fifteen stitches, on this work 25 double stitches; chain 11, loop in, leaving 3 stitches between, repeat 6 times; 2 single, 9 double, 2 single on each of the 11 chain; 1 double, 8 chain, loop in to the center stitch of the 9 double of last row, repeat all round; 1 double, 3 chain on every other loop all round; 2 double, 3 chain, 2 double, 3 chain between every other double stitch of last row; 1 row over the last, with 3 double, 3 chain, 3 double.

A knotted fringe tied into every loop forms a

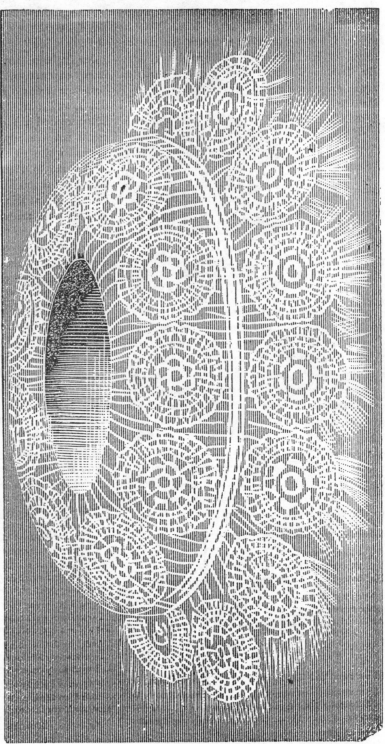

pretty finish to this very ornamental pin-cushion.

The silk lining and the ribbon should match in color. Crochet cotton, No. 16, is a suitable size. The Pincushion, when finished, makes one of the prettiest things of the season.

STAR FOR PINCUSHION.

VARIETIES.

IN SILK EMBROIDERY.

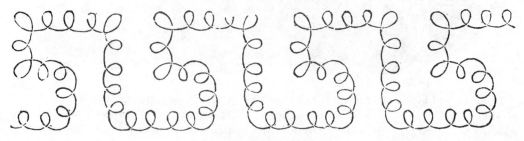

BRAIDING PATTERN.

EDGING.

POLONAISE DINNER DRESS.

BY EMILY H. MAY.

THIS new and fashionable dress is to be made of silk. On the next page we give diagrams, which, when enlarged, will enable any lady to cut out the dress. These diagrams represent half the dress.

No. 1. FRONT.
No. 2. SIDE-PIECE.
No. 3. SIDE-BACK.
No. 4. BACK.
No. 5. GORE FOR SKIRT.
No. 6. SLEEVE.
No. 7. GORE FOR SLEEVE.

As we have already observed, there are two fronts, two side-pieces, two backs, etc. But there are six gores for the skirt, or one to go between every seam, except the seams down the back and up the front. In putting the pieces together, join the front and side-piece at D D, as far down as X X, at which part insert the gore, No. 5, putting in the fullness at the top, in a large box-plait, and then joining the gore to the front down to B B. In the same manner, insert the other gores, between the side-piece and side-back, the side-back and back, and so around. Join, under the arm, the side-piece to the side-back, at E E as far as X X, where,

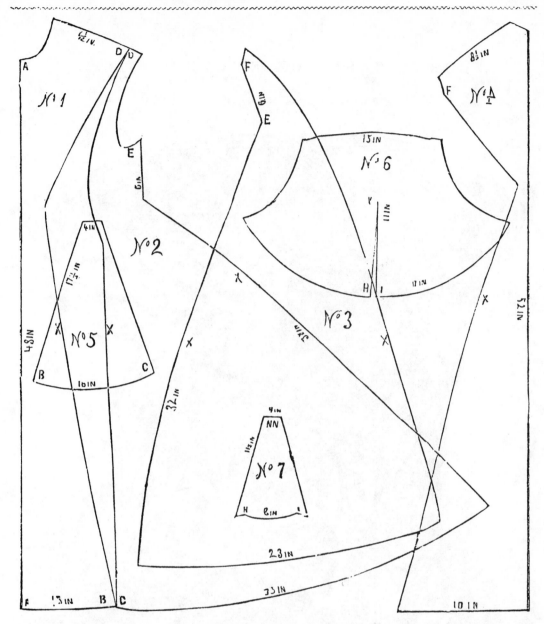

DIAGRAM OF POLONAISE DINNER DRESS.

as we have just said, another gore is put in. Join the side-back to back at F F, as far as X X, where insert a gore as before.

This completes half of the skirt. The length of the skirt is to be determined, of course, by the size of the wearer. The diagram is prepared for a person of ordinary size.

To make the sleeve, insert the small gore, No. 7, at Y Y, with a box-plait, and continue the seam to H H, on one side, and I I on the other. This gore comes on the back of the arm, in the center of the sleeve.

This Polonaise is to be trimmed with ribbon, as seen in the engraving. The ribbon should be of the same color as the dress. A quilling of ribbon is put on around the sleeve.

NUMERALS FOR MARKING.

1 2 3 4 5 6 7 8 9 0

CORAL CASE FOR FLOWER-POTS.

BY MADEMOISELLE ROCHE.

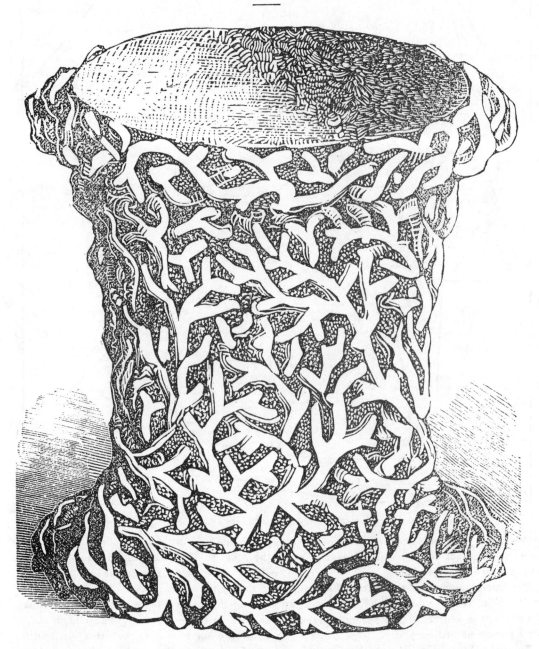

SOME short time back we gave a pretty design for a Coral Shell Stand, executed in a similar way, and intended to form a set of the same ornaments. The shape must be formed of strong covered wire, and it is commenced by twisting the wire into a circle, from whence rows of irregular loops are formed by linking it through and giving it one tie, making the loops rather larger in each round, to allow for the spread of the flower-pot toward the top, and making the last row the largest, so as to bend back in the way of a rim. Having finished the upper part, recommence again at the wire circle at the bottom, and work a wider piece sufficiently large to spread over the flower-pot saucer, giving it a sort of arch for that purpose. When this framework has been thus far advanced, fit it on to a flower-pot, so as to give it perfect regularity of shape, in the way of a mould, bending the rim back in the desired curve, and fitting the lower part over an inverted saucer of the required size. After this, short lengths of cotton cord are to be tied on to some of the more open parts, so as to give the irregular appearance of the coral branches. All this being done, some white wax is to be melted and a sufficient quantity of Chinese vermilion mixed in, so as to give it a rich color, and this must be poured on the wire framework with an iron spoon, holding it up and down and every way until the whole is perfectly covered. After having thus given the first coating, the ends of the cotton cord may be bent out in various positions and finally arranged, and a second coating of the wax be added, to give the thickness of the coral. In making these coral cases, the framework of wire must be fitted on to a flowerpot two or three sizes larger than the one which it is intended to accompany, both because the wax partially fills in the interior, and also to have space for a lining of the green moss, which is to be introduced between the earthen pot and the coral case.

TATTING.

Cast on eight stitches, purl one, eight more, and purl until there are thirty-two; then draw up closely. Continue until the tatting is as long as is required, then turn back and make eight stitches, purl one, eight more, and join to the center purl, and continue so until completed.

CHILDREN'S FASHIONS FOR JUNE.

HEART-SHAPED SCENT-SACHET.

BY MADEMOISELLE ROCHE.

THESE pretty little sachets should be made by every lady, to be scattered through her drawers, so as to impart a general fragrance to the various articles of her wardrobe. The trouble is very slight, and the material no more than any trifling remnant of silk of the size shown in our illustration, and three-quarters of a yard of ribbon to form the bow. The little group of flowers which we have given is to be embroidered on the sides as lightly as possible: the two parts are to be laid face to face, and stitched together with accuracy to their shape, leaving an opening at the top; after this they are to be turned and filled with fine cotton wool, impregnated with any perfume most agreeable to taste; after which the aperture is to be closed, and the rosette of ribbon laid upon the place. Ladies who are not inclined to undertake the embroidery may take any piece of fancy silk, or even such as are quite plain, and make them up in the same way, without this decoration.

ALPHABET FOR MARKING.

CROCHET FOR CUSHION.

BY MRS. JANE WEAVER.

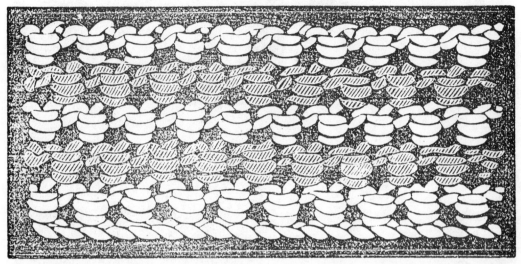

This must be done in bands, the wool must be broken at the end of each band. If one wishes to make lamp-mats, the work must be begun by several chain-stitches joined in a circle, augmenting the ball at each row without breaking the wool.

Do a row of chain-stitches to begin the work.

Turn the wool three times around the needle, take your stitch in the third stitch, it must not be tightened; keep a good hold; draw your crochet, drawing at the same time the ends of the wool above it. Make a plain stitch; begin again in the second stitch, turning the wool three times around the needle.

IN CROCHET.

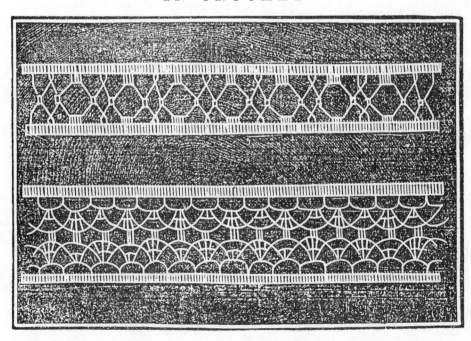

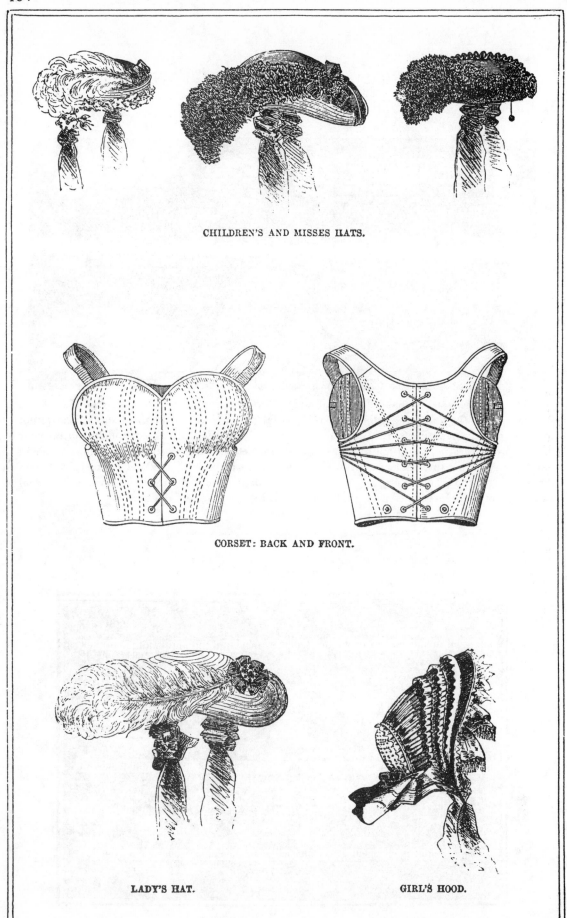

104

CHILDREN'S AND MISSES HATS.

CORSET: BACK AND FRONT.

LADY'S HAT.

GIRL'S HOOD.

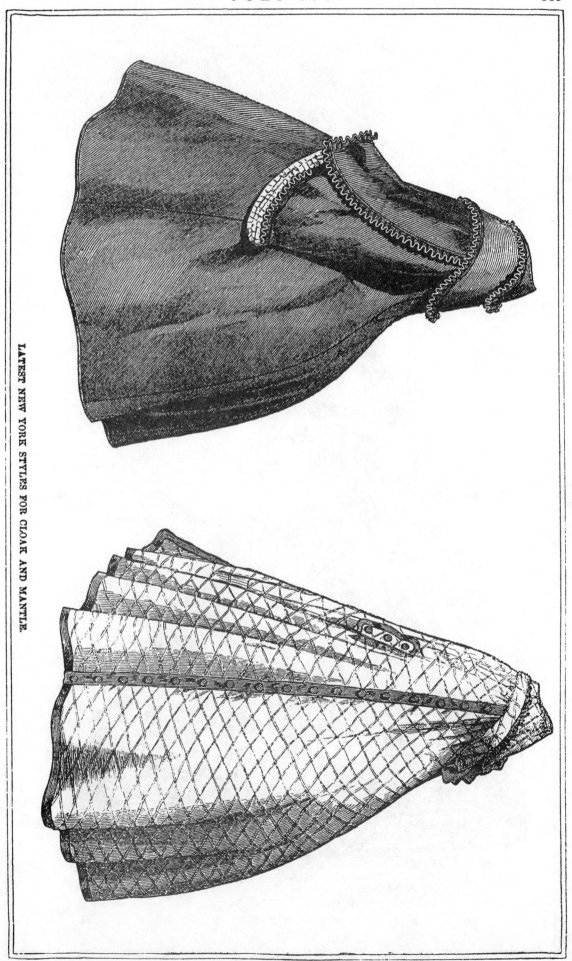

LATEST NEW YORK STYLES FOR CLOAK AND MANTLE.

106

INITIALS FOR MARKING.

THE DUCHESS.

Fanny

NAME FOR MARKING.

THE CHRISTIANA.

HEAD-DRESS: NO. I.

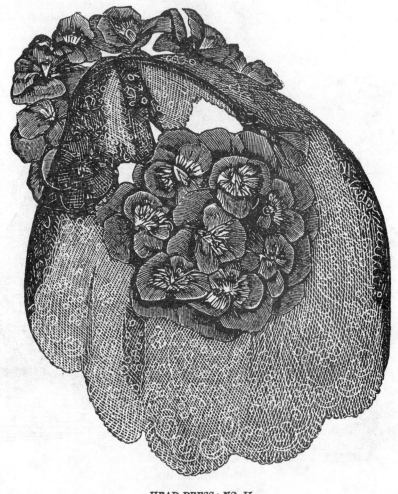

HEAD-DRESS: NO. II.

Engraved & Printed by Illman Brothers.

AT MAMA'S TOILET

Engraved expressly for Peterson's Magazine.

THE RUY-BLAS MANTLE.

BY EMILY H. MAY.

THIS is made of a light fabric, of a white ground, with small stripes. The trimming may be either a ruche fastened by a narrow cherry velvet, or a small headed flounce with narrow velvets also.

The size of the page not allowing us to give the pattern of this cloak full length, our readers are requested to add ten inches at the bottom of the back and of the front.

No 1. FRONT.

No. 2 and 2 *bis.* BACK; the corresponding letters mark the places where the pattern joins the front. The middle of the back is cut on the bias and made without a seam.

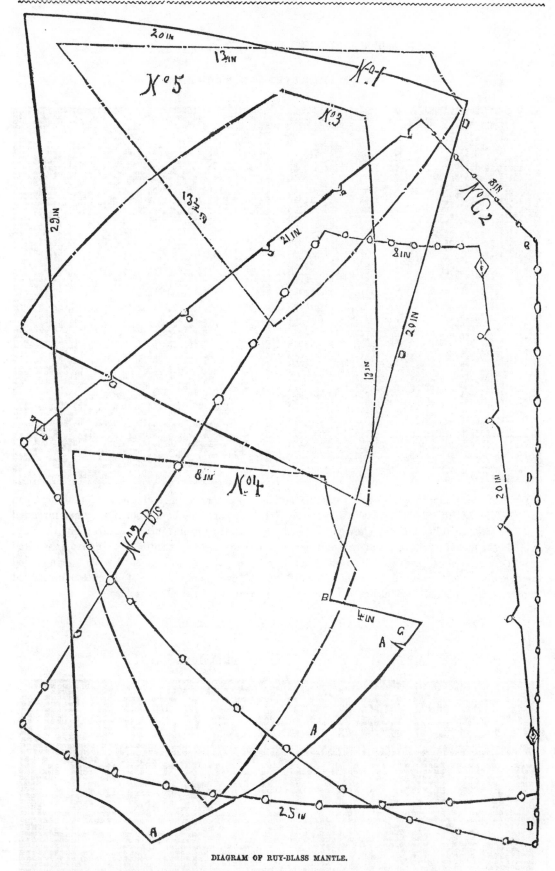

DIAGRAM OF RUY-BLASS MANTLE.

No. 3. Piece of the Back cut on the bias in the middle and made with a seam.

No. 4. Front of the Pelerine.

No. 5. Back of the Pelerine.

PATTERNS IN CROCHET.

BY MADEMOISELLE ROCHE.

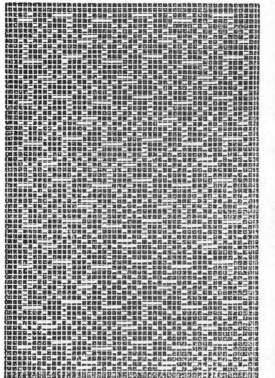 

WE have this month given two patterns for the centers of either antimacassars, berceau-nette covers, or toilet mats. They are worked in solid and chain crochet, and are extremely durable, as well as pretty. The cotton used for working them should be about No. 10. They may be finished with either a fringe or a lace. A border round them, of a light, open description, can be added, if they are intended for drawing-room antimacassars; but they are more simple to execute if a square is worked of the pattern, and finished with a fringe tied in to every loop, a row of crochet being added all round for the purpose.

ALPHABET FOR MARKING.

DESIGN FOR SUBURBAN RESIDENCE

BY ISAAC H. HOBBS.

THIS design contains many advantages over buildings usually of this size and cost. The building is thirty-four feet square, with a small projecting wing, and is built upon a slope of a hill, with basement for kitchen, pantry, cellar, heater, water-closet, and other conveniences. The principal story contains a parlor, library, dining-room, and a fine hall with large and easy stairs. The hall is of such a size and shape as to render it desirable as a place of resort for the family. There is a water-closet on this floor with private stairs to the second-story. The second-story contains four rooms and bath-room; the third-story four rooms. A house of the above design has been built near this city of painted rubble stone, in very substantial and correct manner, at a cost of a fraction over $4,000, and has

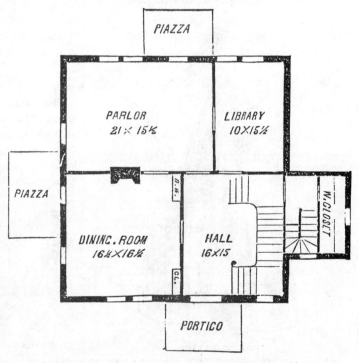

been generally admired; the accompanying plan gives the interior arrangement.

VARIETIES FOR THE SEASON.

BY MME. DEMOREST.

MANY very beautiful patterns are out, not only for July, but generally for the whole season also. We give quite a variety.

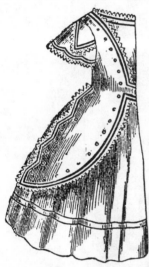

THE LADY ELGIN.

The Lady Elgin dress is for a stately little lady of five or six years, and consists of a plain waist attached to a full gored skirt. Upon the front of the waist is a little fly jacket which terminates in a gored medallion, extending down upon the side skirt. A curved strap joins the jacket at the shoulder, and ornaments the back part of the body, terminating in pendent ends at the waist. The sleeve is short and slightly full, with a pointed cap. The dress should be made in some solid color, the trimming contrasting.

PLAIN NIGHT DRESS.

The above illustration of a plain Night Dress will recommend itself to our lady readers by its richness, simplicity, excellent fit, and durability. The yoke is made double, and fits perfectly to the shoulders, while the curved front gives a rounded and graceful outline to the form. The fullness in the sleeve renders it not only more becoming than the plain, straight sleeve, but adds to the strength. The cuff and collar may be worked on the edge, and the garment closed two-thirds the length of the skirt, the buttons being placed on the upper side of a false hem, an inch in width, which is laid over in front. This Night Dress requires six yards of material, four widths in the skirt.

THE JULIE SLEEVE.

The "Julie" Sleeve is in the half-flowing style, which is just now so much in vogue. It is plain at the top, and has a pointed cap which extends down upon the front of the arm. It is very handsome made in silk or poplin, and trimmed with quilled velvet or ribbon.

THE SPANISH WAIST.

The Spanish Waist is a simple bodice, made in velvet or silk. It is cut very low in the neck, and runs over the shoulder just sufficiently to set in a small cap; should be laced in the back, and also trimmed in front with the cord in imitation of the back. A narrow lace is the prettiest finish for this bodice, which should be worn over a full Swiss waist.

COAT SLEEVE.

The "Stella" Sleeve is a very simple and becoming style, particularly adapted to the fine French cloths, and English mixed poplins, which will be the popular spring wear. It has a double-pointed cap at the top, arranged so that the points of the upper cap fill the spaces of the one below, and a pointed cuff at the wrist. A narrow binding of silk and velvet, with a scalloped edge, ornaments the cap, and cuffs, and the hollows of the points are occupied by small flat velvet buttons.

To be worn with knee pants or skirts, according to the age of the child. The prettiest shirt for this is linen cambric, amply gathered, with an embroidered hem, finished with a narrow ruffle. The skirt is laid in deep box-plaits, and sewed to a band, a sash of the same material as the dress, and simply knotted at the side, finishes the waist. The jacket should be quite short, a simple cut-away, prettily ornamented.

BOYS' COAT.

For a girl of five years—plain, but very pretty, has a plain waist, buttoned up at the back; sleeve plain; the skirt is sufficiently circular to fit easily over the dress; a jacket cut nearly diamond shape, with one joint turned over the whole, neatly trimmed with edging. Will require two and a half yards of material.

SELLA APRON.

Has a sack front, cut rather full, and the yoke in the back is cut with the front; there being no seam on the shoulder, the back is fitted on at yoke and confined at the waist by a belt of the same material as the apron. Will fit a child from six to eight years of age, and requires two and a half yards of material.

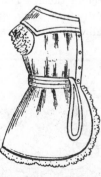

EUGENIE: BACK VIEW.

LAURA APRON.

This has three box plaits in front, one in the center, and one on each side. These give fullness to the skirt, which is cut all in one, with the front. The armhole is also cut in the front, as the waist has no back. The skirt is finished with a plain piece cut sufficiently circular to set well over the hip and joint as represented in the figure. A band finishes this at the waist. Suitable for a child seven years. Takes one and a half yards of material.

Willie's Apron may be made in linen or gingham. It is simple in shape, and laid in box-plaits—back and front—which are trimmed down the center with two rows of narrow braid terminating in a small flat button. Small bishop sleeves finished with a square cuff turned over, and trimmed with braid to match the body.

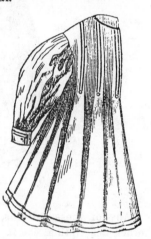

WILLIE'S APRON.

The "Pet of the Parlor" is a simple and charming style of low corsage for a Miss in her teens. It is equally adapted to silk, muslin, barege, or French calico. The waist is plain, with the exception of the puffings, which at the side cross the shoulder and extend down the back to the belt. The sleeves are composed of two puffings, edged with needle-work or lace, according to the material of which the dress is composed.

THE "PET OF THE PARLOR."

The "Venitienne" is one of the latest and most stylish novelties in lady's cloaks. It is of rich lustrous black silk, with gores of lilac silk inserted, ornamented with elegant crochet designs, with fine open centers, through which the color is distinctly visible. The sleeves are wide and box-plaited. The skirt is box-plaited on a tight-fitting waist, over which is placed a crochet cape, of the pelerine form.

THE VENITIENNE.

Any of these patterns, or patterns of any other description, cut in paper, full-size, may be had by addressing Mme. Demorest, No. 473 Broadway, New York. Letters, in all cases, to be post paid. The money to accompany the order.

SLIPPER PATTERN.

BY MRS. JANE WEAVER.

THIS slipper, given in the front of the number, is made of black velvet, with colored pieces in applique, and braided with gold braid. Cut some pieces of silk or merino, the same color and shape as indicated in the pattern, tack them firmly on to the velvet, run the gold braid neatly round them, and work the bars and dots in coarse purse-silk or twist. Our design shows the toe-piece and half the side, the other half being exactly similar. The easiest way to work this is to trace the pattern on tissue paper, to tack the paper on to the velvet, then the various pieces in their respective places, and so braid round them. The paper should then be carefully torn away, and the palms, crescents, etc., filled in with coarse purse-silk.

EDGING.

CROCHETED TIDY.

BY MRS. JANE WEAVER.

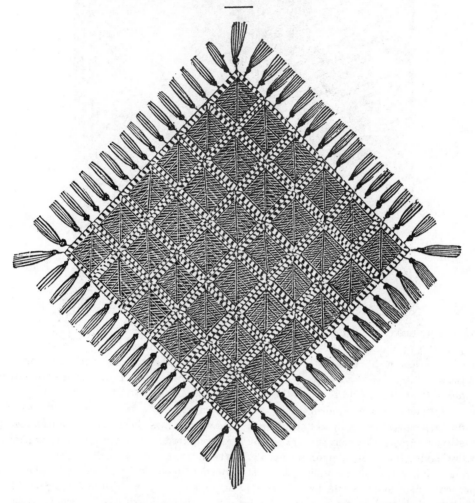

MATERIALS.—Four spools white crochet cotton, No. 16; small hook.

Make a ch of 3 stitches, pass the hook through the last stitch and work backward.

1st Row.—Work in sc, widening by working 3 stitches in the center stitch.

2nd Row.—Work in sc, widening by working 3 stitches (as before) in the center stitch made by widening in 1st row. Always observing to work into the under loop of ch made by previous row.

Repeat this for 30 rows; then work 1 row in dc all around; 1 ch between every dc stitch; 3 stitches at the corner. This completes the block. When enough blocks are finished join with sc stitch. Finish with tassel fringe.

NEW DESIGN FOR AN AFFGHAN.

BY MRS. JANE WEAVER.

MATERIALS.—Double zephyr in eight colors, red, blue, orange, purple, green, brown, white, and black, half pound of each color. To be done in princess royal stitch.

The long crochet needle is used for this stitch.

This design is in blocks, which are crocheted together.

FOR A BLOCK.—Make a ch of 25 stitches as in common crochet.

1st Row.—Place the needle under the first

loop of chain, make the loop, retaining the stitch upon the needle. Repeat this until all the 25 stitches are in this manner taken up on the needle.

2nd Row.—Draw the thread through the first two stitches upon the needle; drop them, and retain the loop upon the needle. Repeat until all the stitches are in this manner worked off the needle, leaving the last loop upon the needle.

3rd Row.—Place the needle under the first long perpendicular loop, (made by 2nd row,) draw the thread through it, retaining the stitch thus made upon the needle. Repeat until all the long loops are in this manner taken up.

4th Row.—Same as 2nd.

5th Row.—Same as 3rd.

Work in this manner until a square is complete. Then work 1 row all round (with the black wool) in sc stitch.

Every block to be finished in the same way. The number of blocks to be determined by the size required. In the arrangement of the colors, care must be taken that they harmonize. Every alternate block to be white. The blocks are to be joined together with the black wool in sc; or if preferred, join with yellow wool. Finish with small balls of wool, white and black, as seen in the design.

PATTERNS FOR HEAD-DRESSES.

BY MRS. JANE WEAVER.

In the front of the number are two patterns for new and stylish head-dresses, the manner of making which we shall now describe.

HEAD-DRESS No. 1.—*Materials.*—Two shades rose-color silk, half yard each; some ribbon wire, and black net.

Cut the silk bias in strips four inches wide, point on both sides, then quill in double box-plaits. Arrange upon the head-piece as seen in the design. This pointed quilling has the effect of flowers, and is very easily made.

HEAD-DRESS No. 2.—*Materials.*—One yard black trimming lace; two large bunches pansies, or soft-crushed roses.

Make a bandeau to fit the head large enough to come well on the head in front, passing under the knot of hair at the back of the head. Cover with black silk or velvet. Gather the lace, sew it upon the bandeau, letting the greater part of the fullness fall at the back. Cut a circle of black net, place it on the back of head-dress quite down upon the lace, plaiting it in as you would the crown of a cap. Cover this entirely with the flowers, reserving enough for the bandeau across the top of the head-dress.

TOILET MAT IN CROCHET AND BEADS.

BY MRS. JANE WEAVER.

THIS is a very pretty pattern, which can be ⸮ description. It will be seen, easily, where the worked from the engraving, without further ⸮ beads are to go.

BRAIDING PATTERN FOR CHILD'S DRESS.

BY MRS. JANE WEAVER.

120

THE COZY NOOK.

WORDS AND MUSIC

BY ALICE HAWTHORNE.

PUBLISHED BY PERMISSION OF SEP. WINNER, PROPRIETOR OF THE COPYRIGHT.

1st. A co - zy nook, A mountain brook, That wan - ders toward the sea; A I
2d. Whene'er I meet The eyes that greet My com - ing un - a - ware,

lit - tle cot In the qui - et spot, Have all a charm for me. A
then re - joice, To hear the voice That gives me wel - come there. And

Chorus.

FASHIONS FOR AUGUST.

COTTAGE TOILET-TABLE.

124

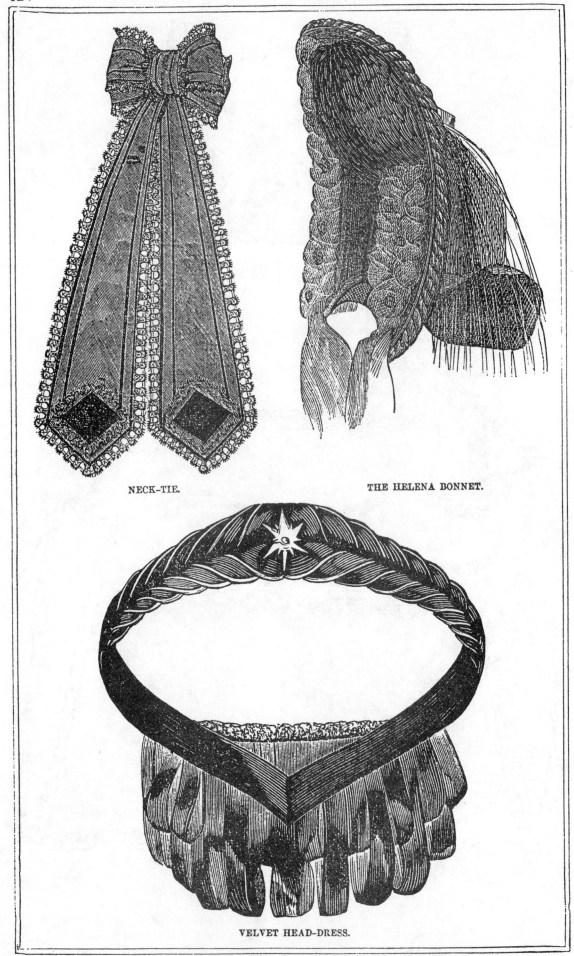

NECK-TIE.

THE HELENA BONNET.

VELVET HEAD-DRESS.

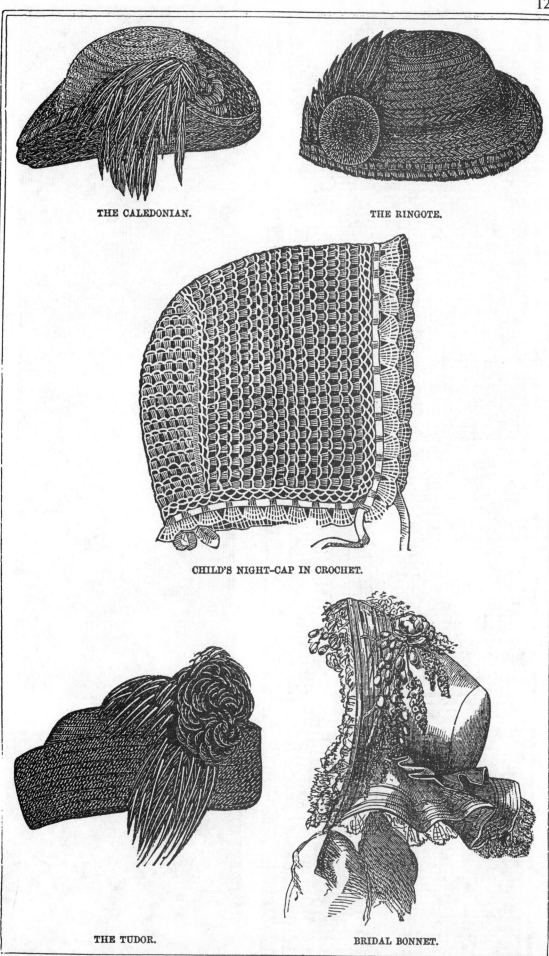

THE CALEDONIAN.

THE RINGOTE.

CHILD'S NIGHT-CAP IN CROCHET.

THE TUDOR.

BRIDAL BONNET.

126

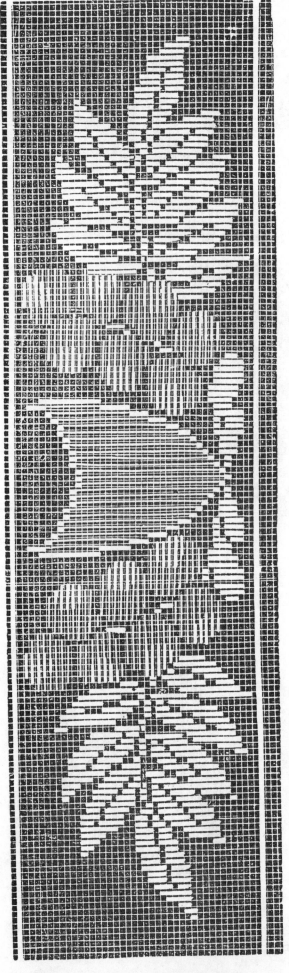

PATTERN FOR DINNER NAPKIN-RING.

PATTERN FOR BRAIDING.

HANDKERCHIEF CORNER.

THE USE AND ABUSE OF COLORS IN DRESS.

BY MRS. MERRIFIELD.

OF the two attributes of ornamental art, namely, color and form, color has always been the more attractive, especially to the uneducated eye. An appreciation of the beauty of form is generally the effect of cultivation; but the love of color is innate. There are few eyes possessed of the blessing of sight which are not affected by it, more or less. This is true of animals as well as of men. The effect of red upon the bovine race is well known. In Spanish bull fights, the agile *matador* rouses the courage of his four-footed opponent by waving before his eyes a red scarf or flag. The terror shown by wild beasts at the presence of fire—the traveler's protection—has been ascribed to the sight of the ruddy glare of the flames. In infants, one of the first acts of consciousness is the recognition of artificial light when concentrated, as in the flame of a candle, and contrasted with surrounding gloom; or of bright colors displayed before the eye. Grown older, the child loves colored toys, and colored pictures, and generally prefers the more gaudy colors, such as red and yellow, to the sober ones. The South Sea Islander robes himself in a mantle of feathers, gay with all the colors of the rainbow. To many races a string of colored beads is a coveted decoration. The American Indian is terrible in his war-paint; with glaring contrasts of red and yellow, black and white, he thinks to add to the deadly effect of his arms. Who can say whether the blue pigment with which the ancient Briton dyed the exposed parts of his body may not have been applied with similar intentions?

Among some nations color was significant of rank or condition. The Romans permitted none but those of the highest rank to wear the Tyrian purple; and the pigment vermilion was reserved for the statues of the gods. With the Mahommedans, a green turban denotes a descendant of Ali, the kinsman of the prophet. In the Romish Church the cardinals wear scarlet; and in European countries may be seen the servants of the bishops clothed in regal purple. The religious societies, renouncing the pomps and vanities of the world, clothe themselves in quiet gray and brown, black and white. Colors are the outward and visible signs of mourning. The Euro-peans mourn in black; the Chinese in white; the Egyptians in yellow; the Turks in blue or violet. Colors also have emblematical significations; but into these I cannot now enter.

In tropical countries, where the birds and insects are brilliantly colored, the inhabitants have a peculiar delight in decorating their persons with bright colors. If we examine relics of art, not only of early date, but those of the best period—the era of Raphael for instance—we find draperies of the primitive (red, blue, yellow) or secondary (green, orange, and purple) colors. The same remark is applicable to architectural decoration, where colors are enhanced by opposition to white and black. The Egyptian and Assyrian courts of the Crystal Palace will supply us with examples.

But bright colors, though they may gratify the savage, will not please the educated eye, unless they be combined in harmonious proportion. The skill of the artist—especially the decorative artist, under which term is included the *modiste*—will accordingly be shown in combining the various colors in such proportions and apposition as will produce the most pleasing effect to the eye. Nor will the modifying influences of light and shade, as shown in the rounded forms of the human figure and the relieved surfaces of architecture, escape the attention of the true artist. It will be seen how the colors are vivified by light and saddened by shade; and how the brilliant colors are intensified by contrast with the more somber ones.

In process of time artists became aware of the value of the various shades of gray and brown—"the broken colors," as we call them—in producing harmonious effects, and giving value to the purer colors by contrast. These tints are called "broken colors," because they are compounded of two or three others.

The Oriental nations—namely, the Chinese, the Indians, and the Saracens—have always been remarked for their exquisite taste in colors; so much so that Mr. Owen Jones, and other artists who have made colors their study, have analyzed with great care the decorative works of these people, and have discovered the principles which govern their various combinations of color. It has been ascertained that the peculiar effect of

Oriental coloring is produced, not by the mixture of one color with another, but by their harmonious juxtaposition in proper proportion—so that a surface which, when placed near the eye, appears to be covered with a symmetrically-arranged mosaic of the primitive or secondary colors, presents, at a distance, or when modified by light and shade, a kind of neutralized bloom; thus producing, but by a different process, the broken tints employed by the European painter. In the one case, these broken tints are merely an optical effect, varying as they are viewed from different distances; in the other, the painter combines the tints on his palette, or the dyer in his vat, and the positive colors of which they are composed are no longer capable of being distinguished by the eye. In both cases great skill is required to produce harmonious effect.

Although we hear of "an eye for color" and "an ear for music," as if the power of appreciating harmonious colors and sounds were a peculiar gift from nature, yet we know that both faculties may be cultivated to a considerable extent. And, considering that every one employs colors, either in dress or household decoration, while only a limited number of persons learn music, and that chiefly as an amusement; it does seem almost indispensable that every one should understand the general principles which regulate the harmonious combination of colors. It is just as reasonable to expect persons who "have not an eye for color"—or, speaking more correctly, who do not understand the laws which govern the employment of colors—to use them harmoniously, as it would be for those who have no ear, natural or acquired, for music, to produce harmony by striking at random the notes of a musical instrument. Every color has a distinct effect upon the eye, as every note has its distinct sound to the ear: but the beauty of both consists in their harmonious combination, and this is always the result of refined taste—sometimes innate—and of cultivation. Discordant colors are as painful to the educated eye as discordant notes to a musical ear.

I wish I could impress this truth upon the reader—that I could induce every one to study harmony of color in its application to personal and domestic decoration. It is a study which must interest everybody, and which is not difficult to master. And yet, how few understand it! How few think there is any art at all in the arrangement of colors! To satisfy oneself of these facts, it is only necessary to walk for half an hour along some public thoroughfare and observe the glaring contrasts of bright colors by which the dress of many persons is distinguished. Children, especially, seem the sport of caprice in this way. On their little persons frequently meet all the colors of the rainbow, without their harmony. The mantle—the dress—the bonnet, with its trimmings—the stockings; all of divers colors, and no two of them in harmony! Verily, Jacob is not the only parent whose darlings have coats of many colors! These good people probably think that fine feathers make fine birds.

There is one class of persons, possessed of more money than taste, who estimate colors by their cost only, and will purchase the most expensive merely because they are expensive and fashionable. Of this class was a certain lady, of whom it is related that, in reply to Sir Joshua Reynolds' inquiry as to what color the dress of herself and husband, who were then sitting, should be painted, asked which were the most expensive colors? "Carmine and ultramarine," replied the artist. "Then," rejoined the lady, "paint me in ultramarine, and my husband in carmine!"

We hear constantly of fashionable colors, and these fashionable colors are forever changing; moreover, we hear more of their novelty than of their beauty. All who wish to be fashionable wear these colors *because* they are fashionable, and *because* they are new; but they do not consider whether they are adapted to the complexion and age of the wearer, or whether they are in harmony with the rest of the dress. What should we say to a person who, with the right hand, plays an air in C major, and, with the left, an accompaniment in F minor? The merest novice in music would be conscious of the discord thus produced; yet, as regards colors, the educated eye is constantly shocked by combinations of color as startling and inharmonious.

As regards dress, inharmonious combinations of color may arise from two causes: namely, first, from employing at the same time two or more colors which do not harmonize with each other; or, secondly, one color alone which does not harmonize with the complexion of the individual. The former is most annoying to the spectator, and actually sets one's teeth on edge; the latter is chiefly prejudicial to the personal appearance of the wearer. When we employ colors merely *because* they are fashionable, and without reference to complexion, age, or their vicinity to other colors, one of these effects is sure to arise. It would require considerably more space than is allotted to this article fully to illustrate the effect of colors in their application to dress only, to say nothing of their employment in the internal decoration of houses. I must, however, endeavor to give the reader some idea of the importance of cultivating "an eye for colors," in their relation to the first of these subjects.

As the object of all decoration in dress is to improve, or set off to the greatest advantage, the personal appearance of the wearer, it follows that the colors employed should be suitable to the complexion; and, as complexions are so various, it is quite impossible that the fashionable color, though it may suit a few individuals, can be becoming to all. Instead, therefore, of blindly following fashion, as a sheep will follow the leader of the flock, even to destruction, I should like to see every lady select and wear the precise shade of color which is not only best adapted to her peculiar complexion, but is in perfect harmony with the rest of her habiliments, and in accordance with her years and condition.

I have stated that the Orientals, and other inhabitants of tropical countries, such as the negroes of the West Indies, love to clothe themselves in brilliant and positive colors—reds and yellows, for instance. They are quite right in so doing. These bright colors contrast well with their dusky complexions. With us "palefaces" it is different: we cannot bear positive colors in immediate contact with the skin without injury to the complexion.

Of all colors, perhaps the most trying to the complexion are the different shades of lilac and purple. The fashionable and really beautiful *mauve* and its varieties are, of course, included in this category. In accordance with the well known law of optics that all colors, simple or compound, have a tendency to tint surrounding objects with a faint spectrum of their complementary color, those above-mentioned, which require for their harmony various tints of yellow and green, impart these supplementary colors to the complexion. It is scarcely necessary to observe that, of all complexions, those which turn upon the yellow are the most unpleasant in their effect—and probably for this reason, that in this climate it is always a sign of bad health.

But, it will be asked, is there no means of harmonizing colors so beautiful in themselves with the complexion, and so avoiding these ill effects? To a certain extent this may be done; and as follows:—

Should the complexion be dark, the purple tint may be dark also, because, by contrast, it makes the complexion appear fairer; if the skin be pale or fair, the tint should be lighter. In either case the color should *never* be placed next the skin, but should be parted from it by the hair and by a ruche of *tulle*, which produce the neutralizing effect of gray. Should the complexion still appear too yellow, green leaves or green ribbons may be worn as trimmings. These will often neutralize lilac and purple colors, and thus prevent their imparting an unfavorable hue to the skin.

Scarcely less difficult than *mauve* to harmonize with the complexion is the equally beautiful color called "magenta." The complementary color would be yellow-green; "magenta," therefore, requires very nice treatment to make it becoming. It must be subdued when near the skin, and this is best done by intermixture with black; either by diminishing its brightness by nearly covering it with black lace, or by introducing the color in very small quantity only. In connection with this color, I have recently observed some curious effects. First, as to its appearance alone: if in great quantity, the color, though beautiful in itself, is glaring, and difficult to harmonize with its accompaniments. Secondly, as to its combination with black: if the black and the magenta-color be in nearly equal quantities—such, for instance, as in checks of a square inch of each color—the general effect is dull, and somewhat neutral. If, on the contrary, the checks consist of magenta and white, alternately, a bright effect will be produced. Again, if the ground be black, with very narrow stripes or cross-bars of magenta-color, a bright, but yet subdued effect, will result. This last effect is produced on the principle that, as light is most brilliant when contrasted with a large portion of darkness—like the stars in a cloudless sky—so a small portion of bright color is enhanced by contrast with a dark, and especially a black ground.

LOVE'S CREATIVE POWER.

'TIS true that to the sons of earth
  The curse of death was given;
Yet love, through some mysterious power,
  Fled to its native Heaven.
And so it is when ties of earth
  Are sundered by grim death,

They reunited are above
  By love's creative breath;
And there the soul can roam with joy,
  Through every fairy bower,
And feel that death is conquered by
  Love's pure mysterious power.

F. J.

PATTERN FOR NIGHT-CAP.

BY EMILY H. MAY.

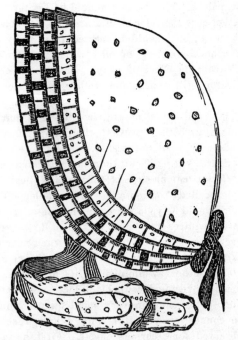

from where the fullness commences (which will be seen in the illustration), run that and the head-piece together, letting the raw edge come on the right side, and then lay a very fine cording over the join.

Cut out the strings, join them on to the head-piece, and then carry one row of lace all round the cap and strings, putting it quite plain on the latter except round the ends. Put the other three rows of lace on, the last row being run on close to the cording, and so hiding the raw edges. A narrow piece of muslin should be

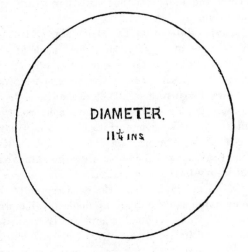

DIAMETER.
11¼ INS.

CROWN OF NIGHT-CAP.

WE give, in this number, by way of variety, a pattern for a Night-Cap. This Night-Cap is made of spotted muslin, and trimmed with lace and narrow satin ribbon. Fifteen inches of muslin, six yards of lace one inch wide, six yards of narrow satin ribbon, and three-quarters of a yard of ribbon one inch wide, will be required to make one cap. Of course, if five or six were made, so much muslin would not be required in proportion, as the material could be cut to better advantage. Cut out the crown the exact size of the pattern, and cut out the head-piece, allowing sufficient turnings for a broad hem down the front. This hem should be quite half an inch wide. Gather the crown

run on the head-piece behind from string to string to form a runner, into which the broad ribbon should be placed to draw the cap in to the size required. Cut the narrow ribbon into lengths of rather more than two inches, and arrange the bows in the lace about one inch apart.

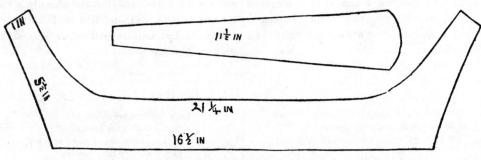

1 IN

11½ IN

5½ IN

21¼ IN

16½ IN

STRING AND HEAD-PIECE OF NIGHT-CAP.

HANGING PINCUSHION AND NEEDLE-BOOK.

BY MADEMOISELLE ROCHE.

THIS little article is extremely ornamental when completed, and possesses the advantage of being also useful. A little case, like a book-cover, is cut out in cardboard; a similar-shaped piece of velvet or silk, a little larger, is also required, on which is worked the sprig given in the illustration. This may be done in white beads, or embroidered in colored silks, or worked in gold thread. This is then stretched over the cardboard, brought over the edge, and gummed down. A little square mattress cushion, covered in silk, is then gummed to one side of the cover; two or three cashmere leaves are stitched to it at the top edge, and the other half of the cover, which is loose, is lined and brought over them. It is now in the form of a book. A bow of ribbon is placed at the back, and it is suspended by a chain of either gold or white beads, to correspond with the sprig. A fringe of the same beads is attached to the two sides, and two tassels are added from where the chain proceeds. This forms a pretty little article for a fancy fair sale, as it may be made very showy; it is also very easy to execute.

INFANT'S HOOD IN CROCHET.

BY MRS. JANE WEAVER.

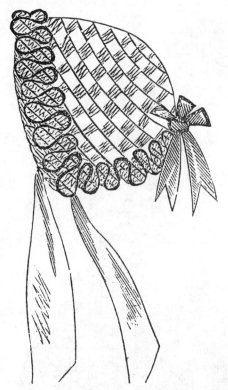

MATERIALS.—One oz. colored split zephyr; half oz. white Shetland wool; fine hook.

FOR THE CROWN.—With the white wool, make a ch of 6 stitches, join. Work in dc, widening enough to keep the work flat for two rows; then work 4 dc stitches in group with 3 ch between, into every stitch for 3rd row.

4th Row.—4 dc into center of every group, 3 ch between. Continue these shells until the head-piece is large enough for child; increase the number of ch stitches between the groups if the work draws. Run an elastic in the edge to fit the head.

FOR THE BORDER.—With the colored wool, make a ch three-quarters of a yard in length.

1st Row.—Work in 1 dc stitch into every ch stitch, 1 ch between.

2nd Row.—2 dc into every stitch, 2 ch between.

3rd Row.—3 dc into every stitch, 3 ch between.

4th Row.—2 dc into every stitch, 2 ch between.

5th Row.—Tie on the white wool and work in dc, 2 dc between every stitch in 4th, 1 ch between. This border will make a very full frill, which is to be disposed all round the hood, sewing it down to keep it in place. Finish with bow and ends at the back of ribbon to match.

A DARNED TIDY.

BY MRS. JANE WEAVER.

CENTER OF DARNED TIDY.

We give, here, a pattern by which a tidy may be darned. The first engraving represents the center: the next the border. The pattern is easy. These are, moreover, about the prettiest tidies that are made; and are always useful.

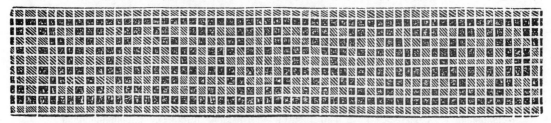

BORDER OF DARNED TIDY.

ALPHABET AND NUMERALS FOR MARKING.

BY MRS. JANE WEAVER.

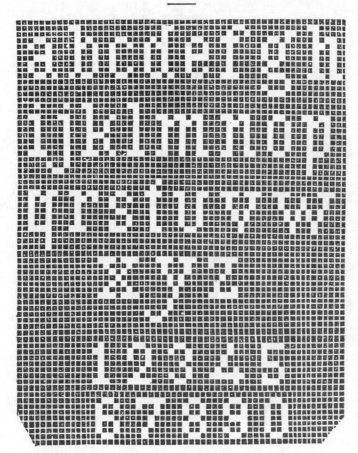

EDGING.

134

CROCHET PURSE.

BY MADEMOISELLE ROCHE.

THESE purses are very pretty worked in any one rich bright color, with the pattern in gold thread; but they allow many varieties, as three or four colors may be introduced. The lower part may be in crimson, the ground on which the pattern rests in a rich violet, with the pattern in gold, and the upper part again in crimson. This arrangement has a very handsome effect. The colors of any piece of work are generally chosen to suit individual taste, but there are certain combinations which are always good. In working any pattern in crochet in two colors, the one not wanted is carried at the back and worked in, being brought to the front again when required. These purses may be completed by either a clasp or a gold cord passed through a row of open crochet, having a little heading of two or three rows. Two tassels of either silk or gold must be added to the sides.

COTTAGE TOILET–TABLE.

BY MRS. JANE WEAVER.

In the front of the number is given a design for a Cottage Toilet-Table, for which we have received numerous requests. The design is original.

MATERIALS.—Twelve yards white Swiss muslin; twelve yards pink or blue; three yards ribbon.

Make the table of pine wood, in shape either a half-circle, square, or curved edged top, as seen in the design. Cover the top with the colored muslin, also make the skirt of the same, quite full; then cover with the white Swiss, which may be braided with linen or colored worsted braid; if colored, it must correspond with the under covering. The frill around the top of table is separate, quarter of a yard in depth, which is also braided and the edge scalloped. Swing the glass; then hang the side curtains, which are fastened to a bracket in shape to correspond with the table, twelve inches in width, to be made of wood, covered with colored muslin, and suspended from the wall. The frill is separate, braided and scalloped on both edges, gathered in the center. Finish with bows of ribbon, disposed as seen in the design. The glass should be small, with narrow gilt frame. Dotted Swiss muslin may be substituted for the plain, and needs no braiding.

VARIETIES IN EMBROIDERY.

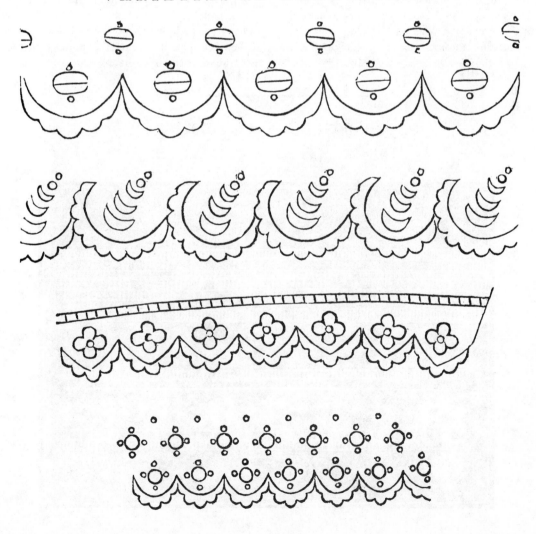

CHILD'S NIGHT-CAP.

BY MADEMOISELLE ROCHE.

FOR this engraving, see front of the number.

MATERIALS.—One oz. of knitting cotton, No. 24, with hook No. 18.

Begin by doing the crown, which is in the form of a horse-shoe. Make a chain of 38 stitches.

1st Row.—† Miss 2, 3 dc in the next, 1 ch, † 12 times. End with miss 2, 3 dc in the last chain.

2nd Row.—Turn the work. 2 ch, † 1 sc under 1 ch, 3 ch, † repeat to the end. Finish with a sc stitch on the first of 2 missed, at the beginning of the last row.

3rd Row.—Turn the work. 2 ch, † 3 dc, on center one of 3 ch, 1 ch, † repeat to the end. Finish with 3 dc on the first, and 2 ch in the previous row.

Repeat the 2nd and 3rd rows 13 times more. Then for 4 times omit the last repetition of the pattern, so as to decrease at each edge 3 stitches in every row. Fasten off.

FOR THE FRONT.—Sc on the original chain, before the last 3 dc of first row. † 3 ch, sc under the stitch in which 3 dc are worked, † repeat all round the crown except the original chain which forms the neck, * turn 3 ch, † sc on center of 3 ch, 3 ch, † to the end of the row, * repeat between the stars.

Having the work now on the wrong side, repeat the 3rd and 2nd rows of the crown until fourteen of each are done. Then three rows completely round the cap, like the first part of the front.

OPEN HEM.—1 dc under chain, † 2 ch, 1 dc under next chain, † repeat all round.

BORDER.—5 tc under 1 chain, † 4 ch, miss 2 ch and 2 dc, 5 tc under the next, † repeat all round.

2nd Row.—† 1 dc after 1 tc, * 1 ch, 1 dc after next tc, * 3 times, 2 ch, † repeat.

3rd Row.—† 1 sc under the chain of 2 in last round, and the chain of 4 in 1 ch, 3 ch, 1 sc under 1 ch, 3 ch, 1 sc under each ch, 3 ch, 1 sc under next, 3 ch, † repeat all round. Run narrow ribbon in the open hem.

CROCHET PATTERNS.

BY MRS. JANE WEAVER.

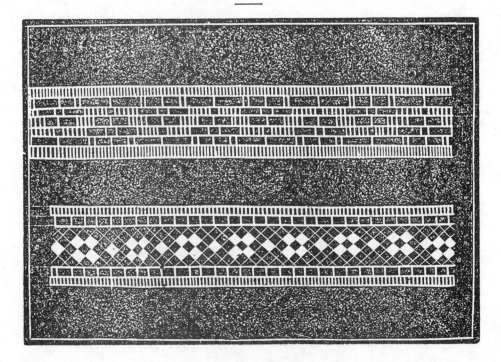

VARIETIES IN EMBROIDERY.

BY MRS. JANE WEAVER.

HANDKERCHIEF CORNER.

LETTERS FOR MARKING.

INSERTION.

NAME FOR MARKING.

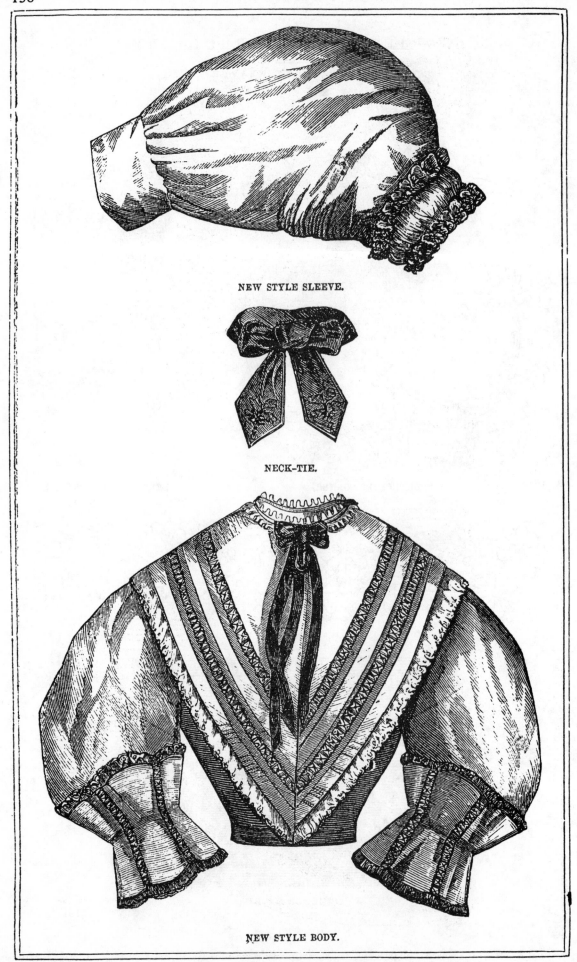

NEW STYLE SLEEVE.

NECK-TIE.

NEW STYLE BODY.

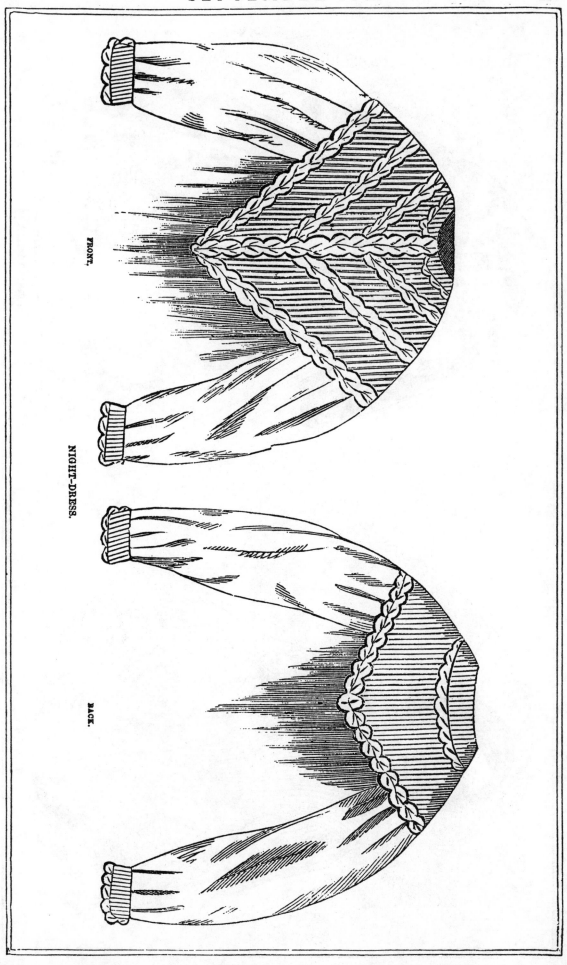

FRONT.

NIGHT-DRESS.

BACK.

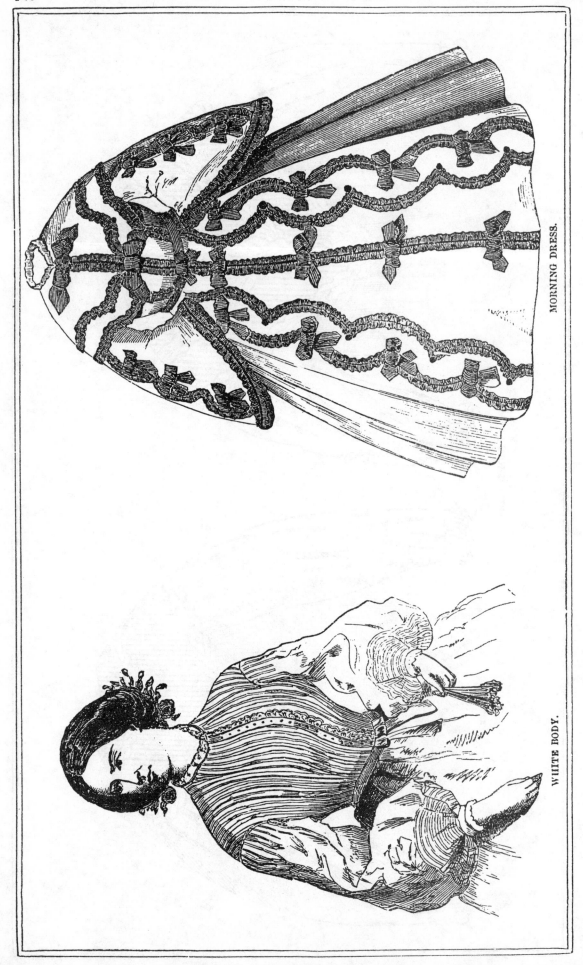

MORNING DRESS.

WHITE BODY.

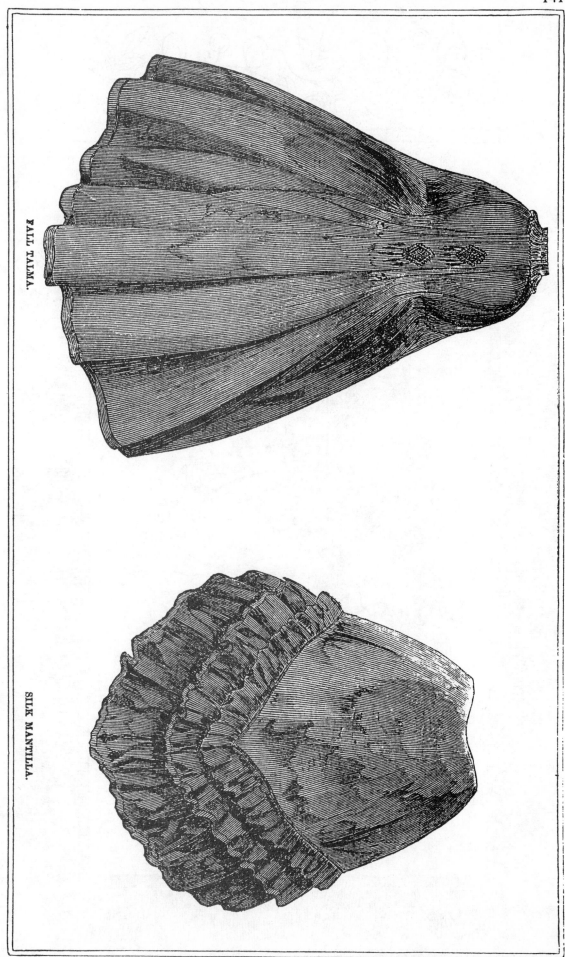

FALL TALMA.

SILK MANTILLA.

142

INSERTION.

ILLUSTRATED D'OYLEY.

THE NOSE OUT OF JOINT

Engraved expressly for Peterson's Magazine.

TOILET–MAT.

BY MRS. JANE WEAVER.

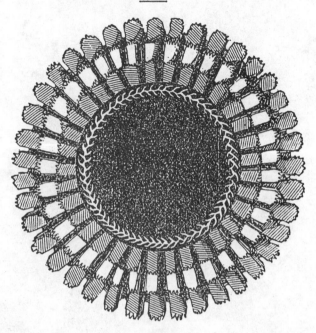

MAKE the center of black velvet, of any size you choose. The little vine, running around this center, is to be done in chain-stitch, with gold thread. The border is to be made of three rows of quilled ribbon, or silk that is pinked on one edge. There are to be two colors employed in this border: crimson for the outside and inside, and white for the center. Line the mat with paste-board covered with silk.

BRAIDING PATTERN.

BY MRS. JANE WEAVER.

KNITTED HOOD.

BY MRS. JANE WEAVER.

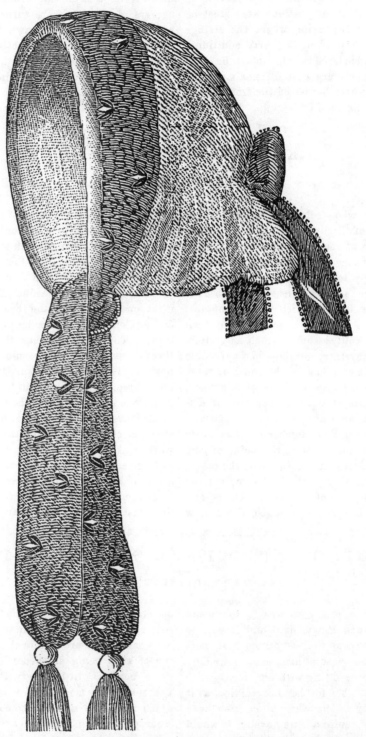

THIS hood is made of plain knitting, in white nd blue Shetland wool. To commence, cast on seventy stitches. Knit sixty rows. Knit twenty rows, increasing one stitch at the end of every row. Cast on at each end forty addi- tional stitches. These form the strings. Knit sixty rows. Cast off at each end the forty ad- ditional stitches. Knit twenty rows, taking two stitches together at each end of every row. There will now be seventy stitches on the needle. Knit sixty rows. Cast off. This piece of knitting is folded in the middle of the strings, and forms two thicknesses of the hood the proper shape; but as four are required, a similar piece must be knitted according to the same directions, only a blue wool must be used instead of the white, where the strings commence—that is, when the forty additional stitches are added. The blue must be continued until these are cast off again. This forms the turn-over border of the front of the hood and the outside of the strings. These two portions of the knitting which we have been describing are folded in the same manner, tacked together, and the blue border ornamented with three long double stitches, two in black and one in white wool, to imitate ermine. The square corners of the back are turned in to form a round. The back is drawn in about three inches in depth from the bottom to form the curtain, and a blue ribbon bow is placed in the center behind. The ends are finished with blue and white wool tassels. No. 4 wooden pins of the bell gauge size are used for this knitting.

KNITTED CUSHIONS.

BY MADEMOISELLE ROCHE.

EVERY lady who feels an interest in the various sorts of Berlin wool-work finds that her box or bag of remainders goes on accumulating to an inconvenient extent, and we are, therefore, happy to offer the suggestion of a kind subscriber for the application of these increasing stores to some pretty and profitable use. With this view, it is proposed to turn them into the knitted shells, which may afterward be sewn together, forming most agreeable and comfortable cushions for the couch or easy-chair. Each shell may be either of one color, of several shades of the same color, or of distinct contrasts, according to convenience and taste. When a sufficient number has been made they must be sewn together, the point of one being placed exactly in the center of the other, and half-shells being knitted to complete the vacancies at the ends of each row. The colors, as in patchwork, must be arranged with a view to good contrast. The edge of the cushion may be finished with a twisted cord of the various colors. The following is one of the best modes of knitting these shells:—Cast on three loops, knit, increasing one each row, until there are seven loops upon the needle. Then knit three, make one by bringing the thread forward, knit one (which is the center loop), make one, knit three. The back row has the first and last three loops knitted, the middle loops being purled. The front row, knit three, make one, knit three, make one, knit three. This completes one stripe or rib of the shell, each stripe being formed of three rows of loops. The next stripe is commenced by knitting the back row, which makes them alternate. When the shell is as large as may be desired, it is to be finished by a row of holes, and three rows of knitting, and must then be cast off. The three first and the three last rows of every row are always knitted.

SHIELD-SHAPED HANGING PINCUSHION.

BY MADEMOISELLE ROCHE.

THIS is a very pretty variety to the usual square and round Pincushion, and it will be found very useful as well as ornamental, as it can be suspended close at hand wherever a lady may happen to be sitting with her work. It is also equally suitable for boudoir service, as it is a very pretty article when hung from bead chains. As it is quite a little novelty, it would be found appropriate for a contribution to any charitable bazaar. The materials of which it is composed are colored velvet and beads; these are the two sorts of white opaque and transparent, and a few gold to terminate the sprays. Steel may be substituted if preferred. The flowers are in the transparent beads, with gold centers, the leaves being in the opaque white; the small sprays are also in the clear white, the end of each being finished with three opaque white beads, a little larger than the others. The cushion is made with a mattrass edge, on which is worked a border to correspond. The lower part is finished with a fringe of beads, made gradually deeper toward the center of the cushion, and formed of the two different sorts of beads. The chains are also made of the two sorts. The bow at the top of the chains may be made either as a rosette—that is, by threading the beads on fine wire, and arranging them as

a flower—or they may be rich tassels of beads, whichever is preferred. If these are found to take too much time, a bow of ribbon the same color as the velvet, with a few loops of gold beads in the centers, will look very pretty. We recommend this cushion for its ornamental appearance.

WATCH–CASE IN CROCHET.

BY MRS. JANE WEAVER.

MATERIALS.—Twenty-six small size brass curtain rings; two skeins China blue purse twist; one spool gold thread; one string large gold beads.

Cover all the rings with the blue silk, working in single crochet; then with the gold thread cross the rings as seen in the design, darning a small spot in the center, in the same manner as in working wheels in cotton embroidery; on this spot sew one gold bead. Sew the rings together neatly as arranged in the design. The back of the pocket is to be made of cardboard, with silk to correspond with the color of the crochet work. Finish with bows of blue ribbon.

ILLUSTRATED D'OYLEY.

BY MADEMOISELLE ROCHE.

THE only material necessary for this very pretty D'Oyley (for which see the front of the number) is white satin; and it is to be worked thus:—Draw the design with indelible ink and a quill pen, and press with a hot iron as soon as finished.

THE FALL PALETOT.

BY EMILY H. MAY.

THE pattern for the present month is that of the half-tight *paletot*, called the *Fall Paletot*: the skirt of each piece will have to be lengthened about 20 inches; when lengthened, the seams

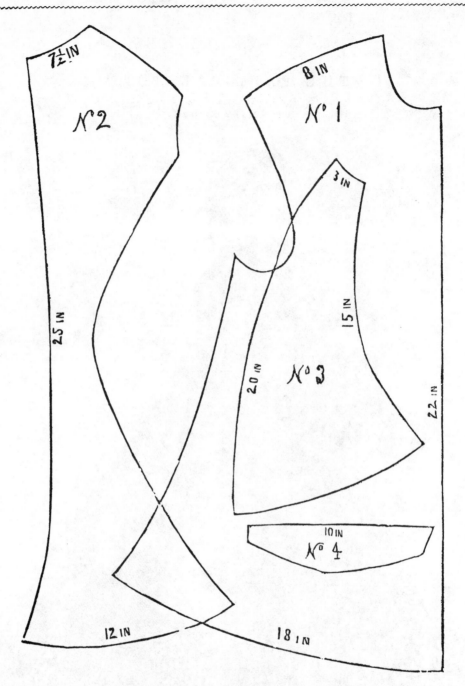

DIAGRAM OF FALL PALETOT.

may all be continued in straight lines, taking care to give the following widths to the bottom of each piece: when lengthened, the bottom of front should measure 34½ inches wide; the bottom of side-piece 30 inches, and the bottom of the back 28½ inches, making the total width of *half* the *paletot* 93 inches: when finished, the width at the bottom will be five yards and six inches. We have given the top part of sleeve only, the required slope for the under side being indicated by a pricked line: the remainder of sleeve may be cut like the engraving, or as a wide *Isabel* or *pagoda* sleeve, or shaped at the elbow, with deep *mousquetaire* cuff, the same as that in our first plate.

This pattern will be found very useful, as it serves as a base for all half-tight *paletots* and *pardessus*, varying the style of trimming, as the pattern is made up in silk or velvet.

No. 1. ONE FRONT.
No. 2. HALF THE BACK.
No. 3. SIDE-PIECE.
No. 4. TOP OF SLEEVE.

WAIST-POUCHES.

BY MRS. JANE WEAVER.

WE have just received two patterns from Paris of the little Pouches, which still continue to be

worn, suspended from the waistband by a chain and hook, and sometimes by a cord. They are made in all kinds of materials, and are embroidered in gold, silver, and jet; or they are

made of the same material as the dress with which they are worn, and trimmed in the same manner.

Last year, it will be remembered, we gave a pattern of one of those Pouches, when they first came up. Both of these patterns are new.

CHILDREN'S FASHIONS FOR SEPTEMBER.

ZOUAVE SCHOTTISCH.

BY F. E. GARRETT.

154

EDITOR'S TABLE.

EDITORIAL CHIT-CHAT.

WHAT IS, AND WHAT IS NOT LADY-LIKE IN DRESS.—Fashion is seldom seen to exceed the bounds of nature and of grace; at least among those who possess a good taste, and are, therefore, the truest standards of style and elegance. It is an excessive ambition for novelty, and a too great eagerness for display, among the affluent, that leads to eccentricity and produces extremes. A *lady* is always distinguished by the unaffected simplicity of her dress, the chasteness of her ornaments, and the grace and ease of all her movements; and an elegant simplicity is an equal proof of taste and delicacy; and the most *perfect* elegance of dress appears always the most easy and the least studied.

Although Paris is the soil in which every fashion takes its rise, its influence is not so general there as with us. They study there the happy method of uniting *grace* with *fashion*, and never excuse a woman for being awkwardly dressed by saying her clothes are made in the mode. They conform to general fashion only when it happens not to be repugnant to private beauty. Our ladies, on the contrary, seem to have no other standard for grace but the run of the town. If fashion gives the word, every distinction of beauty, complexion, and station ceases. Bonnets all of a side, long cloaks and trailing dresses, make them as much alike as if their dress had been all fashioned by the same modiste, or ordered by the drill-sergeant of some marching regiment. The most admirable costume is not that which is most expensive, nor in the extreme of the fashion; but it is that style which is best adapted to the wearer, conveying to the mind of the observer the combined ideas of grace and comfort.

Nature for each has a different style, and each should choose what best becomes her, whether in her character of maid or matron. She should cultivate her taste by experiment and observation. She should educate the eye to the chaste and beautiful, and thus she would become more competent to judge what is most judicious and tasteful for herself, without copying, as we are too prone to do, the dress of others, whose different style, manners, and appearance, render them wrong arbiters of the dress we wear.

Art has of late made rapid progress amongst us. We require handsome patterns in our prints, room papers, table-cloths, etc., and the splashy patterns which eternally repeated the same ill-executed designs upon our walls, our curtains, and our carpets, have given place to light and graceful tracery. We used to tread on gigantic roses growing without leaves or branches from scarlet or blue baskets, while flowers of unknown species curled in distorted wreaths around. In all this we now follow nature and simplicity; and so it should be in our dress, for a multiplicity of colors distracts the eye, and though it may dazzle for awhile, it fails to convey the idea of gentility or refinement.

All nature is intensely beautiful; it appeals to us in every form and in every color; yet, whether we behold her in the gorgeous drapery of summer, or in the still richer glories of the early autumn time, with its golden grain and mellow fruit, there is nothing vulgar in the rich robe she wears, for she stands before us, glorious and beautiful, in simple majesty, and Solomon in all his glory was not arrayed like one of the starry gems that glitter on her verdant mantle. Chesterfield judiciously observes that we should study good taste in our dress as well as in our manners, seeing we are invariably judged by our appearance by those who have no means of judging of us otherwise.

It is often, indeed, the only thing observed during a casual interview or first meeting. "Appearance is something to every one, and everything to some people," and they who present a genteel exterior are mostly treated with deference and respect—always so, indeed, if to good dress they unite good manners and a courteous demeanor.

Young ladies, when they get married, should not relax their habits of personal neatness and graceful deportment, always so charming and becoming in their girlish days, and which were thought *indispensable* then in aiding them to create an agreeable impression, and setting off, in the most engaging light, their natural advantages. No fear of a young lady presenting herself before her lover, in the days of courtship, when each is solicitous to please, in a slovenly or tawdry condition. Yet too often does she drop into careless, slipshod ways in the home to which that same young man has taken her to share with him; and he is indeed an object of the greatest commiseration, whose domestic feelings cannot be gratified by the neat and lady-like appearance of her whom he has selected from the rest of her sex to make his home a bright and pleasant one.

Some will tell you their husbands raise such a "fuss" about the expense of dress. "They had rather want than ask;" but few men now-a-days refuse their wives the means of dressing genteelly, if not expensively; and if they can afford to do no more, surely it is the interest and the duty of the wife to consider so, and to turn to best advantage what she has.

To be agreeably and prettily dressed it is not necessary to be expensively so; it is all a matter of taste and judgment. An over-dressed woman is never a well-dressed woman. How many richly-dressed people do we see who, from the ill-adjustment of colors and material, we pronounce positively vulgar—gaudy paroquettes in their high-colored plumage—literally female Josephs, in their coats of many colors. A becomingly-dressed woman, no matter how cheaply so, beside such, presents by far the most lady-like appearance of the two. Excellence of dress does not mean richness of clothing nor conspicuous attire. Perfect harmony—refined simplicity—these are the charms which always fascinate.

It is too often the case that when ladies get married they cease to practice the niceties of dress, and that care and neatness in their persons which always bespeaks a refined and well cultivated mind; they "give it up," as they do their drawing and their music, and for the same reason too, implied, if not expressed, that now they have succeeded in obtaining a husband, they are *settled in life*, and need no longer worry themselves about such things; besides, *they have no time now*. *Nil questio*, the little elegancies and accomplishments, and romance of youth, have to be laid aside, and duties of plain and sober cast claim almost incessant attention, and yet never more truly than in this instance might the old adage be quoted, "Where there's a will there's a way. Ah! if genuine taste were there, and nothing but genuine taste will wear, marriage would not spoil the harmony of music, nor the simple elegance of dress.

Then, again, a great many women excuse their own carelessness by saying, "Oh! it don't matter whether we make ourselves fine or not, our husbands never perceive the difference. They don't care a fig." But the woman who acts on this shallow principle treats neither herself nor her husband with respect; she underrates her own importance. It turns out that hitherto she has been living but for appearance, and dressing but as an art to please, and now that her point is gained, she throws it aside, as a graceful appendage no longer necessary; and however oblivious her husband may appear to be on the score of her personal negligence, he is not so much so as she imagines; though he may *say* little about it, yet he likely *thinks* a great deal; he naturally draws comparisons between her and those more orderly, and in consequence more economical, than she. His observations are not likely to result in her favor, and she must not be surprised if his disappointment eventually recoil upon herself in indifference. Men are naturally anxious that their wives present a becoming elegance of dress and deportment. They are justly proud of them when they do so; but the slovenly woman is not calculated to excite either affection or respect.

But whilst lady-like manners, neatness, elegance, and order, cannot be too highly inculcated, nothing should be more guarded against than a vain and frivolous taste for finery and personal decorations. It is a dissipation of money and of mind. It leads away from home and home duties into scenes of gayety and expense, in the dissipating tendency of which, in the fashionable uproar, and constant whirl, dress and fashion become a passion, and she who gives herself up wholly to the cares of the toilet and its accompanying amusements, becomes little else than a well-dressed bundle of accomplishments.

CHESS FOR THE BLIND.—In some blind schools the game of chess is taught by means of a set of crooked pins being used instead of the ordinary pieces, so that a blind person may play the game on his own board, while his antagonist can use the ordinary board. Each can be considering his game without interrupting the other, as each names his move, which the other copies. There are few things more interesting than to see the numberless clever and humane arrangements which are practiced in these truly benevolent institutions for enabling those who are afflicted with blindness to use those faculties which they still possess to the greatest advantage, so that the deficiency may, as far as possible, be compensated for by mental education.

CORPULENCE.—With proper regard to diet and abundant exercise in the open air, the unpleasant consequences of an accumulation of fat may be avoided. Dr. Radcliffe recommends that the mouth should be kept shut, and the eyes open; or, in other words, that corpulent persons should eat little food, and that the quantity of sleep should be diminished. These precautions may be followed with discretion, but it may be dangerous to carry them too far.

MILK.—It is common to regard milk as little else than mere drink. But this is an error. Milk is really an article of solid food, being coagulated soon after reaching the stomach. New milk contains thirteen per cent. of digestible solids, and skim milk ten per cent.; that is, the former fully one-half, and the latter above a third, of the nutriment contained in the lean part of mutton and beef.

ORIGIN OF BACKGAMMON.—Backgammon is certainly one of the oldest games practiced still in these modern times. Two parties dispute the place of its parentage; one contending that it was invented in Greece, at the beginning of the thirteenth century, and the other that it was in Wales previous to the Conquest. These two different opinions show how old the game must be.

DESCRIPTION OF NIGHT-DRESS.—The yoke of this night-dress is composed entirely of narrow tucks and insertion. The collar and cuffs are also tucked and trimmed with edging.

TO PROTECT VINES.—The water in which potatoes have been boiled is a sure preventive of the destruction of vines by the striped bug and other insects.

REVIEW OF NEW BOOKS.

Tom Brown at Oxford. By the author of " School-Days at Rugby." 2 vols., 12 mo. Boston: Ticknor & Fields.—At last we hail the completion of this novel, which has been running through "M'Millan's Magazine" for nearly two years, and which Ticknor & Fields have been reprinting in monthly numbers as fast as it appeared abroad. At any time, its genial spirit, its graphic pictures of English country life, and its deliciously told love-story would have attracted interest; but in the present dearth of fresh reading, for our book-publishers print hardly anything except what relates to war, it should be sought with avidity. The author of "Tom Brown" is one of the healthiest writers of the day, as well as one of the most agreeable; and on the whole we consider this the best of his works. The American publishers reissue the book in excellent style, and with a portrait of the author.

Explorations and Adventures in Equatorial Africa. By Paul du Chaillu. 1 vol., 8 vo. New York: Harper & Brothers.—This is a narrative of explorations in that portion of Africa, lying immediately north and south of the river Gaboon and extending into the interior, a portion never before explored by any traveler. The book has created an astonishing sensation. Part of the scientific world pronounces it full of falsehoods; but another part thinks it entirely veracious. One of the chief points of interest in the work is its description of that gigantic ape, the Gorilla, an animal that more closely resembles man than any other of its kind.

Great Expectations. With Illustrations by McLellan. By Charles Dickens. 1 vol., 8 vo. Philada: T. B. Peterson & Brothers.—We have here a handsome octavo edition of Dickens' new novel. The book is spiritedly illustrated, from designs by McLellan, the well known American artist. We regard this as one of the best of Dickens' later fictions. In it, indeed, he returns, more or less, to his earlier style. The interest of the story is intense, and well-sustained; and the characters more natural than usual with this author. The volume may be had in cloth or paper covers.

Hints on the Preservation of Health in Armies. For the use of Volunteer Officers and Soldiers. By John Ordronaux, M. D. 1 vol., 16 mo. New York: D. Appleton & Co.—The author of this work is professor of medical jurisprudence in Columbia College, New York. The treatise seems to be thorough. We should think its general circulation would save many valuable lives and prevent a vast deal of sickness in camps.

The Gipsy's Prophecy. By Mrs. E. D. E. N. Southworth. 1 vol., 12 mo. Philada: T. B. Peterson & Brothers.—Those who admire Mrs. Southworth's writings—and is not their name legion?—will be glad to welcome this novel from her pen. It is printed in handsome type, in duodecimo form, and may be had bound in cloth, or paper, at the choice of the purchaser.

The Sea (La Mer). From the French of M. J. Michelet. Translated from the latest Paris edition. 1 vol., 12 mo. New York: Rudd & Carleton.—As the London Athenæum well says, this is a dreamy book, half-science, half-fancy, with a blending in both of sensuous imagination. It is handsomely printed.

Volunteers' Camp and Field Book. By John B. Curry. 1 vol., 16 mo. New York: D. Appleton & Co.—Full of useful and general information on the art and science of war. Of many recent publications, similar in character, we regard it as one of the very best.

FEMALE EQUESTRIANISM.

THE management of the reins is the greatest difficulty in horsemanship, and, by some persons, it is a difficulty never altogether overcome. Do not pull at a horse's mouth. Work the reins continually very gently and easily; but let there be no strain on him, or he will certainly learn to pull, and lose the graceful, easy carriage of his head. A thoroughbred horse should have his mouth so light, that he may be ridden with a piece of pack-thread. But a bad rider may teach him to pull in a very few lessons. By working the mouth I mean a light, wavy motion of the hand, not tiring to the rider, and pleasing to the horse—to be acquired by practice and attention only.

The reins should never be required to assist the seat—I mean that perfect balance that enables the rider to do what she will, without interfering with the action of the horse. The perfect rider should be able to bend her body down to the stirrup on the left side, or down to the girth on the right, to throw her arms over-head, and yet her horse not swerve in the least. A lady who has a perfect seat, may throw her stirrup aside, and her reins across her horse's neck, and yet be able to guide him by the mere balance of her body, whether in walking, cantering, trotting, or galloping. I had almost forgotten to mention the whip. It should be carried in the right hand, and simply as an ornament. A good rider never requires it; a kind rider will never use it. The man who strikes the willing creature that carries him through heat and cold, through rain and wind, in spite of fatigue or thirst, degrades himself by the act. A lady—a *lady*—uses the hand that holds the whip but to pat and encourage. "Poor fellow! Good horse!" will do more with the noble animal than the blow.

CANTERING.—On first setting forth, the horse should be allowed to walk a short distance. Some riders gather up their reins hastily, and, before they have secured them properly, allow the animal to trot or canter off. Such a proceeding is often productive of mischief, sometimes of accident. A lady's horse should canter with the right foot. The left produces a rough, unpleasant motion and ungraceful appearance. The whole body is jerked at every stride. Should the animal have been trained to canter with the left foot, a little perseverance will soon teach him better. Hold the rein so as to tighten it slightly on the left side of the mouth, touch (not hit) him gently on the right shoulder, with the whip, and sit well back in the saddle, so as not to throw weight on the shoulder. The horse will soon understand what is required of him; but if he does not, try again after an interval of a few minutes. Straighten the reins immediately he throws out the right foot. Pat and encourage him with kind words, but repeat the operation should he change his feet, which he may do before getting accustomed to his new step. The considerate rider will not compel him to canter too long at a time, for it is very fatiguing. That it is so, is easily proved by the fact that the steed of a lady too fond of cantering becomes weak in the forelegs, or what is commonly called "groggy."

TROTTING.—Trotting, if well performed, is very graceful, but is more difficult to acquire than cantering. The rider should sit slightly more forward than for cantering, on, but not more forward than, the center of the seat, pressing the knee firmly against the saddle, and keeping the foot perfectly straight (rather turned in than out) in the stirrup. She must rise slightly, with every step of the animal, taking care to keep the shoulders quite square with the horse. To lean over one side or the other, be the inclination ever so slight, or to bring forward one shoulder more than the other, has a very bad appearance. A good horsewoman will avoid the common error of leaning forward when trotting. It is not only very ungraceful, but in the attitude nearly all power is lost. The arms are comparatively useless. Should the horse stumble, the rider risks being

thrown over his head. Her position deprives her of the power of assisting her horse to rise, whilst the additional weight thrown on his shoulders prevents him from helping himself. At all times, the broad part of the foot only should rest on the iron of the stirrup.

SHYING.—Should a horse shy, he does it generally from timidity. The common practice of forcing a horse to approach very near the object of alarm, is a foolish and useless abuse of power. He should be encouraged by words and patting on the neck, and, above all, by the fearlessness of his rider. A horse soon learns to depend greatly on his mistress. Should she start, or feel timid, he perceives it immediately, and will prick up his ears and look about him for the cause. On the other hand, I have known many real dangers encountered with safety, through the rider having sufficient presence of mind to break out into a snatch of song (all horses like singing), which has diverted his attention from the object of fear.

REARING.—Should a horse rear, lean the body forward, loosing the reins at the same moment; press both hands, if necessary, on the mane. Should, however, a horse rear so as to endanger the safety of the rider, loosen well the reins, pass the whip from the right hand to the left, double up the right hand into a fist, and hit him between the ears. Show no fear, but trot on as though nothing had occurred. Turn his head toward home, and he will be certain to repeat his feat on a future occasion. The above is rarely necessary, and should only be done in a case of urgency.

KICKING.—Should a horse kick, take care to keep him well in hand. He cannot kick unless he throws his head down, and he cannot do that if the reins are not held carelessly loose. A practiced rider can always tell when a horse is about to kick, by a peculiar motion of his body. It is instantaneous, but unmistakable. The best-tempered horse may kick, occasionally, from a rub of the saddle, or pressure on the withers. The animal should not be beaten, but the cause of his misconduct inquired into.

DISMOUNTING.—The ride being over, the horse should stand in the stable, with the girths loosened, but the saddle untouched on his back for at least twenty minutes, until cool, when it may be removed without inconvenience. Should the animal, if usually quiet, have misbehaved in any manner, the cause will generally appear as soon as the saddle is removed. Snatching the saddle from the horse's back, while it is still heated, often produces swellings, particularly if the skin be at all irritated by friction. The saddle should be sponged and dried, either in the sun, or by the harness-room or kitchen fire, before being put away. This precaution prevents the stuffing from hardening. A humane rider will always attend to the lining of the saddle; for a wrung back must be sad pain. A horse will shrink from the slightest touch of a finger on the injured part; what must, then, be the torture of the weight of a saddle and rider? We owe much pleasure to our saddle-horse; should we not do all we can to preserve him from pain?

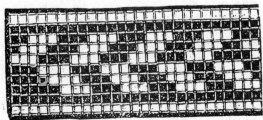

CROCHET.

CHILD'S CLOAK.

CHILDREN'S FASHIONS FOR OCTOBER.

THE AGNES.

THE CATHARINE.

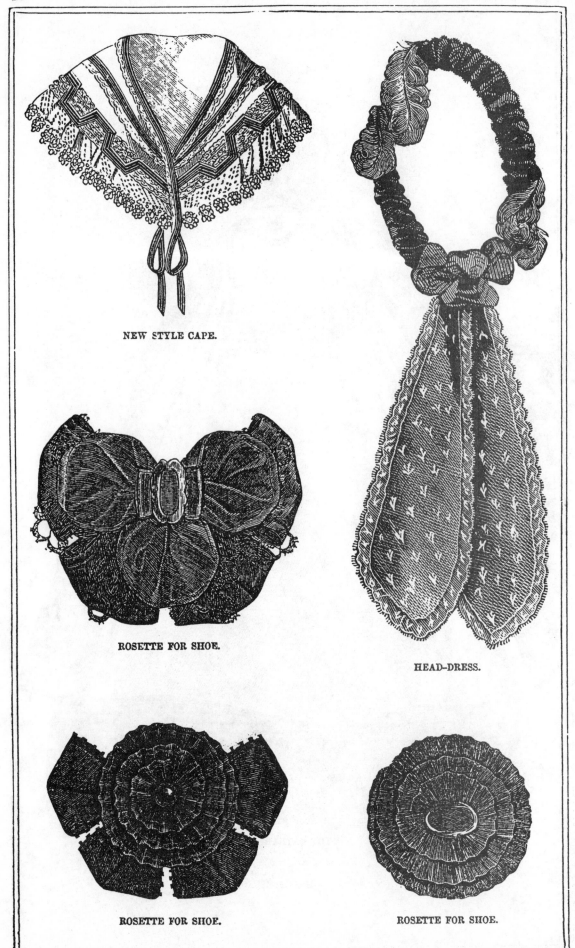

NEW STYLE CAPE.

HEAD-DRESS.

ROSETTE FOR SHOE.

ROSETTE FOR SHOE.

ROSETTE FOR SHOE.

LITTLE GIRL'S CASAQUE.

BOY'S CLOAK FOR FALL.

THE CLOTILDE.

THE FRIENDS: FROM A PICTURE BY LANDSEER.

CHILDREN'S FALL DRESSES.

BY MME. DEMOREST.

THE fall styles are unusually pretty, as will be seen from our engravings for this month.

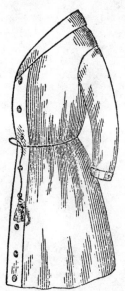

GENTLEMAN'S WRAPPER.—Cut sack shape, with a seam in the center of the back, which fits it sufficiently to have the garment plain in the back. Confined by a cord at the waist, plain coat sleeve. Requires seven yards of cashmere, if the figure is such that it cannot be reversed; if it can be, six yards will do for a person of ordinary height.

SERENA APRON.—For a Miss of nine years—made in chambre. Would require five yards. The waist is carried down the skirt, and forms a gore. Both front and back are alike. The sides are a plain breadth gathered to a band. This is a low neck apron, simply joined at the shoulders with a bow and ends.

ELVA DRESS.—This dress, for a child of eight years, is something in the same style as the "Nellie" dress, excepting that the gore terminates in tabs, which extend over the short puffed sleeve: upon the waist, and also upon the skirt. The body is plain; the skirt plaited. Requires eight yards of silk.

BOY'S SUIT.—Of plain light French cassimere, for a boy of eight years. The pants are laid in box plaits, and finished with a wide waistband. The jacket is plain, slightly cut away, and rounded off from the front, in the most approved French style, and finished with side pockets. Neatly tucked shirt, with a single row of embroidery, turn-down collar, and Prince of Wales neck tie, such as is furnished by Devlin, Hudson & Co., New York.

THE PRAIRIE FLOWER.—The "Prairie Flower" is as charming, when made up in suitable materials, as the blossom whose name it bears. It is simply a small bishop, with cuff and cap, and a sort of scalloped cap laid over the front of the sleeve. It may be made in rep silk, or any rich goods, but is not adapted to thin materials.

UNION COAT.—This little coat is proper for a child from two to five years. Made of poplin; the back is in plain sack fashion, and the front partly covered by a fancy jacket, which extends to the side-seams under the arm, and is fastened in the front by straps across the breast. The sleeve is plain, excepting a cuff, which terminates at its center in rounded tabs. The trimming may be velvet or flat braid, and buttons. The quantity of material required is three yards, three-eighth yard wide.

WARREN DRESS.—Dress for a child of three to five years, and may be worn with either skirts or knee pants. It is cut in three pieces, front, back, and sleeve; the skirt and waist are cut all in one, cut two-thirds of the way across the waist, both back and front, to allow the additional fullness required in the skirt, there are two box plaits in the front, and in the back of the skirt each side. Of double width material, it requires one and a half yards.

EMPIRE COAT.—A pleasant coat for boys of five to seven years. Any light material will do for this coat, which has a jacket waist, box plaited behind, over a full skirt. In front the jacket is plain, and turned back *en revers* from the waist beneath, which buttons down the front. Trimming of flat braid. Plain loose sleeve, with cuff turned back. Four yards of poplin will make it.

WALKING COAT—FRONT VIEW.—Walking Coat for a boy from five to seven. Is sack front, with box plait running from the shoulder, and tacked down with buttons to bottom of waist; buttons down the front; back of waist plain; skirt laid on in box plaits; with a little pointed polka, sleeves half-wide, with a cuff ornamented with buttons. A small square collar. Is pretty in plain woolens or plain poplin. Requires three yards of material.

Mme. Demorest, 473 Broadway, New York, furnishes patterns of all the latest Paris fashions. They can be procured, either by mail or express, in great variety, for either ladies or children, by addressing her, postpaid. Inquiries, in reference to such matters, should be addressed to her, and not to the literary editors of "Peterson."

UNION SOFA PILLOW IN CROCHET.

BY MRS. JANE WEAVER.

MATERIALS.—Six oz. red double zephyr; six oz. white double zephyr; four oz. blue double zephyr.

With the red wool make a ch of 6. Work in Princess Royal stitch a strip long enough for a side of a cushion. The same with the white wool, making 3 long white stripes, 4 long red ones, 3 red, and 3 white a little more than half the length. For the field, make a ch of 42 stitches, work 38 rows, and on it work 34 stars in cross stitch with the white wool. Finish with worsted cord and tassels of red, white, and blue. Both sides of cushion may be alike, or the under side of worsted damask if preferred. The quantity of material given is enough for both sides.

A full description of the Princess Royal stitch has been given in one of the back numbers.

EDGING.

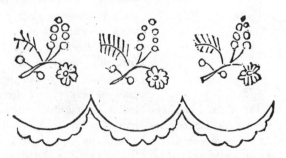

LOOSE JACKET AND WAISTCOAT FOR BOY.

BY EMILY H. MAY.

This is a pretty pattern for a boy of three or   of cloth suitable for the season.   The sleeve is
four years old.   The material may be any sort   arranged with a turned-back cuff, as will be

BRAIDING DESIGN FOR THE TURNED-BACK CUFF AND WAISTCOAT.

BRAIDING DESIGN FOR TRIMMING ROUND THE JACKET.

seen in the illustration, and the waistcoat is stitched in the seams under the arms, so forming one garment. The broad braiding design which we also give is for trimming round the jacket,

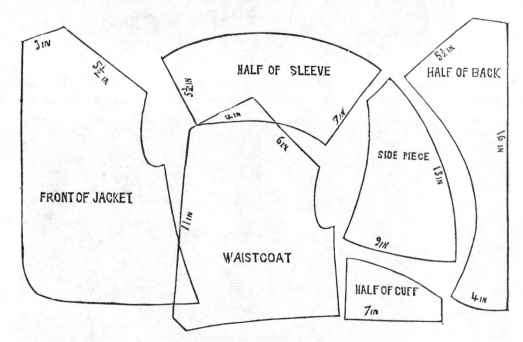

DIAGRAM FOR CUTTING OUT JACKET AND WAISTCOAT.

and the narrow one for the turned-back cuff and waistcoat. The braiding design would be equally suitable for ladies' loose or tight jackets. We annex also a diagram by which to cut it out.

LADY'S PURSE.

BY MRS. JANE WEAVER.

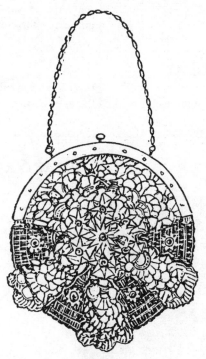

THIS beautiful purse is composed of two circles, which are made as follows. Do seven little roses separately, of the size of the one given opposite, of gold thread. In the center of each a bead is placed. Then join them together, as in the following engraving, surrounding them by a chain-stitch in black silk. Finish the circle by following the pattern, using red silk. We repeat, two of these circles are to be thus made.

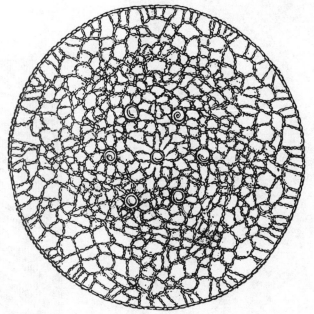

the foregoing, in black silk; the eyelet in gold thread, with a white bead in the center. Join the flaps to the circle. Between these flaps, put three festoons, like the following, in gold

thread and a chain-stitch, passing over the flaps, so as not to break the thread.

Next make four, or eight, double flaps, like

VARIETIES FOR THE WORK-TABLE.

EDGING.

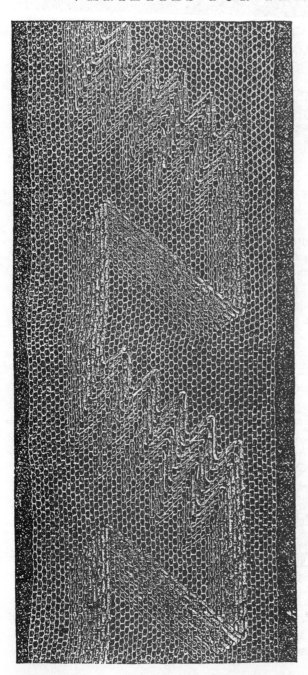

DESIGN FOR DARNING A PATTERN IN BOBBINET LACE.

INSERTION.

COVER FOR A SMALL TRAY,
OR FOR A BREAD OR BISCUIT BASKET.
BY MADEMOISELLE ROCHE.

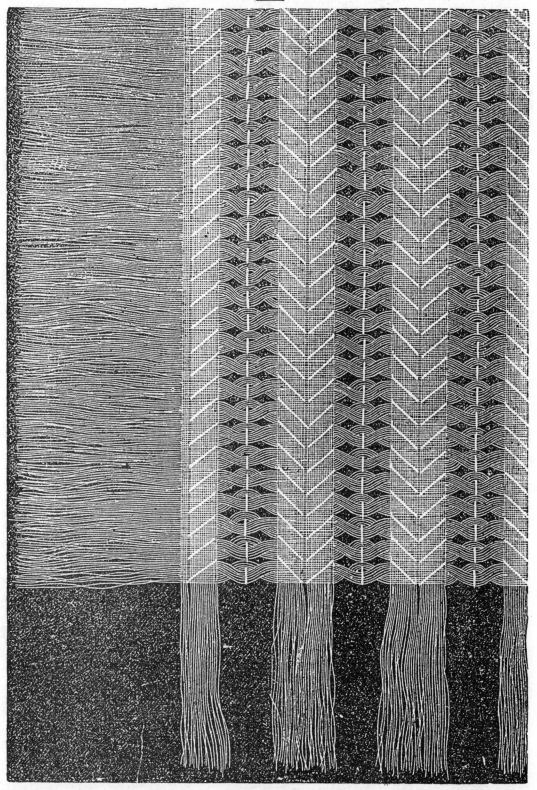

THE materials required for making this cover {cotton. The work is remarkably effective, and are white linen and coarse white embroidery} extremely easy of execution. The linen employed must not be very fine, and should be rather loose in texture. When cut to the required size, the first thing to be done is to ravel out the threads, for the purpose of forming the fringe, which may be about an inch in breadth. It should be at first made only on three sides— viz: along the selvage and the two cross sides, the opposite selvage side being left till the work is nearly completed. For the work, draw out twenty-seven threads close together, then leave a space, and draw out twenty-seven more threads in the same manner. The space from which the threads are drawn is worked in a kind of open-stitch, with coarse embroidery cotton. Twelve threads are taken up with the needle, and fixed by a back-stitch. Six threads are dropped, and then, again, twelve are taken up in the same manner as before, thus forming the sort of chain pattern shown in the illustration. From the middle of the opaque stripe a single thread is drawn, and worked in common hem-stitch, and on each side narrow stripes in satin-stitch form a sort of herringbone pattern. The work consists entirely of a series of opaque and open stripes. When the requisite number of stripes are formed, the fringe should be made on the fourth side, and the cover is completed. This sort of work may be applied to various other objects besides the cover here described.

ANTIMACASSAR.

BY MADEMOISELLE ROCHE.

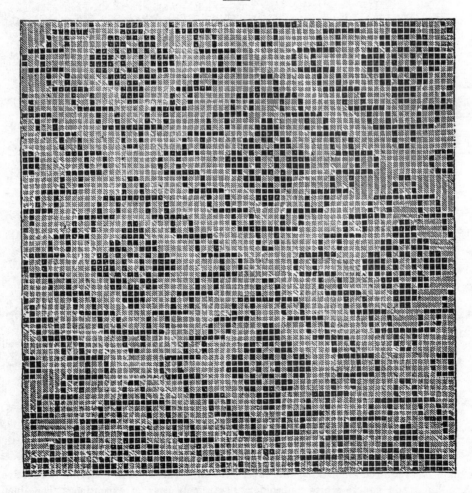

THIS pattern will be found very effective for an Antimacassar or Toilet-cover; or, indeed, any of the many purposes to which crochet and netting may be adapted.

PATTERN FOR A SERVIETTE.

BY MADEMOISELLE ROCHE.

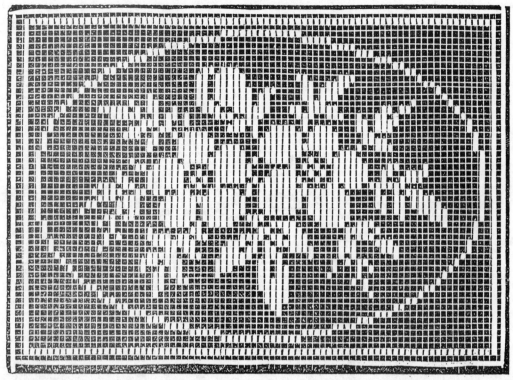

THE Serviette may be worked either in crochet or netting, and it should be bordered by a fringe. The oblong form is sometimes preferable to the square, especially for a tray.

BOOK-MARKER.

BY MRS JANE WEAVER.

FOR this see front of number.

MATERIALS.—1½ yards of dark blue ribbon, the width given in design; 1 bunch of opaque white beads, small size; some fine white perforated cardboard.

With the beads work the crosses upon the cardboard, sewing a bead for every dot given in the design. Work two of each kind, stitch them together back to back, inserting the ribbon as seen in the design. Care must be taken in cutting out the crosses after they are worked, as much of their beauty depends upon the neatness and precision with which they are cut. Confine the three ribbons at the other end with a small piece of cardboard, in the same way as the crosses. The effect of this book-marker is very beautiful, the ribbons seem to be tipped with ivory; and nothing could be prettier than the combination of the Roman, Greek, and Maltese crosses.

EDGING.

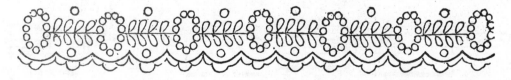

THE FASCINATION SCHOTTISCH.

BY A LADY.

BY PERMISSION OF SEP. WINNER, PROPRIETOR OF THE COPYRIGHT.

VARIETIES IN BRAIDING, EMBROIDERY, ETC.

CIGAR-CASE: IN BLACK VELVET AND GOLD BRAID.

INITIALS FOR MARKING.

INSERTION.

EDGING.

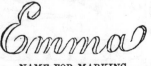

NAME FOR MARKING.

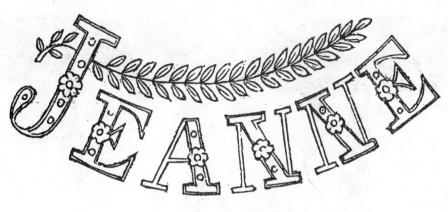

NAME FOR MARKING.

THE AZELINE.

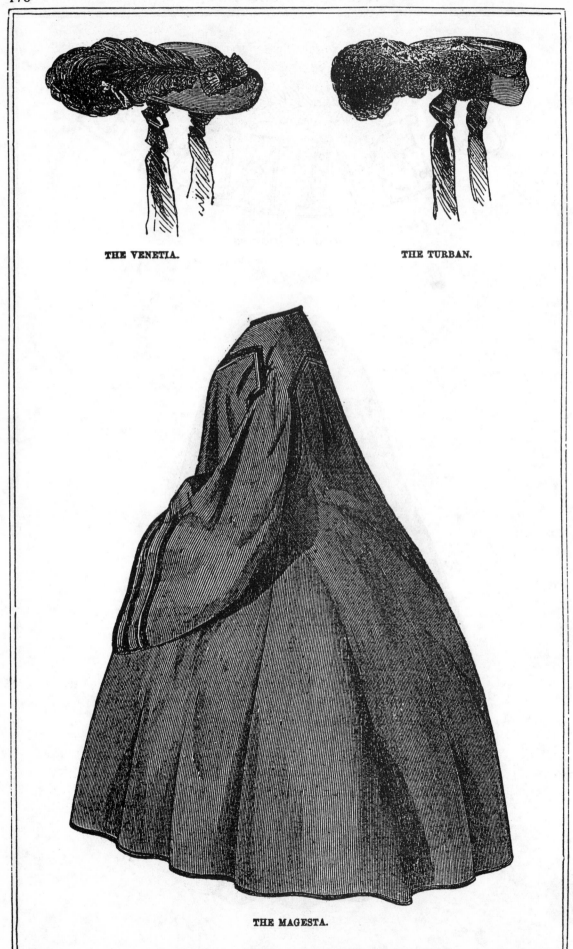

178

THE VENETIA.

THE TURBAN.

THE MAGESTA.

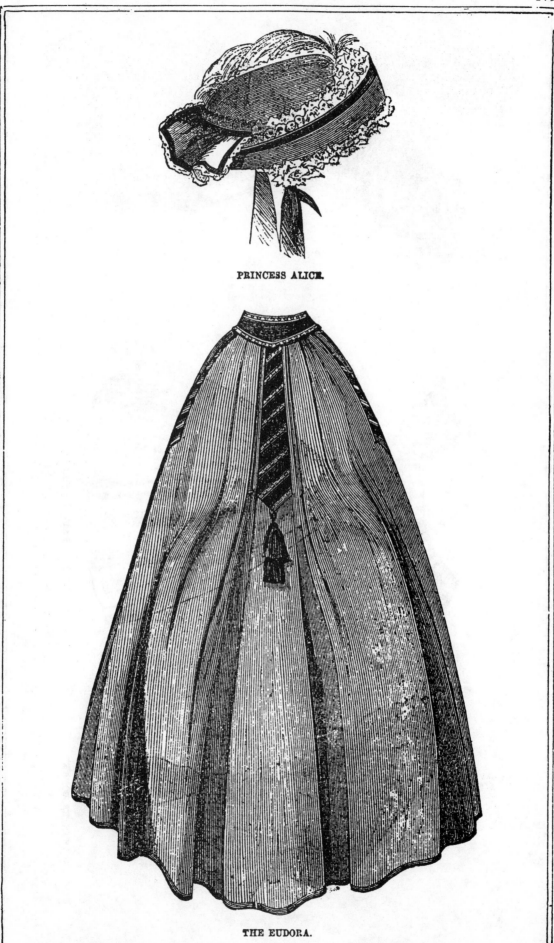

PRINCESS ALICE.

THE EUDORA.

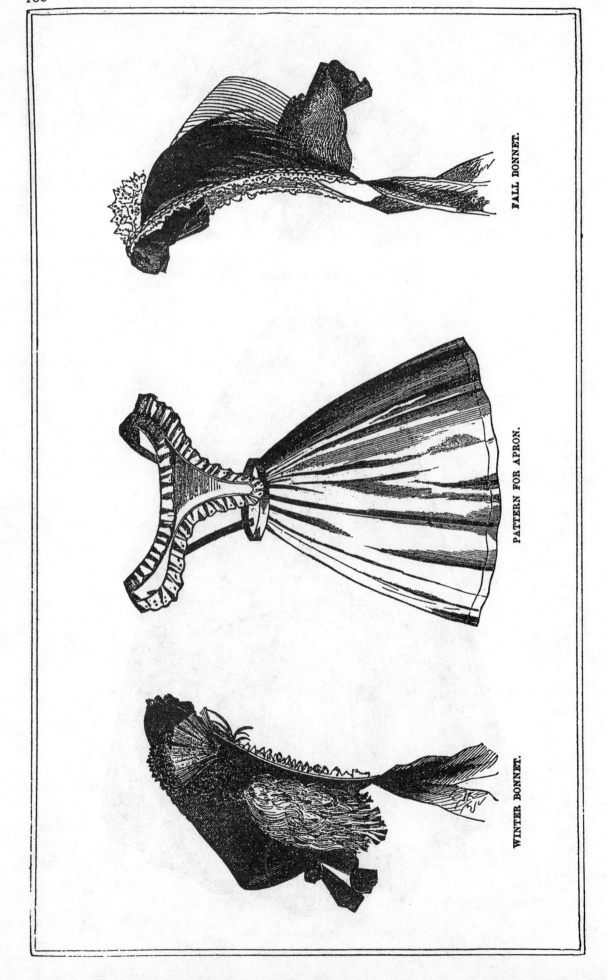

FALL BONNET.

PATTERN FOR APRON.

WINTER BONNET.

181

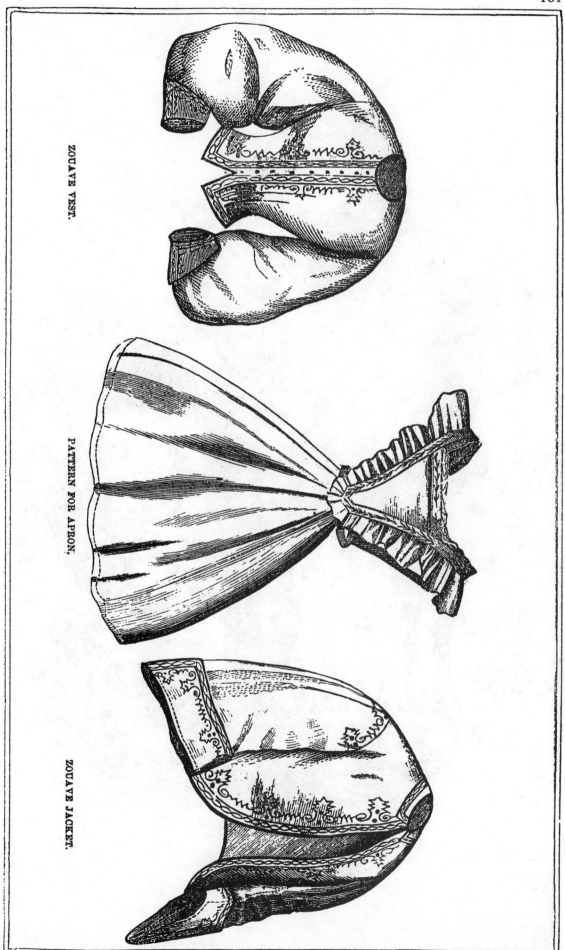

ZOUAVE VEST.

PATTERN FOR APRON.

ZOUAVE JACKET.

LATEST EQUESTRIAN FASHIONS.

PENDANT PIN-CUSHION IN APPLICATION.

BY MRS. JANE WEAVER.

MATERIALS.—A piece of white silk or satin; ditto bright scarlet; one spool gold braid; cord and tassels.

This cushion is intended to be suspended against the wall, by the side of the toilet-glass. It is very easily made. A piece of white silk or satin about four inches by seven, on which the scarlet is applique as seen in the design.

The edges of the pattern are finished with the gold braid, the pattern of which is very simple and easily followed by the eye. Make up the cushion in the usual manner, stuffing with bran.

Finish with a cord of silk and gold mixed, sewing it all round the cushion; also suspend it by some of the same, adding tassels to correspond.

DEMOREST'S PRIZE MEDAL HOOP SKIRTS.

BY MRS. ANN S. STEPHENS.

FIVE years ago when hooped skirts were first introduced, every one predicted for them a speedy decline, and fall; but after encountering the shafts of ridicule and opposition in every conceivable form, they still not only remain a fixed fact, but have become a permanent institution, which no caprice of fashion will be likely wholly to destroy.

The reason of this constant and increased appreciation is found in the acknowledged principle of comfort and utility upon which the idea was based. The first specimens were many of them very imperfect, some of them ludicrously so; but through all the stiff, ill-shaped, clumsy styles, which were the result of first efforts in the hands of ignorant, inexperienced persons, ladies recognized what they needed—something to extend their dresses to proper and becoming dimensions, and save the oppressive weight of a mass of clothing upon the hips.

When a mode, no matter how excellent in itself, becomes a fashion, the tendency is always toward an extreme, and it is not surprising that this was the case with hooped skirts, and that at a certain period the size became absurdly and preposterously large. At the present time a happy medium seems to have been reached; the size near the waist is small, and the circumference increases, bell-shape, to the bottom, thus giving a natural and graceful flow to the outer garments, and affording in the gradually increasing dimensions a fine opportunity for the display of the ample coats and cloaks which form a peculiar feature of present attire.

Many of the former disadvantages in the manufacture of hooped skirts resulted, doubtless, from the fact of the designers and manufacturers being men, who, however well acquainted with mechanical principles, could hardly be expected to perceive at once all the nice adjustments necessary to so important an article of ladies' wardrobe. These difficulties being recognized by Mme. Demorest, she succeeded in producing a skirt, which, according to the testimony of the thousands of ladies who use them, combine, perfection of shape, graceful appearance, and great durability; and especially the advantage of the tapes not slipping on the springs, which is entirely obviated by a process that Mme. Demorest has secured by a patent, and consists in passing the standards through the covering of the springs, making it impossible for them to slip or break away.

The high price of the best kind of hooped skirts has been, also, a great objection to them by many persons of limited means. Skirts with

12 springs, are now retailed at -	$ .50
15 springs, - - - - - - - -	.75
20 springs, - - - - - - - -	1.00
25 springs, - - - - - - - -	1.25
30 springs, - - - - - - - -	1.50
40 springs, - - - - - - - -	2.00

Children's can be obtained from 19 cents to $1.00.

The real excellence of these skirts, combined with the small cost, has established for them an unprecedented success. They took the first premium and prize medal at the Fair of the American Institute, and are now well and widely known as Mme. Demorest's Prize Medal Skirt.

BORDERING FOR MATS, CURTAINS, ETC.

BY MADEMOISELLE ROCHE.

THE want of a simple border for various articles is, we are quite aware, often felt by many ladies, and we are happy to supply one that can be produced with great rapidity, that is extremely economical, and well suited for many purposes. It makes a good edging for all mats that are wanted for real service, being very durable; and it also makes a good finish for Morocco curtains. The material is merely a worsted braid of the best quality, the color, of course, depending upon the article for which it is intended. The work is commenced in the following way: Double the braid into two equal lengths, and make a slip-loop in the middle; then pass a second loop through the first, drawing down the cord of the first, so as to fix it in its right place. Continue to work in this way, making the loops alternately of the two lengths of the braid, first on one side and then on the other, keeping the work as regular as possible, as on this its good effect entirely depends. When the required length has been made, draw the end of the braid through the last loop without forming a fresh loop. This bordering, being very elastic, easily adapts itself to the curves of any article to which it is appropriated, although, at the same time, it is equally good as a straight line when intended for window curtains.

KNITTED SHAWL: STAR STITCH.

BY MRS. JANE WEAVER.

MATERIALS.—¾ pound of colored zephyr; 1¼ pound of black zephyr; medium wooden needles.

With the black wool, cast on four stitches.

1st Row.—Make one stitch by taking up the loop under the first stitch upon the needle. Knit this loop, then throw the thread forward and knit three stitches. Bind the first of the three stitches over the last two knit. (This makes the cross stitch.) Knit the remaining stitch.

2nd Row.—Purl all the stitches.

3rd Row.—Make one stitch as in first row, then throw the thread forward and knit three, binding the first stitch over the last two knit, as before; again throw the thread forward and knit the two remaining stitches.

4th Row.—Purl.

5th Row.—Commence as in first row. Work in the same way, observing when there is but one stitch upon the needle, after knitting the last star stitch, to knit it off plain. If there are two stitches, then throw the thread forward and knit the two stitches off plain. Knit ten rows of star, or pattern stitch, for the width of stripe. Tie on the colored wool at the beginning of the purl row. Knit the colored stripe the same width as the black one. Continue the stripes until you have the shawl long enough. End with the colored stripe. Bind off.

FOR THE BORDER.—With the black wool, cast on one stitch. Knit plain, placing the needle at the beginning of the row, under the thread, making one stitch.

2nd Row.—Knit plain, without making the stitch at the beginning of the row.

3rd Row.—Same as first row.

Repeat until there are thirty stitches upon the needle. Then knit a piece long enough to border two sides of the shawl as seen in the design. Finish with fringe tied into the border, alternate colored and black.

This is an original design.

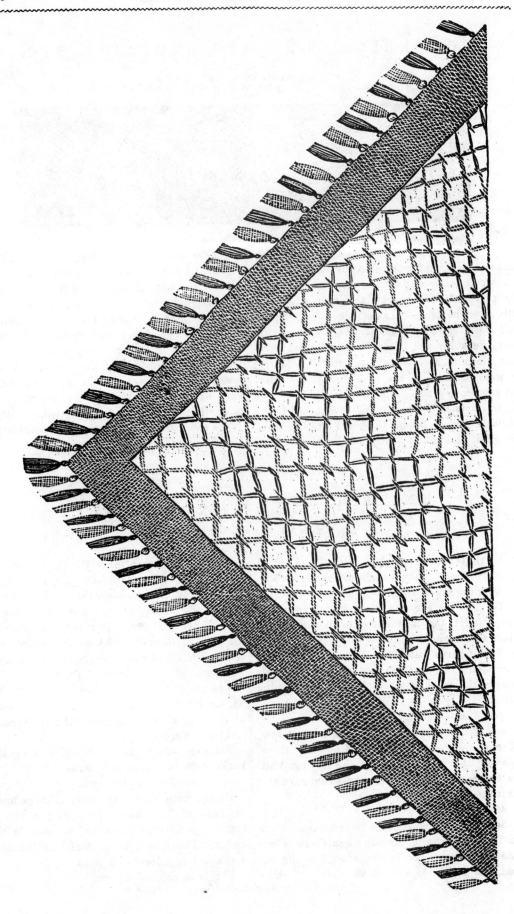

VARIETIES IN LINEN.

BY OUR "FASHION EDITOR."

WE gave, last month, various patterns for children's clothes. These patterns enable handy mothers to make up the clothes of their little ones at home, or tell them where to buy them.

We now give some new patterns in linen, which have been sent out to us from Paris. As everybody is talking of economy, many ladies, who have heretofore put out their linen work, will now make it up for themselves: hence we shall give hereafter, much more frequently than before, such patterns. In this way, in 1862, every subscriber for "Peterson" will be able to save three, four, five, or even ten times the price of subscription.

Our first pattern is a chemise, with a yoke richly tucked in plaits, the top of the yoke is edged with narrow embroidery: it is finished with full infant sleeves.

Our next pattern is a night dress, cut high in the neck, and with long sleeves. Down the front are two rows of insertion. The cuffs, which are comparatively deep, are also embroidered in the same pattern.

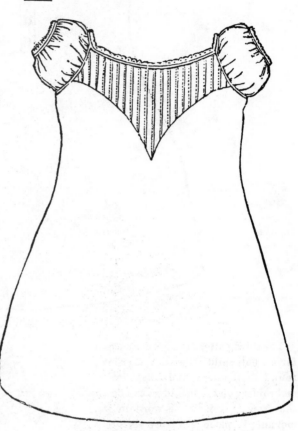

CHEMISE.

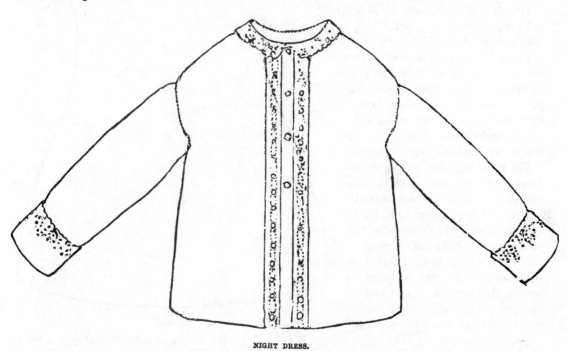

NIGHT DRESS.

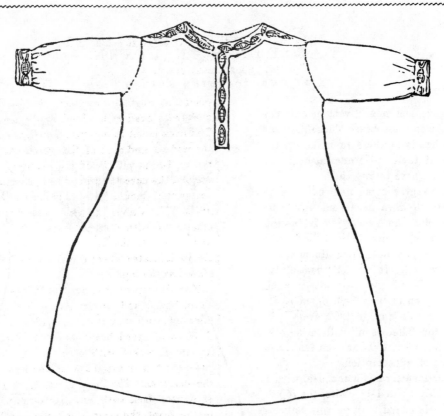

FRENCH SACQUE FOR A SMALL CHILD.

The third pattern is a French sacque for a small child. It is cut rather low, round in the neck, and finished with embroidery on the shoulders and down the front. It is to be worn in the morning in place of a more elaborate dress.

The fourth is a chemise, with a yoke and sleeve, tucked and edged with embroidery.

Under-bodies, or spencers, as they are sometimes called, for keeping the bodies of dresses clean, retain their place much better, if made with a skirt coming down below the waist. These under-bodies should be cut something like old-fashioned basques.

The latest style for making pillow-cases is to run six or eight tucks around the edge, and embroider the initials, in large letters, not on the end, but directly in the middle of the pillow-case. If the pillow-cases are made with a plain hem, or ruffled, the stud-holes are prettier for being embroidered: for which we give patterns on a preceding page. The embroidery looks better on the pillows, if pink paper muslin is put over the ticking. But pillow-cases can be marked in indelible ink, if preferred.

CHEMISE.

It is customary now to embroider sheets, table-cloths and napkins, with red embroidery cotton.

THE KNICKERBOCKER SUIT.

BY EMILY H. MAY.

THE Knickerbocker costume is now the favorite style of dress for boys, when they are of that awkward age, too young to be breeched, and too old to wear frocks and pinafores. This costume has a great many recommendations: it can be made in almost any material; it always looks neat and tidy; and for the play-ground is peculiarly suitable, as it leaves boys the free use of their limbs, besides being rather more manly than petticoats, which used to be (particularly at school) a boy's abhorrence. The suit we have illustrated is made of cloth for winter wear. On the next page we give a diagram, as follows:

No. 1. BACK OF KNICKERBOCKERS.
No. 2. FRONT OF KNICKERBOCKERS.
No. 3. HALF OF BACK OF JACKET.
No. 4. FRONT OF JACKET.
No. 5. HALF OF BACK OF WAISTCOAT.
No. 6. FRONT OF WAISTCOAT.
No. 7. SLEEVE.
No. 8. CUFF AND SLEEVE.
No. 9. POCKET FOR KNICKERBOCKERS.

THE JACKET is bound at the edges with broad braid, and is trimmed above that with two rows of narrow; whilst down the front, on each side, nineteen round and stout buttons are placed at regular distances, the jacket being merely fastened with a hook and eye at the top. The back is cut in one piece, with a seam down the middle, and each of the fronts has a pocket put in, bound with braid and trimmed with two rows of the narrow braid; a line, showing where the pocket should be put, is drawn in the diagram. The sleeves are made with a seam at the elbow, and with a turned-back cuff, also bound and trimmed; the line crossing the top of the sleeve indicates where the front half should be sloped at the top.

THE WAISTCOAT.—The fronts are made of cloth, bound and trimmed with braid, and are fastened with ten buttons and button holes. A piece of broad braid, doubled, is run on, to imitate a pocket, with a row of narrow braid run round it in the shape of the line shown in the diagram. The back is made in one piece, of double dark twill, and, in joining the back to the front, the seam is left open as far as the letter A, to give the waistcoat a little play in front, and make it sit well over the stomach. The back has two strings to tie it in behind to the size required.

THE KNICKERBOCKERS.—Each leg is cut in one piece, that is to say, there is no seam down the straight part; but it should be opened as far as the two B's, and a false hem made on each side of the opening. This straight part is trimmed with three straps of broad braid, with a button in the center, the braid being put on in a point at each end. The top of the Knickerbockers is gathered into a band, the length of the band being eleven inches and a half in front, and twelve inches and a half behind, to allow for buttoning over, and each of the bands has three button holes made in them of rather a large size. The bottom of the Knickerbockers is plainly hemmed with a hem half an inch wide, in which a piece of broad elastic should be put, so as to make them fit tightly to the leg, and this elastic should always be taken out, if the suit is to be washed. The pocket shown in the diagram is put in on the right side of the Knickerbockers, and the opening in it should be made as far as the cross. All these three patterns are drawn without allowing for turnings anywhere, or for the hem at the bottom of the trousers. In former numbers, we have explained how to enlarge these patterns.

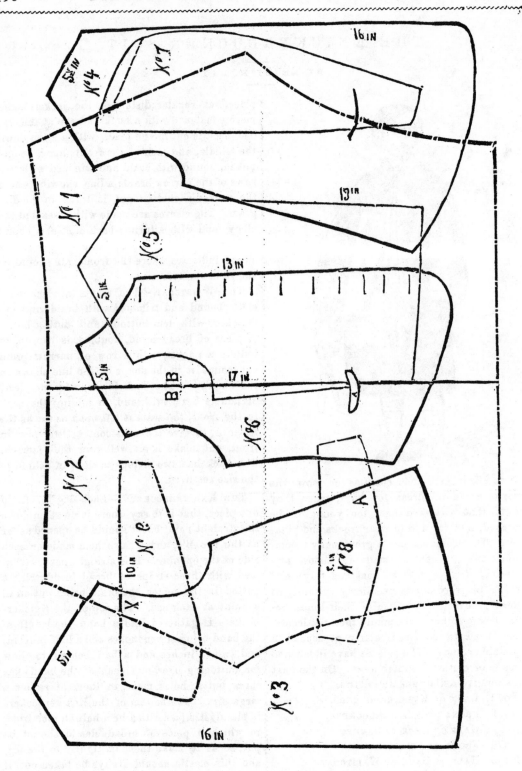

In Remembrance.

PURSE.

BY MADEMOISELLE ROCHE.

THIS sort of Purse can be made with very great expedition, and the materials are extremely simple. Cut the shape given in kid, velvet, watered silk, or satin. Stitch down upon it the number of gilt stars, as seen in our illustration, or any other arrangement or variety of the gilt ornaments, of which there are now so many manufactured. Stitch the back and front together twice, and line with silk. Then, with netting silk, buttonhole all round regularly, but with the stitches a little apart, and on this crochet a row of loops all round. Attach a silk cord at each side of the top, and two tassels. If further ornament is desired, place another tassel at the center of the bottom and one at each corner.

EDGING.

CARD-CASE.

BY MADEMOISELLE ROCHE.

THESE little articles are very useful productions of the Work-Table on various accounts. In the first place, they are inexpensive; in the second, they are more convenient for carrying, being flexible. The design given is to be worked on canvas, the cross bars being in deep maize-color silk; in the places where they cross the nine small squares formed by the crossing they are in a deep crimson Berlin wool, the remainder of the ground being in black Berlin wool. The larger squares, on which the pattern rests, have the upper half of their ground in a medium shade of French blue, and their under half of dark, in Berlin wool, the pattern being in beads alternately of transparent and chalk-white. When this part of the work has been completed, the Card-Case must be closed up at each side, leaving the flap to turn over, lined with silk, and a line of the chalk-white beads carried up the seams and round the edge of the flap, to the center of which a loop must be attached to fasten with a large ornamental button.

BAG PURSE.

BY MADEMOISELLE ROCHE.

A VERY useful sort of bag, being an easy and ready receptacle for all the materials of any moderate-sized piece of work, together with such accompaniments as require to be carried from room to room during its execution, may be made in the style of the Bag Purse, which is a little novelty of its kind. Work a piece of crochet in any simple and open pattern, sixteen inches wide and twenty-four inches long; close this at each end so as only to leave an opening in the middle of the join; line with colored calico, and finish each end with a fringe or a crochet border. The same bag may be made either with silk or a pretty chintz: to the first of these a silk fringe must be attached to each end; to the second a crochet border in a mixture of white and colored ingrain cotton. Sometimes these bags are made a little smaller in crochet silk, either in a slight, open crochet-stitch, or they are netted in silk, and are made to look ornamental by means of a stripe of the loops being ornamented with steel beads; and in both of these last-mentioned styles there is a fringe in which the steel beads are freely introduced.

ALPHABET FOR MARKING.

BY MRS. JANE WEAVER.

"BID ME GOOD BYE."

BALLAD.

ARRANGED FOR THE GUITAR BY SEP. WINNER.

Bid me good bye, mo - ther, bid me a - dieu;

Kiss me a - gain, for I leave thee to - day. Sad is my heart, for its

joys are but few, And less may they be when I'm gone far a - way. It

2d.

Bid me good bye, dearest, bid me adieu;
  Kiss me again for I leave thee to-day.
Sad is the task for my heart, it is true,
  Yet still may I dream of thee when I'm away.
But ere we must part I give thee a token;
  Close to thy heart wilt thou hide it away;
Until I return may its charm be unbroken,
  True be thy heart, tho' far distant the day.

TOILET PIN-CUSHION.

BY MRS. JANE WEAVER.

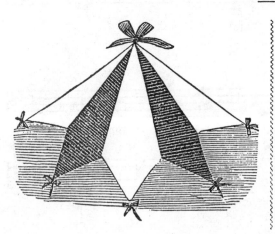

THIS pretty Cushion is to be made of merino, red, white, and blue. It consists of eight points, two red, two blue, four white. These points are made by taking a square of eight inches, fold in half, making a triangle. Sew all around, leaving a small space for turning and stuffing, which latter may be done either with wool or bran. Eight of these points complete the cushion. Arrange the red points opposite, the blue ones the same, the four white ones dispose of between the others, joining all the parts together at the top, as seen in the design. Finish with rows of red, white, and blue ribbon, one at the top, and one at every point.

ALPHABET FOR MARKING: OLD ENGLISH.

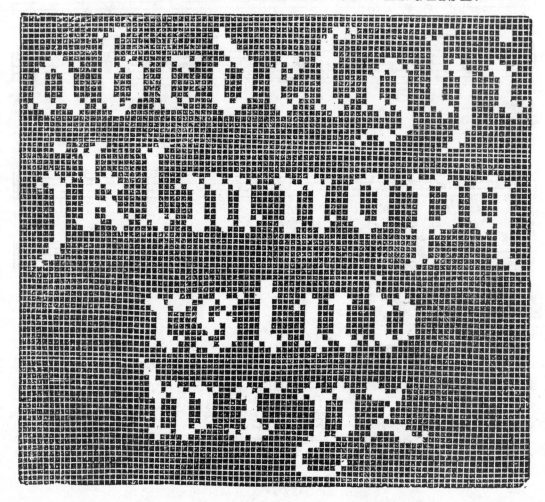

MUSLIN BODY AND SASH: NET FOR HAIR.

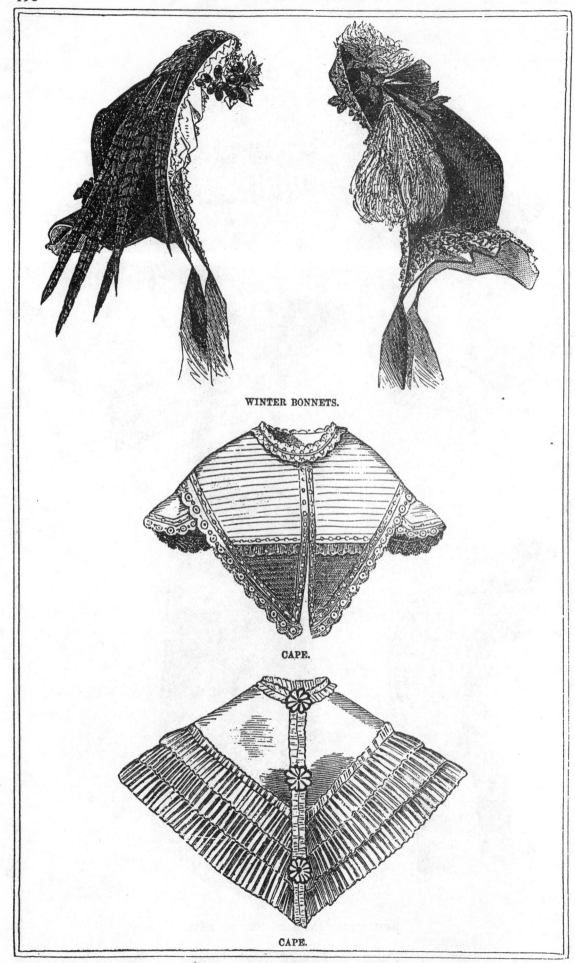

WINTER BONNETS.

CAPE.

CAPE.

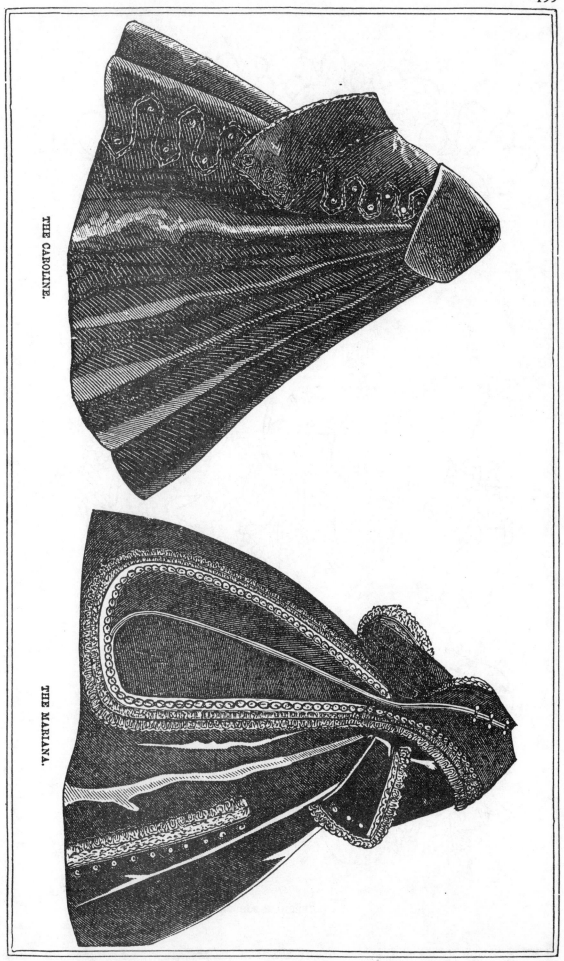

THE CAROLINE.

THE MARIANA.

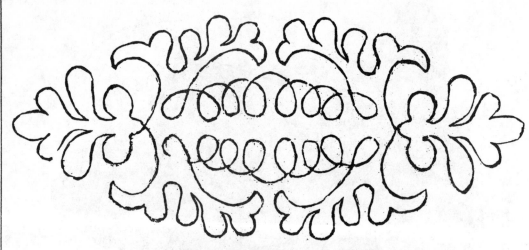

PATTERN IN BRAIDING FOR CIGAR-CASE.

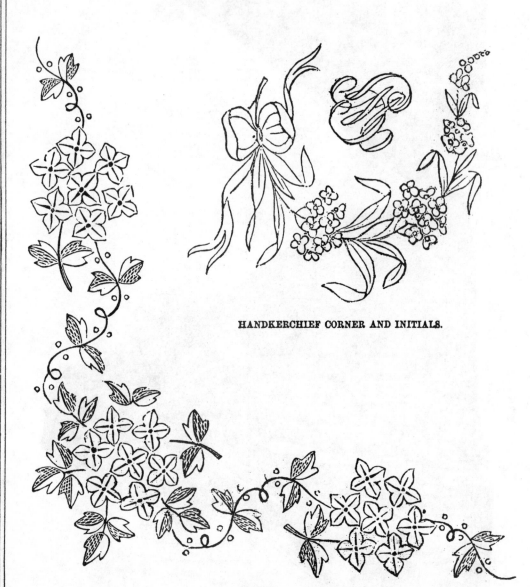

HANDKERCHIEF CORNER AND INITIALS.

HANDKERCHIEF BORDER.

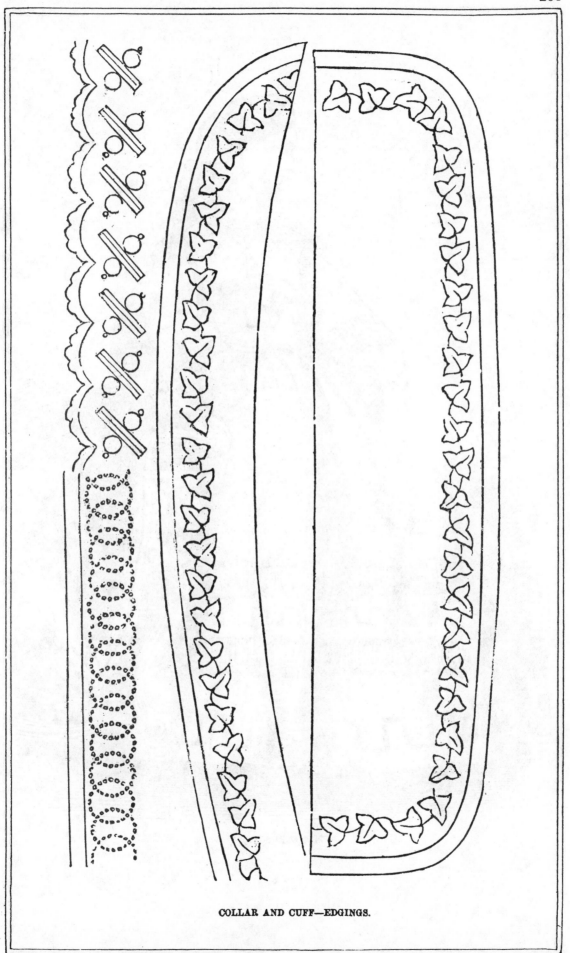

COLLAR AND CUFF—EDGINGS.

THE ETRUSCAN.

THE AUGUSTA.

"Sliding, or One Finger Waltz."

AS PUBLISHED BY SEP. WINNER, PHILA.

Fine.

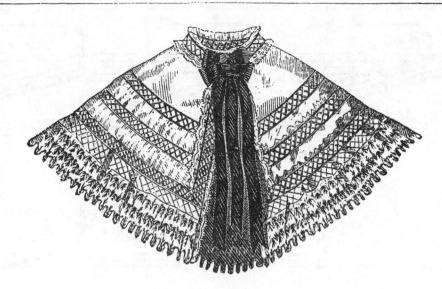

LACE CAPE.

CHILDREN'S FASHIONS FOR DECEMBER.

CASAQUE FOR LITTLE GIRL.

BY EMILY H. MAY.

OUR diagram, for this month, is that of a Casaque for a little girl from six to eight years old; it is cut without seam at waist, the pattern consisting of four pieces, namely, the front, back, side-body, and sleeve. The sleeve is shaped at the elbow, and should be left open at the back seam for about four inches, the corners slightly rounded. It is intended to be made in black silk. Enlarge the diagram to the size indicated.

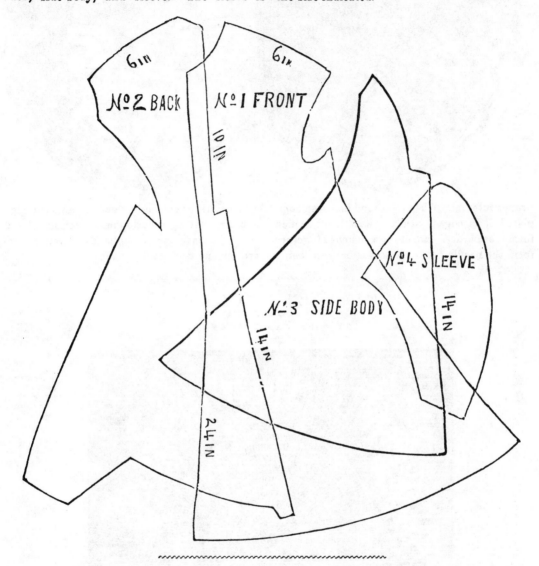

NEEDLE-BOOK IN CROCHET.

BY MADEMOISELLE ROCHE.

THIS little article, so simple and expeditiously made, is extremely pretty when seen completed, and is well calculated for a young lady to present to her friends, or to work a number of them in various colors, as contributions to charitable bazaars. It is nothing more than plain crochet worked over a fine cord, and going round and round until the size of our engraving is reached, or a very trifle larger. Two threads are employed for the crochet, and when one of these is gold the effect is greatly improved. Violet and gold, blue and gold, green and gold, all look rich and handsome: but two silks of well-contrasting colors are also in good taste. Our engraving shows when the dark and light succeed each other, and we need scarcely say that where the one appears it is worked over the thread of the other, which is resumed in its turn after the

proper interval. When the round has been completed, it is edged with a row of loops, which forms the border. Two of these fastened together form the needle-book, the leaves between being of fine cloth or cashmere worked round the edge with a row of open buttonhole-stitch in colored silk. We have rarely published a prettier pattern, or one more easily made.

TIDY IN CROCHET.

BY MRS. JANE WEAVER.

MATERIALS.—4 spools pink crochet cotton, No. 16; 4 spools white crochet cotton, No. 16; fine steel hook.

With the white cotton, make a ch of 6. Join. Work 3 rows in dc stitch, widening enough to keep the work flat. Join the pink cotton, and in every stitch of last row work 2 dc stitches, 1 ch stitch between. Repeat all round the row.

2nd Row.—* work 4 dc between the 2 dc stitches formed by last row *.

3rd Row.—* work 4 dc between the 4 dc stitches of preceding row *.

4th Row.—* 6 dc between the 4 dc of 3rd row *.

Join the white cotton, work * 1 dc (between 3rd and 4th stitches in the group of 6 stitches made by last row), 4 ch, 1 dc between the groups *. Work 3 rows in this manner, widening enough to keep the work flat. Join the pink cotton and work 3 rows of shells, 4 dc stitches to each shell; then join the white cotton and work 4 rows in dc, 4 ch stitches between each stitch, as directed above; then 3 rows of shells as before with the pink cotton, 4 rows in white

cotton as before. This completes the center-piece.

FOR THE BORDER.—With the pink cotton, make a ch of 6, join, into it work 22 stitches in dc for 1st row.

2nd Row.—* 1 dc, 1 ch, miss 1, * all round the row.

3rd Row.—4 dc between every stitch of 2nd row.

4th Row.—White, 4 dc between every 3rd stitch of 3rd row.

5th Row.—Pink, 4 dc between every 4th stitch of 4th row.

This completes one of the small circles forming the border: 20 are required to border the tidy. Into these tie the fringe, alternate white and pink, about one-eighth of a yard in length when tied.

GLASS BEAD MAT.

BY MRS. JANE WEAVER.

MATERIALS REQUIRED.—6 rows dark blue beads; 7 rows middle shade; 10 light blue; 6 rows dark red; 6 middle shade; 7 light red; 2 rows of dark yellow; 2 rows light or amber; 5 rows white; 2 rows black.

Commence working this mat at the center of the left side, marked A, by taking 1 light blue bead upon each needle; draw them to the middle of the thread; then pass both needles through 1 light blue, then take 2 next shade of blue, one on each needle; then pass both needles through 1 dark blue, then take 2 light red, 1 dark blue, 2 light red, 1 second shade blue, 2 light blue, 1 light red, 2 light red, 1 light red, 2 amber, 1 dark yellow, 2 white, 1 dark red, 2 dark red, 1 dark red; then one black on the right hand needle and 1 red on the left hand needle, then 1 black, 2 black, 1 black; 1 black on the left hand needle, 1 white on the right; then 1 white, 1 red on right hand needle, 1 white on left, 1 red, 1 yellow on right hand, 1 red on left, then 1 yellow.

This brings the work back to the center of the mat; and by reversing the work, it will bring you to the opposite side, finishing with two, the same way as the beginning.

LADIES' BRAIDED SLIPPER: TOE AND HEEL.

HAIR DRESSING.

YOUNG BRIDE'S HEAD-DRESS.

An exquisite Head-Dress, of a very graceful style, and well agreeing with a fair or brown complexion, to be worn by a young bride, or at grand assemblies.

EXPLANATION: Comb the hair back and place a set of small loose curls across the forehead; place a diadem plait over the top of the curls, and comb the hair off the temples over the ends of the plait, and form a chignon or bow of the back hair, and place a three-strand braid around the chignon, made either from the ends of hair from the temple or a switch. Add a crown of white blossoms and a veil, as shown in the engraving. If not for a bride, trim to match dress.

HAIR DRESSING.

COURT HEAD-DRESS.

A rich Head-Dress, having a great stamp of distinction, and for that reason will be adapted for a Court Head-Dress, or Grand Evening Parties.

EXPLANATION: Make a parting over the head from ear to ear, two inches from front, and form a row of nine small puffs over the forehead. Comb the remaining hair back, and divide into four partings around the head, and form each parting in a large puff, as in cut. Add a few small friz curls and orange blossoms between the puffs.

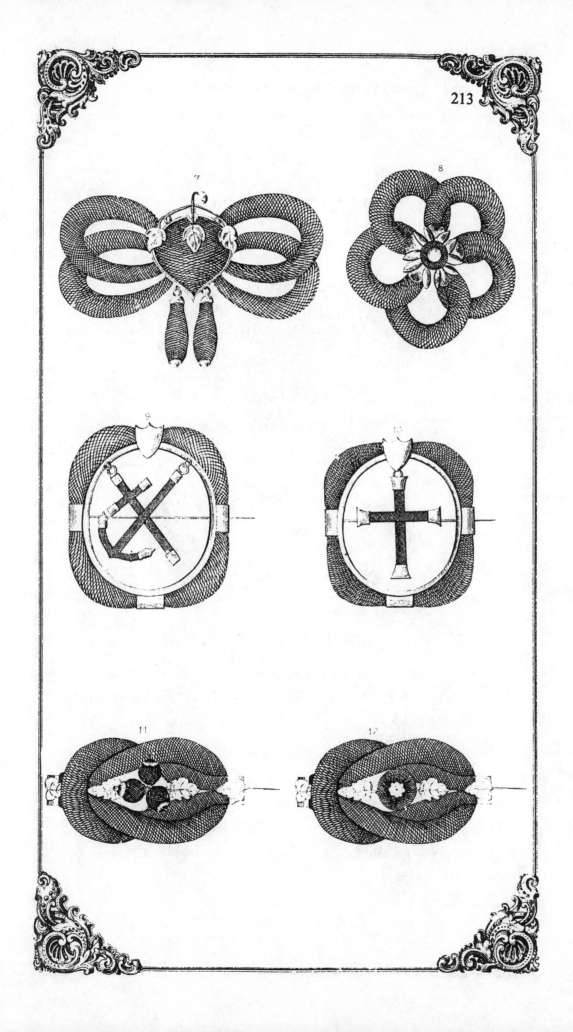

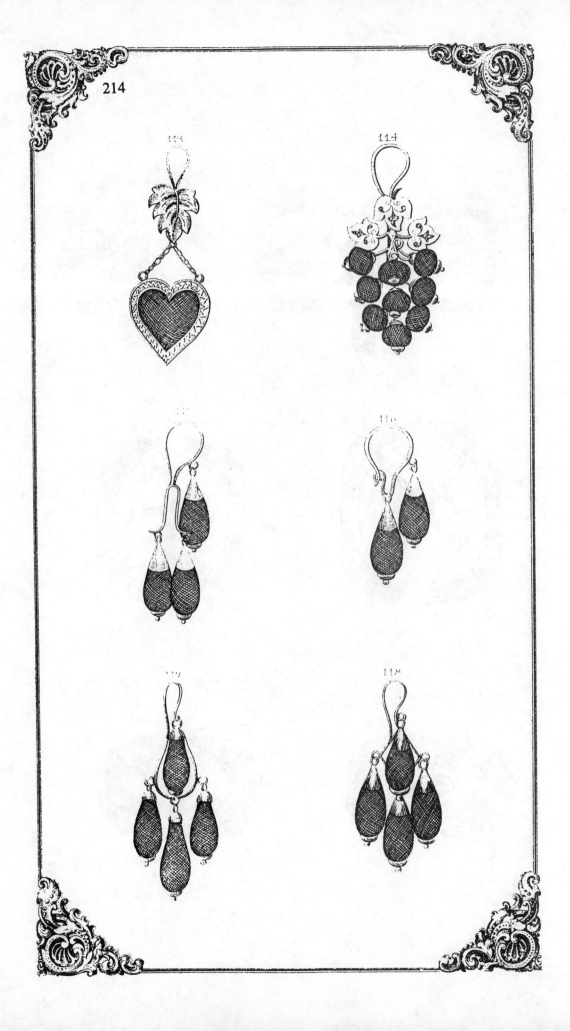

HAIR DRESSING.

GRAND EVENING PARTY HEAD-DRESS.

A very graceful Head-Dress, of a bold style, suited for a young lady of brown or fair complexion, and is in good taste to be worn at the theatre or Grand Evening Parties.

EXPLANATION: Make a parting over the head, from ear to ear, two inches from front; on the forehead, between the temples, curl the hair in small friz curls, and from the temple to the ear, make loose puffs.   Divide the hair in three partings over the head, and roll each in a large puff; then form a large puff of the back hair, round the nape of the neck, as in cut.   Fasten a large set of loose curls over the puff, with a comb or other ornament.

HAIR DRESSING.

SOIREE OR EVENING HEAD-DRESS.

This cut illustrates the Soiree or Evening Head-Dress. It is a very unique and modern style, suited for almost any complexion, and very easily executed.

EXPLANATION: Comb the hair straight back between the temples, tie it, and curl the ends, or use a set of long false curls. Place a diadem plait, made from a switch, across the forehead; then comb the hair back from the temples, over the ends of the plait, twist it, pass it back under the curls, and fasten firmly. Use a fancy back-comb on top of curls, and pin an ornament to diadem plait, with feather and chain attached, as in cut, or trim to suit dress.

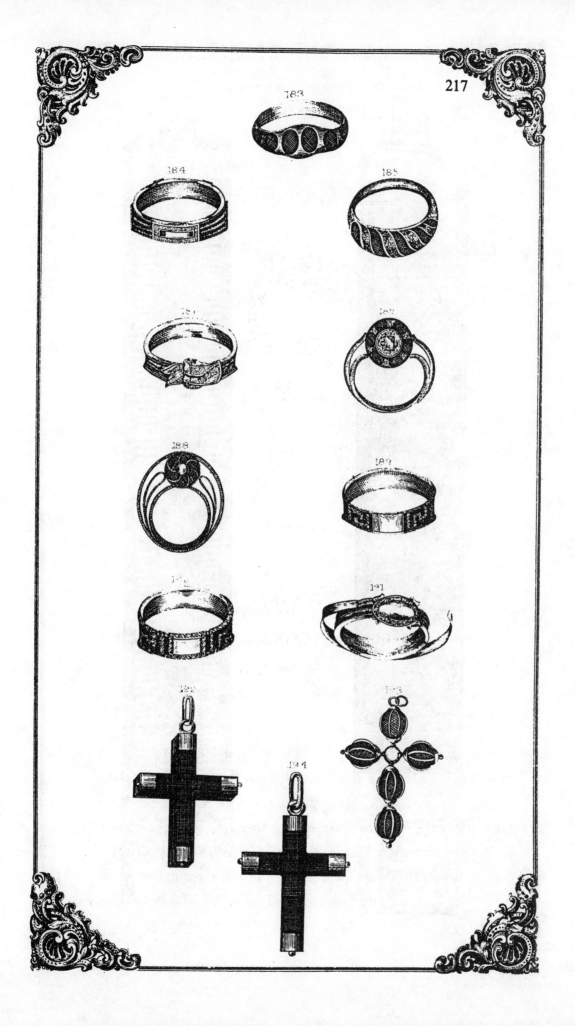

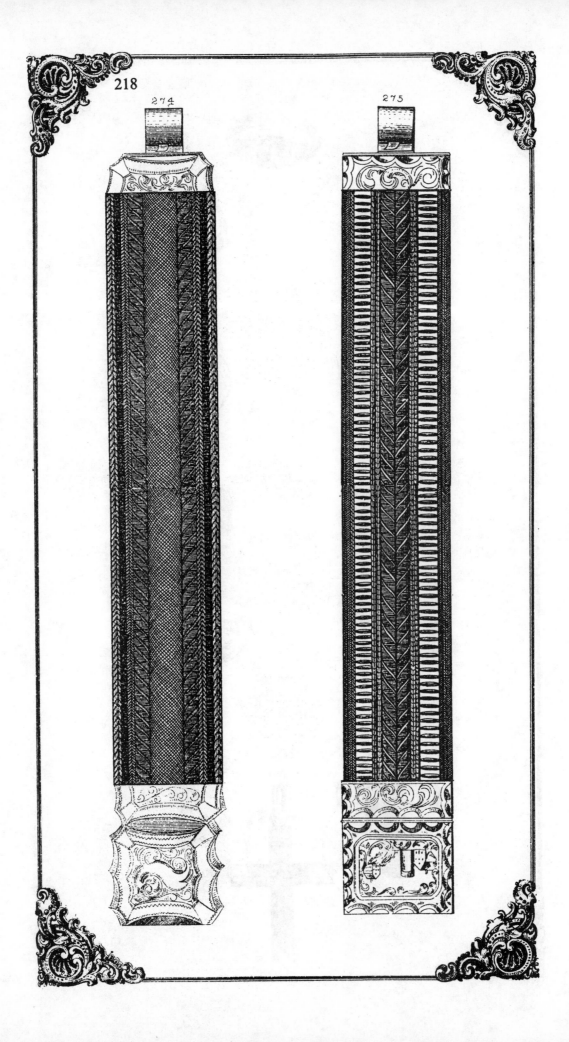

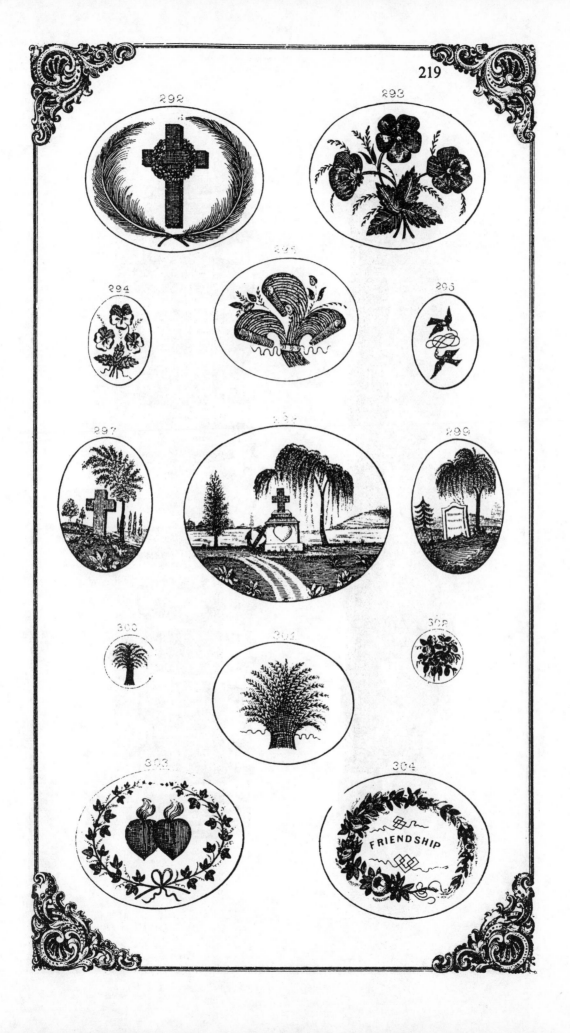

FRIENDSHIP

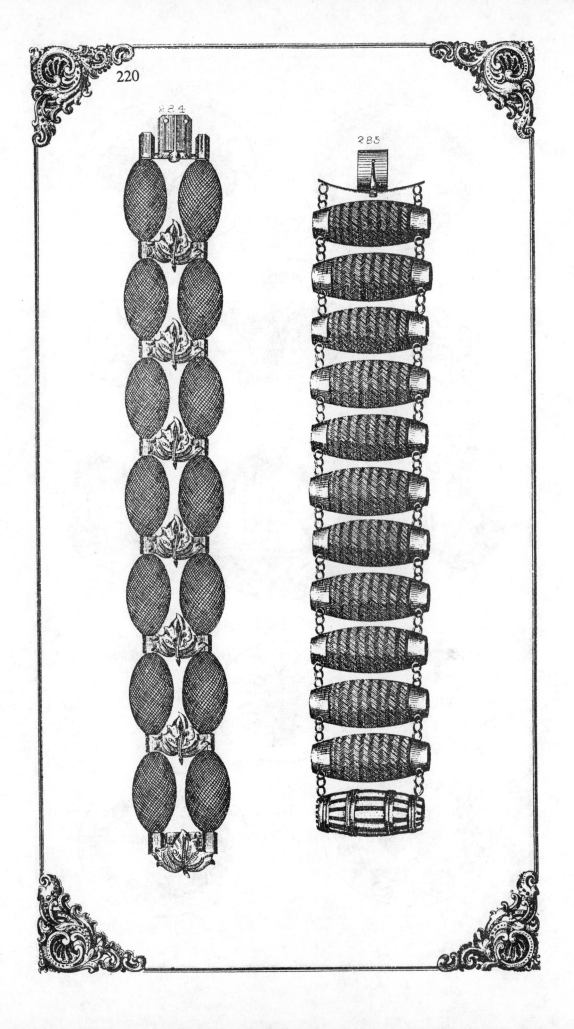

HAIR DRESSING.

RECEPTION HEAD-DRESS.

This Head-Dress is a most charming composition, and entirely new.   It is adapted either for a brown or fair complexion, to be worn at grand dinners or receptions.   Ornamented with pearl or gilt, it is in good taste for evening parties.

EXPLANATION: Curl the hair across forehead, or use false curls, combing the hair straight back, and form a chignon of curls at the back.   Place a diadem plait across forehead, and raise the hair from the temples over the plait.   Trim with roses and ribbans, or to suit dress.

HAIR DRESSING.

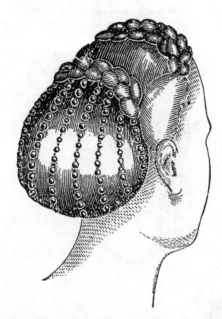

PROMENADE HEAD-DRESS.

Our first cut represents the Promenade Head-Dress, but is worn as frequently in the drawing-room, and even at public and private assemblies—in fact, a common and very pretty style.

EXPLANATION: Comb the front hair between the temples straight back, over a cushion of crimped hair, forming a Chignon; then make two braids of two small switches, and place one of them over the top of the Chignon, and the other across the forehead, forming a diadem, turning the ends under; then comb the hair from temples over the braids, and put back under the Chignon, and fasten. Place a net of pearl or gilt beads over the Chignon, as in cut. You can use false hair for covering cushion, if desired.

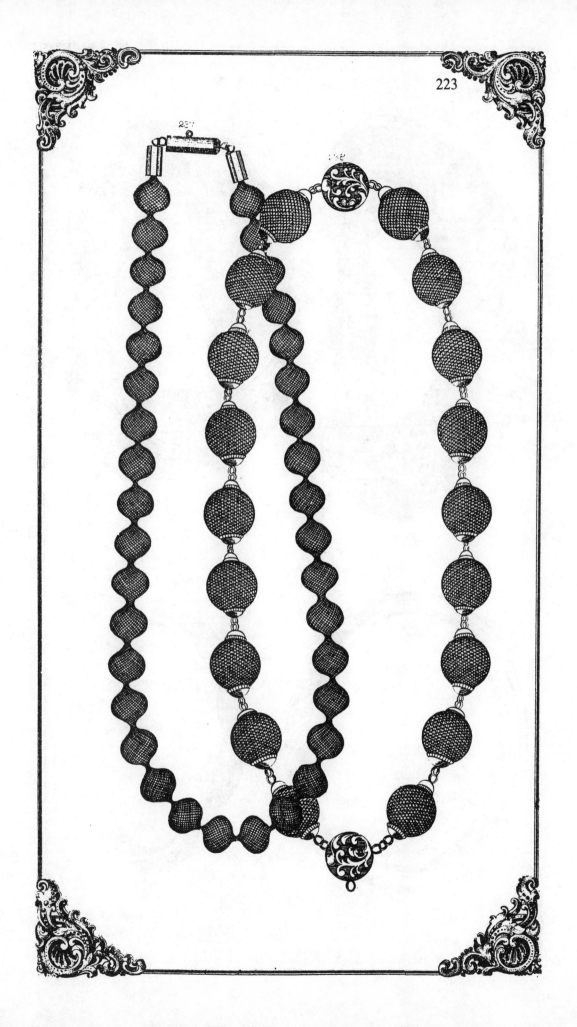

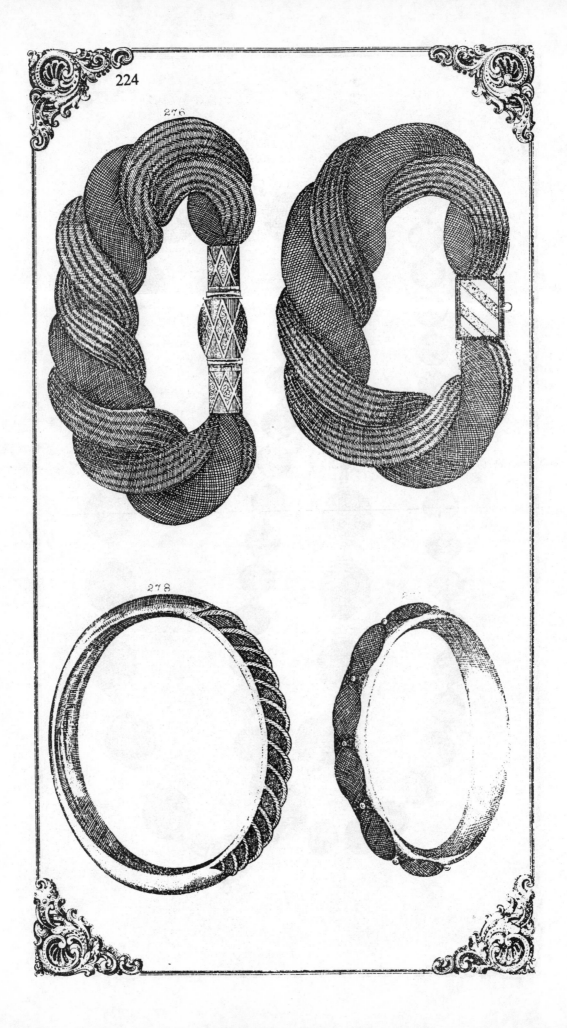

PETERSON'S

CHASED BY THE LOVES

MAGAZINE

1864

CHILDREN'S FASHIONS FOR JANUARY

INITIALS FOR MARKING.

FURRED CLOAK.

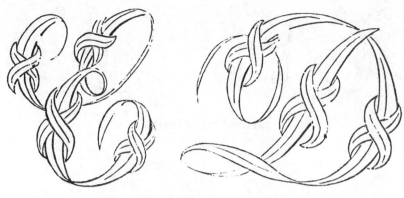

INITIALS FOR PILLOW-CASE.

THE VESTVALI CLOAK.

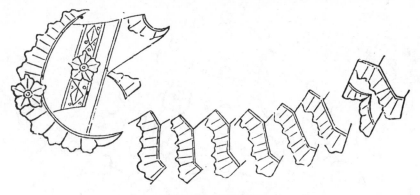

NAME FOR MARKING.

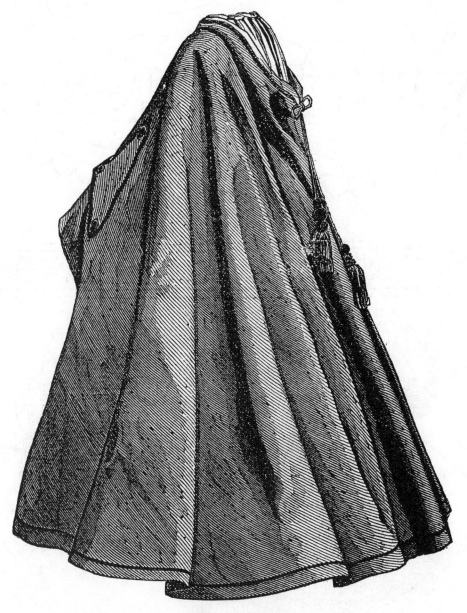

THE PATTI CLOAK.

TOP OF PIN-CUSHION: ONE-QUARTER; EMBROIDERED ON MUSLIN. SILK EMBROIDERY ON FLANNEL. INSERTIONS, ETC.

COLLAR AND CUFF IN EMBROIDERY: HALF OF EACH. HANDKERCHIEF CORNER. EDGING.

232

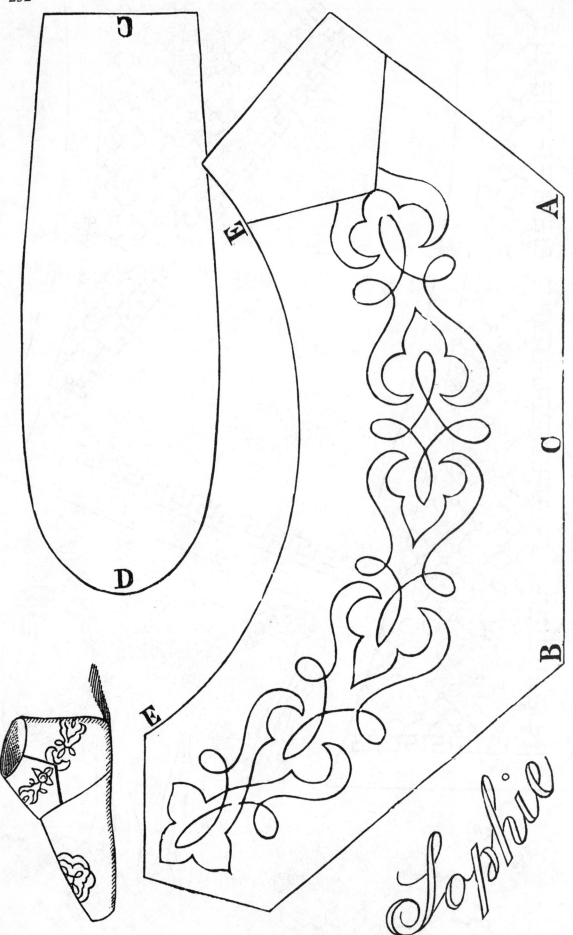

BABY'S SHOE: SOLE AND SIDE-PIECE. NAME FOR MARKING.

TOE OF BABY'S SHOE. HANDKERCHIEF BORDER, AND CORNER, NAME FOR MARKING, ETC.

VARIETIES FOR THE MONTH.

BY EMILY H. MAY.

THERE are very many new things, this month, for the winter promises to be quite gay. We give selections of a few of these novelties. The first is a beautiful body with braces in velvet, one of the latest affairs that have come out in Paris: it is said the empress was the first lady for whom one was made; and it would be especially becoming to persons of similar style and complexion. It has the advantage, also, of being easily made. Any lady, with taste and skill, can copy it, without the aid of a mantua-maker.

The next is a white cashmere jacket, braided in black. The braiding pattern, given in our embellishment, need not be followed, necessarily. Any other pattern, which may be preferred, or may be ready at hand, would do as well. We are constantly giving new patterns for braiding, in

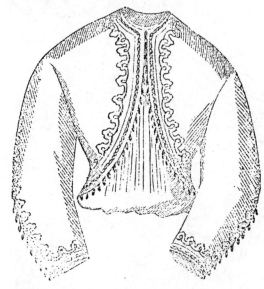

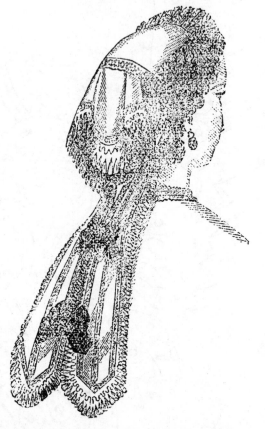

order that our subscribers may use them for this and similar purposes. On certain styles of figures, this jacket is pre-eminently handsome.

Our third illustration is an Italian head-dress; something entirely new, and very charming. This graceful affair has created quite a sensation in London and Paris, and is being introduced, with the greatest success, in the fashionable circles of Philadelphia, New York, and Boston. It has a picturesque air, as will be seen, which very few similar articles attain. On a tall, wil-lowy form it is particularly pretty. It has a careless, artistic effect on such persons, as if a handkerchief had been thrown, lightly, over the head, and the ends allowed to fall down. It is, on all persons, singularly free from the stiffness so common to so many head-dresses.

Raphael bodies still continue popular, and will always look well on certain styles of persons. Our fourth illustration is a very handsome body of this description. The tassels are a particularly noticeable feature of this pattern.

Our fifth engraving is a fichu, trimmed in purple or blue, as the wearer's taste may dictate. Our sixth and seventh engravings are illustrations of caps, which are very far prettier than most of the kind. These articles are always fashionable, and always look well, on almost every lady. They are easily made also, which is another recommendation; and, besides, are not extravagant. We shall continue to give, in this way, new patterns of such affairs whenever anything striking comes out. Many of the articles, thus represented, will be such as only a milliner can get up: but it is necessary, in such cases, to know, at least, what to wear. Most of them, however, will be such as ladies can themselves make.

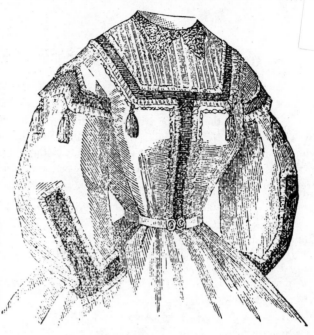

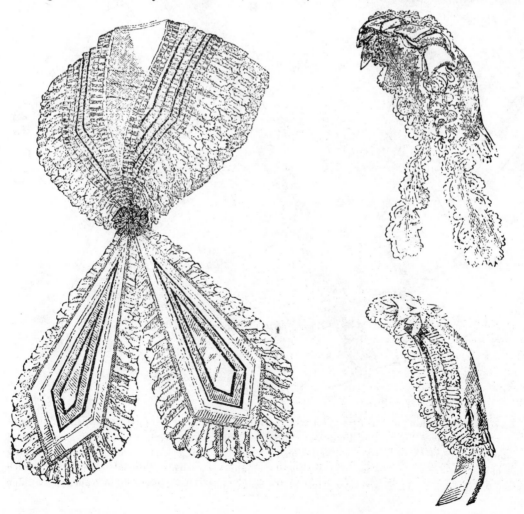

BORDER IN NETTING AND DARNING.

BY MRS. JANE WEAVER.

In the front of the number a pattern is given for a Border in Netting and Darning. Short window-blinds for bedrooms look pretty, darned in stripes like this illustration; it also makes a pretty border to an Anti-Macassar. Care must be taken in darning not to pull the thread too tightly, or the work will have a drawn, puckered appearance. Trafalgar cotton should be used for darning. There are few things, so easily done, which are so pretty.

BOY'S FRENCH BLOUSE.

BY EMILY H. MAY.

The diagram for this popular dress (for which see next page), gives the proper dimensions for the complete dress to fit a boy two and a half years old. The dress is to be made of gray silk poplin, trimmed with black or very dark blue velvet ribbon two inches in width. The front is in one entire piece, opening diagonally from A to B, closing with hooks and loops at the shoulder, or with a button corresponding with those upon the strap reaching from the shoulder

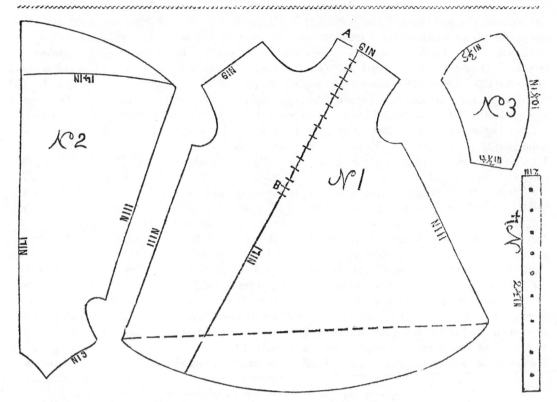

to the bottom of the dress. It is very simple and easily made: in fact, only a loose blouse, confined at the waist with a leather or velvet belt, and large buckle.

No. 1. FRONT.
No. 2. HALF OF BACK.
No. 3. SLEEVE.
No. 4. STRAP FROM SHOULDER.

CROCHET INSERTION FOR PETTICOATS.

BY MRS. JANE WEAVER.

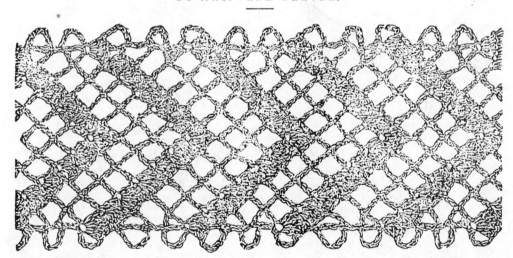

MATERIAL.—Cotton No. 12. Make a chain of 20 stitches, and work backward and forward. 1st row: 5 chain, 5 treble crochet in the last stitch of the foundation, 3 chain, miss 2, 1 double crochet in the next stitch, 5 chain, miss 3, 1 double crochet in the next, 5 treble crochet in the next. Then 1 chain, miss 3, 5 treble crochet, 5 chain, miss 3, 1 double crochet, 3 chain, miss 2, 5 treble crochet in the last stitch. 2nd row: 5 chain, 1 treble crochet in the center treble of the 5 last worked, 5 treble crochet in the first of the 3 chain, 3 chain, 1 treble crochet on the next chain, 5 chain, 1 double crochet in the center of the 5 treble, then 5 treble crochet in the chain placed between two sets of 5 treble in preceding row, 1 double crochet in the center of the 5 treble, 9 chain, 1 double crochet on the chain stitches of preceding row, 3 chain, 5 treble crochet in the last of the next 3 chain, 1 treble crochet in the center of the last set of 5 treble belonging to preceding row. 3rd row: 5 chain, 1 treble crochet in the last treble of preceding row, 3 chain, 1 double crochet in the center of the 5 treble, then 5 treble crochet in the first of the 3 chain belonging to preceding row, 3 chain, 1 double crochet on next chain stitches, 5 chain, 1 double crochet in the center of the 5 treble in preceding row, 5 chain, 1 double crochet in the next chain stitches, 5 chain, 5 treble crochet in the last of the next 3 chain, 1 double crochet in the center of the 5 treble, 3 chain, 1 treble crochet in the last treble of preceding row. 4th row: 5 chain, 1 treble in the last worked treble of preceding row, 5 chain, 1 double crochet in the center of the 5 treble, then 5 treble crochet

in the first of the next 3 chain, 3 chain, 1 double crochet in the next chain stitches, 5 chain, 1 double crochet in the next chain stitches, 3 chain, 5 treble crochet in the first of the next 3 chain, 1 double crochet in the center of the 5 treble of preceding row, 5 chain, 1 treble crochet in the last treble of preceding row. 5th row: 5 chain, 1 treble crochet in the last treble of preceding row, 3 chain, 1 double crochet in the following chain stitches, 5 chain, 1 double crochet in the center of the next 5 treble, 5 treble crochet in the first of the next 3 chain, 3 chain, 1 double crochet in the next chain stitches, 3 chain, 5 treble crochet in the last of the next 3 chain, 1 double crochet in the center of the next 5 treble, 5 chain, 1 double crochet on the next chain stitches, 3 chain, 1 treble crochet in the last treble of preceding row. 6th row: The same as the 1st. The illustration shows where the double crochet stitches should come over the chain stitches, and the position of the sets of five treble crochet stitches. The pattern should be repeated from the 2nd to the 5th row.

VARIETIES IN EMBROIDERY.

SPRIG.

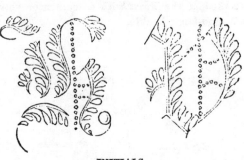

INITIALS.

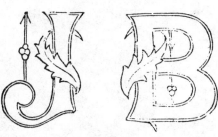

INITIALS.

INITIALS, ETC.

INITIALS.

BRAIDED SMOKING-CAP, ORNAMENTED WITH BEADS.

BY MRS. JANE WEAVER.

MATERIALS required to make one Smoking-Cap: A strip of cloth 6 inches wide: 1 skein of silk Russia braid; 1 bunch of smooth gold beads, No. 9. For lining, a piece of sarsnet and a small piece of demet. A tassel.

The mixture of braid and beads, in the Smoking-Cap we are illustrating, is somewhat novel, and, when worked, has a most charming effect. The pattern should be traced on tissue paper

the crown round to the desired size, and run that and the head-piece together, holding the head-piece next to you. The lining must then be run together in the same way, and fitted into the cap, and the edges of the cloth and lining turned in, and the latter felled down. The tassel should be attached to the top, through the lining, to keep it in its place, and the cap will then be complete.

and tacked on the cloth, and, in cutting out the crown, a six-inch square of cloth must be allowed for. The braid should then be neatly run on over the tissue paper, the beads dotted in where indicated, and, when the work is completed, the paper should be torn away.

The cap is then ready to make up, which is done in the following manner: Tack the demet and sarsnet together, and neatly quilt them; cut

We have not named the colors to be used, as the choice of these so much depends on individual taste, but we can recommend black cloth, with scarlet, blue, amber, or green braid, or a blue cloth, with a gold-colored braid, or a scarlet cloth with black or blue braid, always using gold beads, except when amber braid is selected, when white chalk or steel will be found prettier.

SIDE OF SMOKING-CAP.

PENWIPER.

BY MRS. JANE WEAVER

MATERIALS.—Some pieces of scarlet cloth. Other pieces of black cloth. One large hickory-nut. Cut three circles of red cloth six inches in diameter, notch them upon the edge. Also

old woman's head, take the nut, and display as much genius (with the aid of pen and ink) as is possible under the circumstances, in making her look as much like a cross old woman as you

three black ones in the same manner; fold each circle in half; then make a funnel of each piece so folded, fastening them with a stitch at the point; arrange them, alternating black and red, all the points coming to the center. For the

can. With a little frill of lace or muslin for the cap. and some of the black cloth, bordered with scarlet, for the hood, the old woman's head will be complete. Sew it firmly in the center of the Penwiper.

MARIE STUART CASHMERE HOOD.

BY MRS. JANE WEAVER

This very pretty affair is made as follows. Take a square of cashmere (scarlet, blue, or white), thirty-three inches square, and of the shape as seen in the diagram on the following page.

The front is A. From C to C, following the dotted line, run a casing of half-inch ribbon on the inside. Trim with silk of the same, or contrasting color, pinked on the edges, and quilled, as seen in the design, given above.

If warmth is needed, line the head-piece with silk, slightly wadded. It will take about one yard of silk for the trimming, cut bias. The lower frill is two inches in width, pinked on one edge only, gathered and put on at the other edge.

The upper frill, of the same width, is pinked on both edges, gathered in the center. Nothing prettier than this, or so easily made, has come out, this winter.

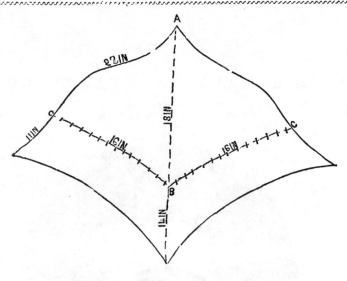

DIAGRAM OF CASHMERE HOOD.

CROCHET EDGING FOR PIN-CUSHION.

BY MRS. JANE WEAVER.

MATERIALS.—Crochet cotton, No. 18. Make a chain, on which work one long, two chain into every other loop. 2nd row: five chain,

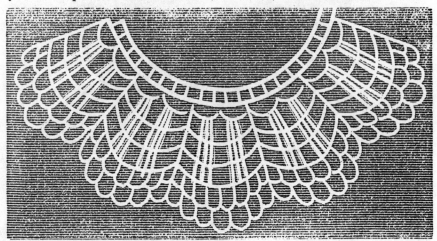

loop in short, leaving four stitches between; continue to the end. 3rd row: three chain, three long, three chain, three long, three chain; loop in short; repeat to the end. 4th row: the same. 5th row: the same. 6th row: one long, two chain in every other loop seven times, loop in short; continue to the end. 7th row: five chain, loop in short; repeat to the end. These rows complete the edging, which is to be tacked round the braided Pin-Cushion.

NAME FOR MARKING.

NAME FOR MARKING.

IMPERATRICE PALETOT: FRONT AND BACK.

INITIALS FOR MARKING.

THE ALEXANDRINE.

INITIALS FOR MARKING.

THE TARTAN.

INITIALS FOR MARKING.

HOUSE DRESS.

INITIALS FOR MARKING.

EVENING DRESS.

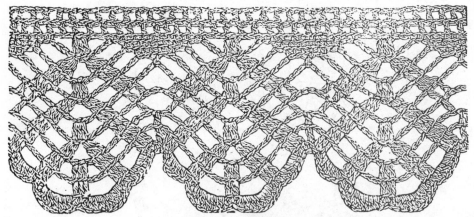

CROCHET PATTERN.

HANDKERCHIEF CORNER.

NAME FOR MARKING.

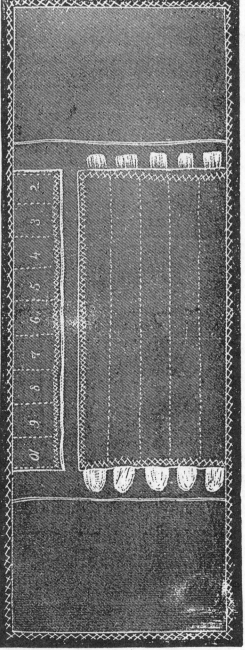

LINING OF NEEDLE-CASE IN BERLIN WOOL.

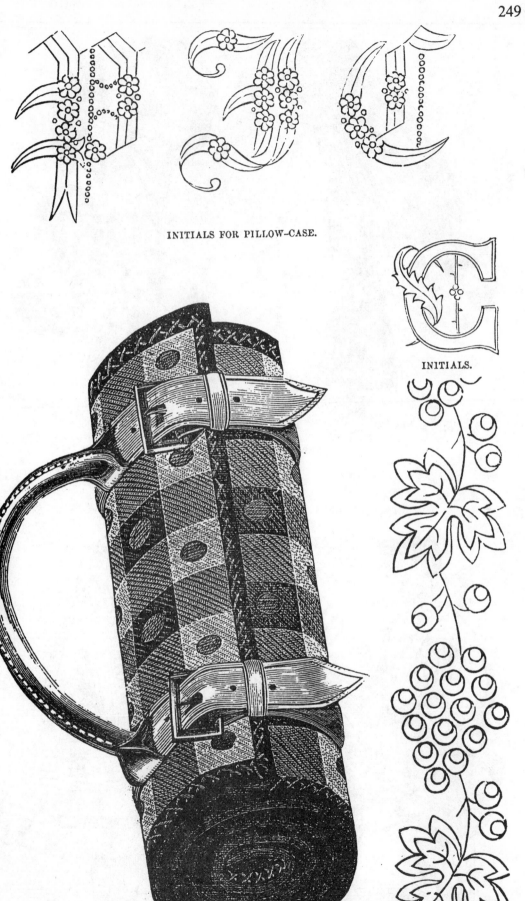

INITIALS FOR PILLOW-CASE.

INITIALS.

NEEDLE-CASE IN BERLIN WOOL.

EDGING.

NEW STYLES OF BONNETS.

CHILDREN'S FASHIONS FOR FEBRUARY.

MISSES' HAT.

BOY'S TROUSERS.

SPANISH BODY.

GIRL'S DRESS.

BRIGHTEST EYES GALOP.

ARRANGED BY

SEP. WINNER.

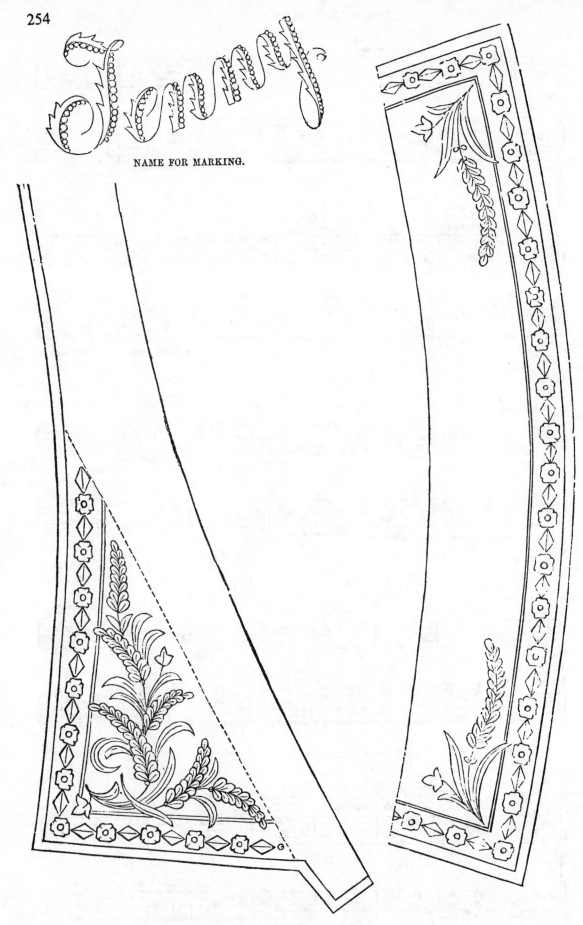

NAME FOR MARKING.

COLLAR AND CUFF.

VARIETIES FOR THE MONTH.

BY EMILY H. MAY.

WE give, again, some of the newest patterns in head-dresses, etc., as we did in the January number. The first to which we call attention is a charming head-dress, one of the very pret-

tiest sent out, from Paris, this winter. The next is also a head-dress, in some respects more elaborate than the last; and of this we give a back view. The next two illustrations are of a prettily trimmed sack-coat, and a set of the fashionable braces, etc.: both of which articles are very desirable, indeed. These two last can be made, after our patterns, by almost any lady. The head-dresses are more difficult, however; but still not beyond almost any lady's skill.

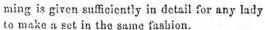

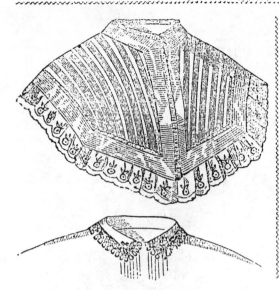

ming is given sufficiently in detail for any lady to make a set in the same fashion.

On the next page, we give a new pattern for a night dress. In some respects, as will be observed, this pattern is an improvement on former ones. It is certainly an unusually elegant affair of the kind.

We give, elsewhere, several very stylish patterns of different things, most of which are suitably described in the fashion department, to which we refer the reader for further information as to the latest novelties.

We also give, in various parts of the number, different patterns for different articles of children's dresses. This is a department to which we shall pay particular attention, this year: more so than any cotemporary.

Our fifth illustration, as will be seen, is a very pretty cape: the ribbon used in trimming which is green. The next is a collar, simple in style, but very elegant. Our seventh engraving is a sleeve, after a new pattern. Our eighth (which see opposite) is a charming cape, in a different style from the

last cape, and better adapted for many wearers. All of these are Paris patterns.

The ninth and tenth illustrations (at the foot of the page), are drawn from a very beautiful chemisette and sleeves. The trim-

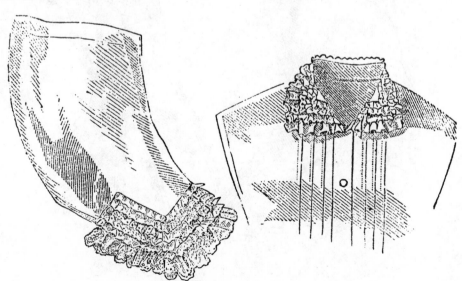

NEEDLE-CASE IN BERLIN WOOL.

BY MRS. JANE WEAVER.

In the front of the number, we give an engraving of a very beautiful Needle-Case in Berlin wool, and also an illustration of the lining. The materials are a piece of fine canvas, 18 inches long and 6 inches wide; some black, scarlet, and white single zephyr; several skeins of yellow embroidery silk; 1½ yard of velvet ribbon, black; some scarlet or black silk for the lining.

Work the canvas in block, 19 stitches and 19 rows to each block. The black blocks, in the design, are done in black, the dark gray in scarlet, and the lightest gray in white. The dots are embroidered (after the blocks are completed) with the yellow silk. Line this outside with the silk, the lining having the places arranged for the thread and needles, as seen in our design, in the front of the number, and bind all round with the black velvet, which is cat-stitched with the yellow silk, both on the inside and outside of the case. Two small straps of black morocco, with a connecting handle, also made of morocco, and two small steel buckles, finish the Needle-Case. If the morocco straps and buckles cannot be procured, black silk elastic and a button will look pretty.

INSERTION.

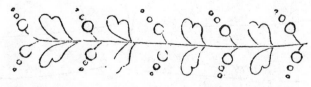

THE IMPERATRICE PALETOT.

BY EMILY H. MAY.

IN the front of the number, we give an engraving of a new winter coat, called the IMPERATRICE PALETOT. In order that our friends may make this stylish article for themselves, if they wish, we give back and front views of it, and also a diagram. The diagram is below, and shows how it may be cut out, and of what size each piece is to be.

No. 1. FRONT.
No. 2. SIDE OF FRONT.
No. 3. SLEEVE.
No. 4. BACK.
No. 5. SIDE-PIECE.

We have not given the full length to these pieces, as the size of our page forbids it. The side-piece and side of front should each be lengthened nine inches at the bottom, (the seam under the arm is indicated by a small cut made in each of these two pieces); this being done, the front must be lengthened to agree with the side of front, and the back must be made to agree in length with the side-piece. The sleeve has a small corner cut off the hind arm at the wrist, which will have to be made good. Nothing has come out, this winter, more stylish than this Paletot.

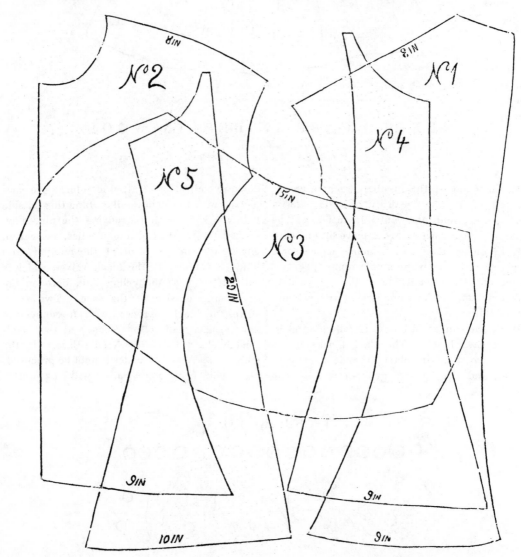

BABY'S KNITTED HOOD.

BY MRS. JANE WEAVER.

MATERIALS.—½ oz. of white single zephyr; 1 oz. of white split zephyr; fine bone knitting-needles.

Make a chain with the white single zepyhr three-eighths of a yard in length—take up every stitch upon the knitting-needle—and knit in ribs, purling six rows and knitting six rows plain, or make wider ribs, according to the taste; narrow one at the beginning of every row, until the work is narrowed down to five or six stitches. For the ruche.—Cast on eight stitches with the split zephyr and knit one row plain. 2nd row: wrap the thread three times round the first and second fingers of left hand, and knit the loops thus made into the first stitch; repeat to the end of the row. 3rd row: plain. 4th row: loop. Continue until the piece is long enough for the face of the hood. The piece at the back is done with four stitches in the same manner.

Four rows of shells form the cape. Draw at the back with narrow ribbon, and finish with a bow of ribbon at the back and on top. Strings of the same.

INITIALS FOR MARKING.

CROCHETED MUFF FOR CHILD.

BY MRS. JANE WEAVER.

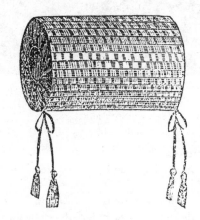

MATERIALS.—From three to four oz. of double zephyr, chinchilla or white and black.

Make a chain ¼ of a yard in length. Work in dc stitch, 2 stitches to a block, 1 ch between each block. Work in rows until the piece is ½ yard in length. If made of white wool, it should be spotted with black in imitation of ermine. Make up the inside of the muff with wadding and silk, (scarlet or blue if the crocheted part is of chinchilla, and if white, the lining should be all white,) and stretch the crocheted work over the foundation muff so made. Finish with cord and tassels.

HAIR-NET.

BY MRS. JANE WEAVER.

THE Hair-Net is a very pretty article of dress, and useful also where the hair is redundant, though the fashion lately has gone rather in favor of curls. It is one of those classical fashions, revived, with advantage, in the present day, when the stiff modes are entirely out of favor. The materials are as simple as possible, being nothing more than of good netting silk.

Brown is the prettiest color for general wear; but if a more dressy style be desired, the color should be selected to suit the costume with which it is to be worn.

To commence—cast on twenty-seven loops on a small piece of its own silk, using a mesh half an inch wide; close it by netting two rounds with a mesh a quarter of an inch wide; then net a row with the wide mesh; then, still with the wide mesh, net round, taking two loops in one, reducing the number to fourteen. Although you have begun with twenty-seven loops, you will have made another loop by passing the silk to the fresh row, which brings the number even. Then net four loops on one all round, using the wide mesh. Resume with the small mesh, and net two rows; then repeat the three rows with the wide mesh exactly the same as already de-scribed; then net two more rows with the small mesh; then the same three rows on the large mesh, which brings the work to the border pattern. After this, a small purse-mesh is to be taken, and one row netted plain round. Another, missing one loop between; and then a third, netting the point-loop only. This forms the edge of the pointed border. These last three rows require a little attention, as it is necessary to leave between each point some little length of silk, both to divide them, and to prevent the work from being drawn up.

These nets are confined round the head by means of an elastic band, passed through the rows of loops immediately above the border pattern. It will be understood that the portions cut off the round are the same as those top and bottom.

VARIETIES FOR THE WORK-TABLE.

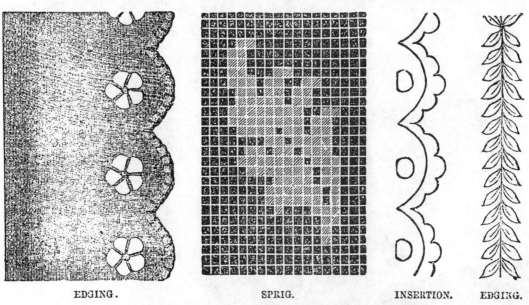

EDGING.   SPRIG.   INSERTION.   EDGING.

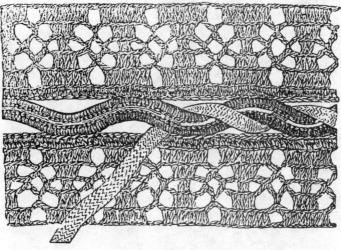

CROCHET TRIMMING.

DESIGN FOR SMOKING CAP--SCOTCH SHAPE.

Crown and Front.

APRIL FASHIONS: HUNTING WILD FLOWERS.

INITIALS FOR MARKING.

WALKING DRESS.

INITIALS.

SPRIG.

HOUSE DRESS.

266

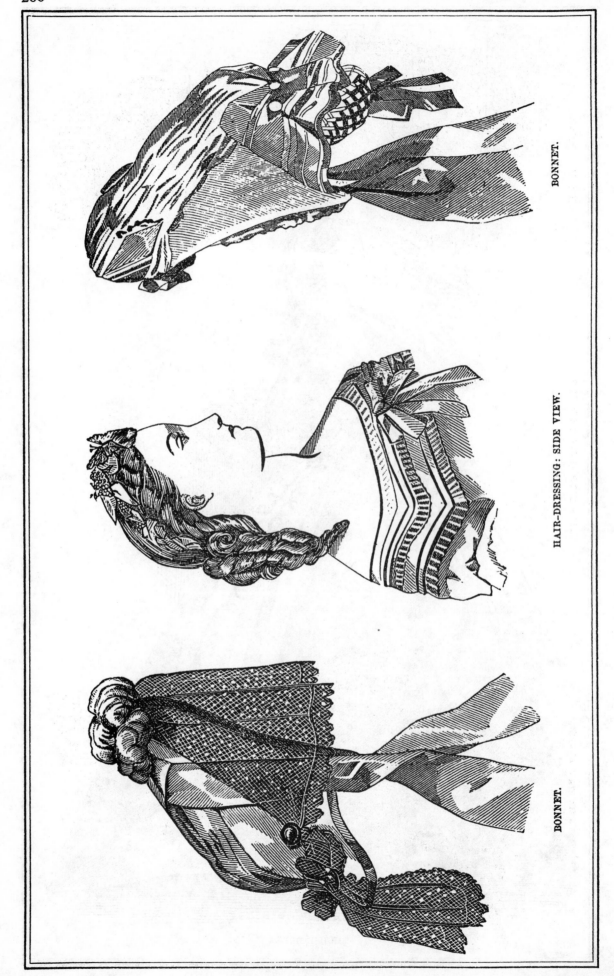

BONNET.

HAIR-DRESSING: SIDE VIEW.

BONNET.

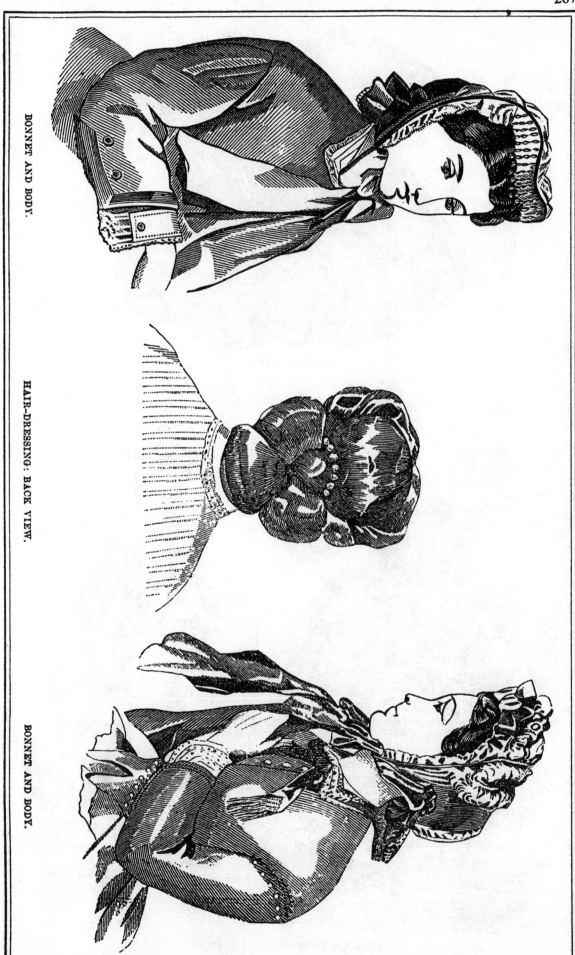

BONNET AND BODY.

HAIR-DRESSING: BACK VIEW.

BONNET AND BODY.

267

CHILD'S DRESS.

CHILDREN'S FASHIONS FOR APRIL.

CAPE.

WHITE BODY.

CRAPE BUTTERFLY FOR HEAD-DRESSES.

BY MRS. JANE WEAVER.

As it is now the fashion to use butterflies for ornamenting bonnets, and head-dresses, our readers will, perhaps, be glad to find the explanation of one. Butterflies are made more or less elegant; but this is one of the simplest and also of the cheapest kind. To form the body, which the following illustration represents, half

finished, twist a piece of wool fourteen times round the forefinger and the middle finger; before taking off the wool from these fingers, take a piece of wire about one inch and a half long, round which some black silk should previously be neatly rolled; bend it in half and place it inside the wool, so that the ends may come out, as shown in the engraving. Next tie the small bunch of wool, in two different places, very tightly with strong thread; the first time the wire must be tightly fastened; this is also clearly shown. Now cover the body over with green crape, or with any color that may be preferred.

To make the wings, you must cut out the crape in the shape shown in the illustration, and, in the outer edge, run a piece of very fine wire. Four similar wings should be cut out, to complete the butterfly.

The places marked with a cross show the place

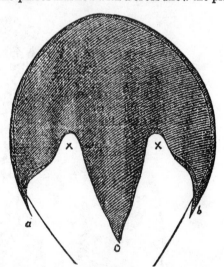

where the folds are to be made; the points *a b c* should be sewn together, and the wings attached to the body, as represented in the complete butterfly. Two beads are added for the eyes, and the top of the head is finished off by a few stitches in black or brown silk.

KNITTED HOOD WITH SWAN'S-DOWN BORDER.

BY MRS. JANE WEAVER.

MATERIALS.—3 ounces of white wool; 1 yard 3 inches of gray worsted fringe, 3 inches wide; 21 inches of the same fringe only 2¾ inches wide; 1 yard 5 inches of swan's-down; and two tassels in wool.   For this hood it is necessary to knit three separate pieces, of which two, exactly alike, and placed one over the other, form the largest handkerchief-corner shaped piece, and a third piece, much smaller, is placed on the top.   Medium-sized knitting-needles should be used, and the knitting should not be done too loosely.   For one of the larger pieces, cast on 159 stitches, and knit plain, backward and forward.   1st row: Make 2 stitches in the first stitch, thus increasing one, knit 34 stitches plain, knit the 3 middle stitches together, then knit plain till only 34 stitches remain, increase one stitch, and complete the row. 2nd row: Make 2 stitches in the first row, then go on working plain, without increasing or decreasing. 3rd row: The same as the 1st, only the second increasing is made after 35 instead of 34 stitches, that it may be continued in a straight line. Now the work is but a repetition of the 1st and 2nd rows. After the 8th row, the increasing at the edge ceases. Ten rows are worked, casting off 2 stitches at the beginning of each row. In the 18 following rows, not only should 2 stitches be cast off at the beginning, but 2 stitches should be knitted together at the end of every row. After the 18 rows you no longer increase in the middle, but continue to decrease in the same manner until the piece of knitting terminates in a point. When you have completed two pieces alike, place them one over the other, and join them by a seam. For the smaller piece, cast on 101 stitches, and knit plain, backward and forward; in every 2nd row knit the 3 middle stitches together, and in every row knit together the 2 stitches at the end until the point is formed, then sew on this piece over the two first. The lower part of the hood is edged with the wider fringe, and the upper part with the narrower. The points are trimmed with swan's-down, the ends of which are finished off with large woolen tassels, white and gray. Two ends of ribbon are sewn inside the hood to tie it under the chin.

HANDKERCHIEF BORDER AND INITIALS.

BY MRS. JANE WEAVER.

QUILTED BED-POCKET.

BY MRS. JANE WEAVER.

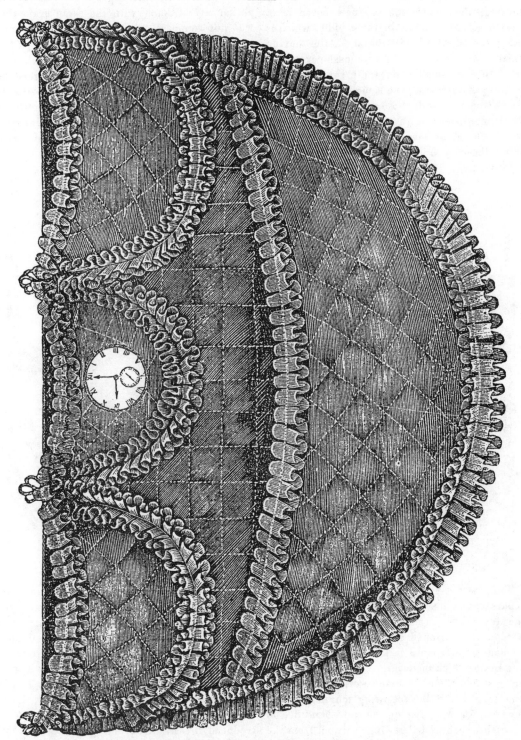

THIS is intended for hanging at the back of the bed. Its three upper pockets are for the watch shown in our illustration, and the others for the smelling-bottle, handkerchief, and so on.

To prepare the pocket, begin by cutting out the foundation or shape in cardboard; cover this cardboard with calico, and then with violet-colored cashmere, lined with muslin, and slightly wadded, before stitching the diamonds with white silk. With the same materials—cardboard, thinner, this time, calico, and cashmere, lined and wadded—prepare the large lower pocket, and the three smaller upper pockets; the center one of these three must have a round opening in the middle, which is to be bound round with braid. After having lined each pocket inside with cashmere, edge each of the smaller ones all round with a quilling of ribbon of the same shade of violet, about one inch wide. Edge the upper part of the larger pocket with the same quilling, and sew it on to the lower part of the large piece of cardboard you have prepared; all round the bottom and sides of the same sew on a quilling of ribbon, stitched, not in the middle, but so as to form a heading; next sew on the three upper pockets, placing them as shown in the illustration. Lastly, bind the upper edge of the watch-pocket, at the back, with the same braid that was put round the opening for the watch, and with this braid form, in four different places, three small loops (see illustration). The center loop of the three should be rather longer than the other two; it serves to fasten the pocket to the bed. Quilted silk may be used, if preferred to merino; this can now be purchased quilted by machinery, which saves much time and trouble.

A KNITTED BORDER FOR WOOLEN COUNTERPANES.

BY MRS. JANE WEAVER.

This border is composed of circles worked separately and sewn together, and finished at the top with a small crochet edging. This border will be found useful for putting round woolen counterpanes in knitting or crochet, or one in any thick material. For each circle cast on 2 stitches, and continue working backward and forward in the following manner: throw the wool forward, placing the right hand needle over the wool, and throwing the wool from the back in front; then take the 2 following stitches slantways. Turn the work, and work as follows on the next needle wool forward the same as before; take the next stitch slantways with the stitch formed by throwing the thread forward which comes next to it. The other rows are knitted the same as this, until you have from 15 to 16 openings on each side of the work: then pass the wool through the last stitch, and tie the two ends of the circle together, so as to hide the joint as much as possible. The circle should be kept flat, and in the opening of the middle a rosette worked with black silk, in the same way as those often introduced in white embroidery. Above the circles the following edging is worked. 3 chain, 3 stitches of double crochet in 3 openings of each circle, and over this 1st row work a 2nd in open treble crochet, (for which see our illustration at the beginning of this article.)

COLLAR IN CROCHET.

BY MRS. JANE WEAVER.

We give here, in answer to numerous inquiries, a pattern for a collar in crochet, which can be worked, from the engraving, without the necessity of further directions.

GENTLEMAN'S DRESSING OR LOUNGING BOOT.

BY MRS. JANE WEAVER.

Before commencing to work this boot, which is warm, comfortable, more elegant than a slipper, and much newer in style, the proper measures should be taken by a shoemaker, who should be told the dimensions the boot should be, so as to leave sufficient space, free of embroidery, for making it up.

Our pattern is made of brown cloth, embroidered in two shades of brown silk, lighter than the cloth. Both shades are clearly marked in the separate illustration we give of the full-size pattern on the upper part of the foot (for which see next page): the same pattern is repeated on the leg.

This pattern may be worked either in herring-bone, in chain stitch, or braiding. In the two last cases, a double row should be worked; these rows may be either of two different colors, or, if preferred, of two distinct shades of the same color.

If a boot is not desired, a slipper can be made, taking the slipper-part for the pattern, supersede the slipper, as many gentlemen catch cold by changing from a boot to a slipper, even

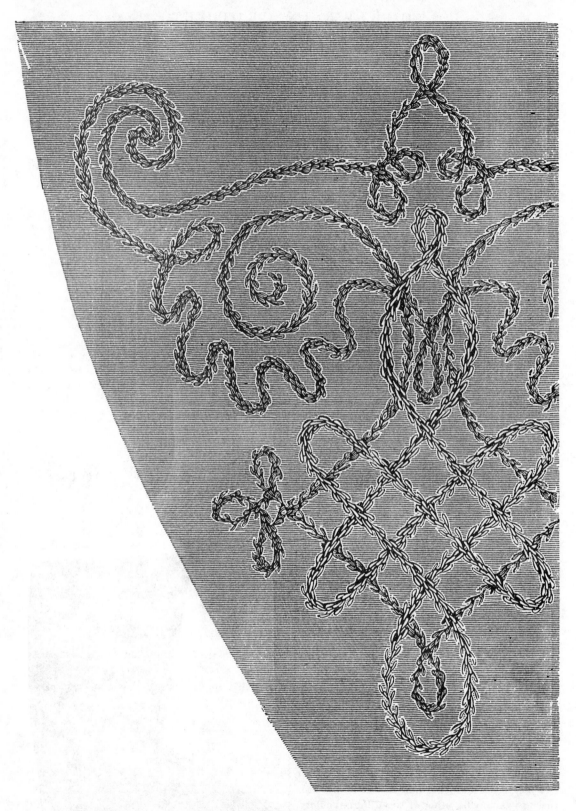

which will be found of a size adapted to the foot of most gentlemen.

The Lounging Boot, however, will almost in the house. The novelty of the Lounging Boot, too, will increase its popularity; and it is easily worked.

SMOKING-CAP IN APPLICATION.

BY MRS. JANE WEAVER.

We give, here, a pretty design for a Smoking-Cap in application of what is called the Scotch shape. In the diagram, accompanying this, we give the proper dimensions for the cap itself. It is to be made of black velvet or cloth, with the design done in blue velvet *applique*, edged with white silk or gold embroidery braid, as the taste may suggest. Line the cap with black silk, wadded and quilted. Finish with a bow of narrow black ribbon at the back.

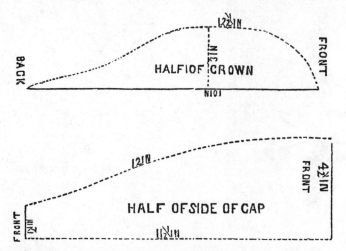

give the proper dimensions for the cap itself. It is to be made of black velvet or cloth, with the design done in blue velvet *applique*, edged with white silk or gold embroidery braid, as the taste may suggest. In the front of the number we give a design, full size, printed in colors, for this very stylish Smoking-Cap, so that any subscriber can make it for herself.

INSERTION.

VARIETIES IN EMBROIDERY.

SPRIG.

VELVET OR CLOTH SPECTACLE-CASE.

HANDKERCHIEF CORNER.

INITIALS.

HANDKERCHIEF CORNER.

EDGING.

CARRIAGE DRESS.

Marie

NAME FOR MARKING.

MORNING DRESS: CHILD'S DRESS.

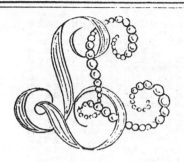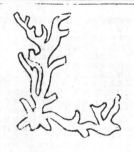

INITIALS FOR MARKING.

WALKING DRESS: CHILD'S DRESS.

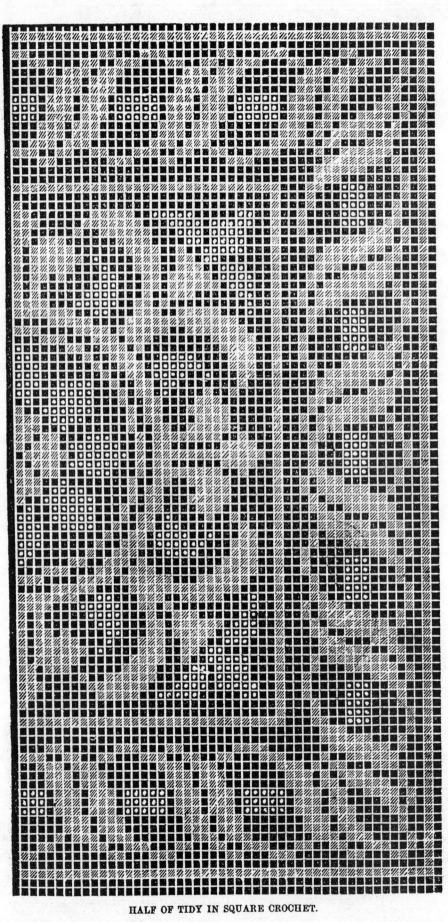

HALF OF TIDY IN SQUARE CROCHET.

WAVED BRAID BORDER.

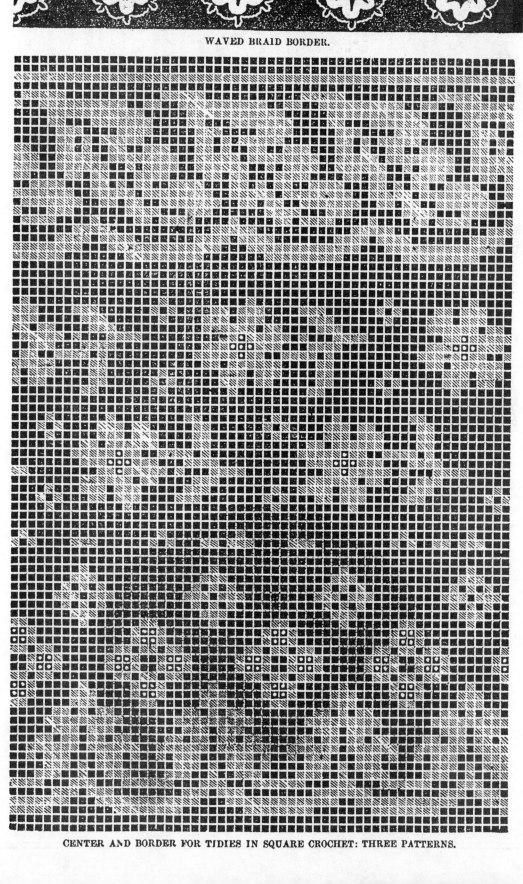

CENTER AND BORDER FOR TIDIES IN SQUARE CROCHET: THREE PATTERNS.

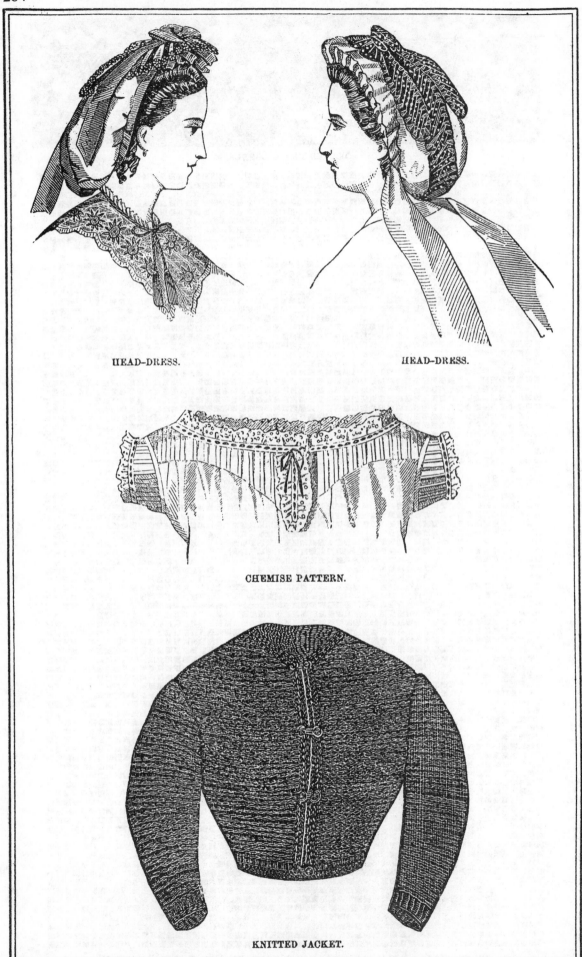

HEAD-DRESS.

HEAD-DRESS.

CHEMISE PATTERN.

KNITTED JACKET.

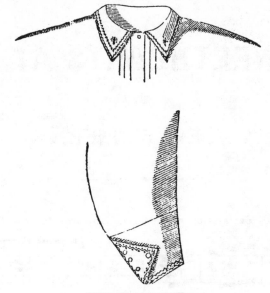

COLLAR AND CUFF.

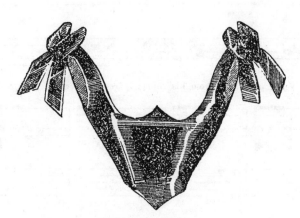

VELVET WAIST.

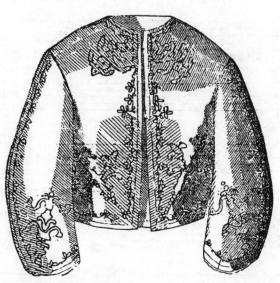

SPANISH JACKET.

OUR SWEETHEARTS AT HOME.

BY

SEP. WINNER.

Allegretto

mf

1. The ro - ver goes forth from his home far - a - way,   And roams o'er the
wide world by night and by day;   For - sa - king his home and the friends that are dear,   Tho'
bid - ding "good-bye" with a sigh and a tear: The hope in his heart, no

vis-ion can mar,   As he wan-ders a - way to some re - gion a - far;   Tho' bright be his

rall.

jour - ney wher-e'er he may roam,   He dreams with a sigh   of his sweethearts at   home

CHORUS.
a tempo.

Our sweethearts at home, be we ev - er so   far,   Live still in our thoughts, wher-ev - er we

are; A - way, far a - way, tho' wild-ly we roam, We dream, ever dream of our sweethearts at home.

2.
The Soldier goes forth to the army afar,
And dares with a firm heart the perils of war;
He braves ev'ry danger, unconscious of fear,
Yet parting at first cannot keep back the tear:
For over the heart a sorrow will come,
As we part from our friends and the comforts of home;
He tries to forget, as he bids them adieu,
But parting is sad to the friends that are true.
Chorus.—Our sweethearts, etc.

3.
The Sailor goes out o'er the waters so wide,
And heeds not the dash of the deep ocean's tide;
He leaves the "sweet home" of his childhood a while,
And drives back the tear as he forces a smile:
He wanders away, but o'er his lone heart
Full many a dream of the future will start;
Tho' reckless and wild o'er the world he may roam,
He dreams, often dreams of his sweethearts at home.
Chorus.—Our sweethearts, etc.

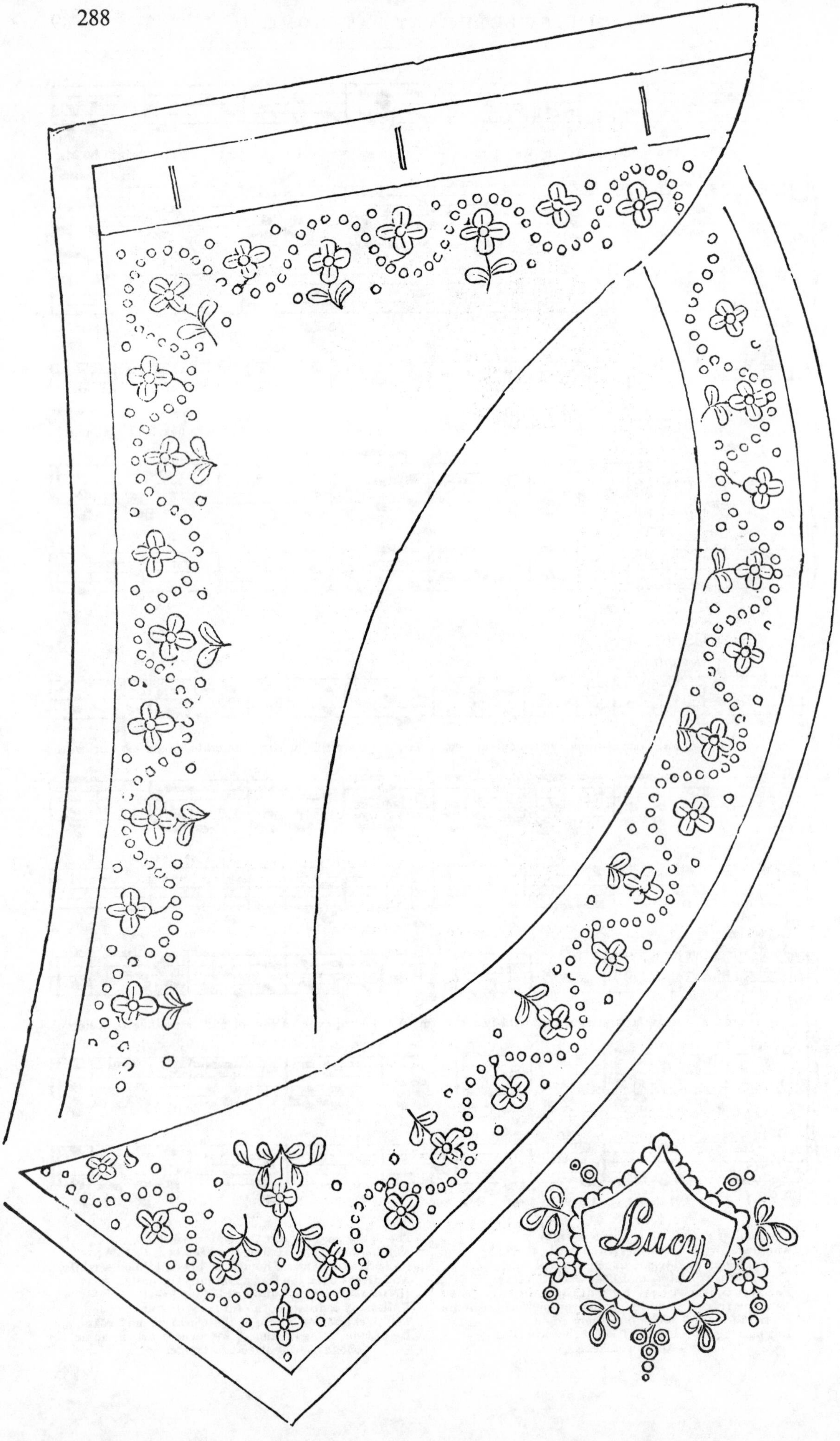
Lucy

CROCHET BEAD PURSE.

BY MRS. JANE WEAVER.

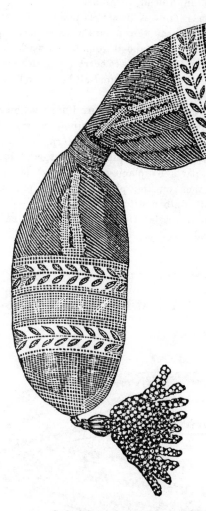

MATERIALS.—2 skeins each of blue and white, and 3 of scarlet fine netting silk; 4 bunches of steel or gold beads, No. 6; a set of slides and tassels; needle No. 4.

This purse is made in plain crochet, and, before commencing the work, the beads are to be threaded on each of the silks. A bead stitch is formed by passing down a bead to the wrong side, and working a plain stitch to secure it. In the following directions this is sometimes called "1 bead," or "2 bead," a plain stitch being worked after each bead.

Commence with the scarlet silk and work 6 chain, then 1 single in the 1st chain to make it round.

1st round—2 bead stitches, both worked in one chain stitch, then 2 bead stitches, 2 bead stitches in one, 2 bead stitches.

2nd round—2 bead stitches, both in one stitch, 8 times.

3rd round—1 bead stitch, then 2 bead stitches in one, 8 times.

4th round—24 bead stitches.

5th round—2 bead, and 2 bead in one, 8 times.

6th round—32 bead stitches.

7th round—2 plain in one and 7 bead stitches, 4 times.

8th round—1 plain, 2 plain in one, 7 bead, 4 times, and at the end 1 plain in the same stitch at the last bead stitch.

9th round—1 plain, 1 bead, 1 plain, 2 plain in one, 5 bead, 2 plain in one. Repeat 3 times, but at the end omit the last 2 plain in one.

10th round—1 plain, 2 plain in one, 3 bead, 2 plain in one, 1 plain, 5 bead. Repeat 3 times more.

11th round—3 plain, 3 bead, 3 plain, 2 plain in one, 3 bead, 2 plain in one. Repeat 3 times more, at the end 1 plain more.

12th round—2 plain in one, 2 plain, 1 bead, 2 plain, 2 plain in one, 3 plain, 3 bead, 3 plain. Repeat three times more, at the end 1 plain more.

13th round—2 bead, 1 plain, 1 bead, 1 plain, 2 bead, 5 plain, 1 bead, 5 plain. Repeat 3 times more, but at the end work only 3 plain instead of 5.

14th round—2 plain in one, 9 bead, 2 plain in one, 2 plain, 3 bead, 2 plain. Repeat 3 times more, but at the end work 1 plain instead of 2.

15th round—4 plain, 2 bead, 1 plain, 1 bead, 1 plain, 2 bead, 4 plain, 2 plain in one, 3 bead, 2 plain in one. Repeat; at the end 7 plain more.

16th round—(1 bead and 10 plain, 7 times); then 1 bead, 9 plain.

17th round—(3 bead and 19 plain, 4 times.)

18th round—(3 bead and 19 plain, 4 times,) at the end 1 plain more.

19th round—(1 bead and 21 plain, 3 times,) then 1 bead.

20th round—2 plain in one, 43 plain, 2 plain in one, 53 plain. It will now be 90 stitches round.

21st round—All beads. Join on the white silk and beads.

Work the wreath pattern, as in the section, the 1st round of which will be all beads. When the wreath is finished, join on the blue silk and beads, and for the blue stripe, work 1 round all the beads: then 20 rounds, working 2 bead stitches and 2 plain alternately. When finished, repeat the wreath pattern, ending with two rounds all beads. Then commence working backward and forward for the opening of the purse, as follows:—

THE CENTER OF THE PURSE.—1st round—4 bead, 85 plain.

2nd round—6 bead, 83 plain.

3rd round—8 bead, 82 plain, 4 bead, turn back so as to work on the wrong side.

4th round—3 bead, bringing them through the stitch to the same side as the other beads, 84 plain, 3 bead, turn back.

5th round—4 bead, 82 plain, 4 bead, turn back; repeat the 2 last rounds for about 3 inches, then make it round, and work the 3rd, 2nd, and 1st rounds to correspond with the other side; then work 1 round all beads and leave it; and for

THE OTHER END OF THE PURSE.—Commence at the 1st part of the direction, and work to the end of the 2nd wreath pattern. When it is finished, work 22 plain stitches, and join the two parts by placing the last round of each together on the plain side, and putting the needle into a stitch of each round, join them with a single stitch, continuing the same all round.

GENTLEMAN'S BRACES.

BY MRS. JANE WEAVER.

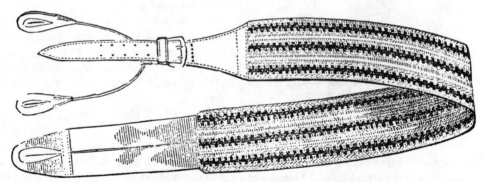

MATERIALS.—10 skeins of cerise, and 5 each of black and maize crochet silk. Make a chain 150 stitches with the cerise. 1st row: Work a stitch of double crochet, make a chain, miss 1 loop, repeat. 2nd row: Turn, make 1 chain, work a stitch of double crochet into the chain of last row, make 1 chain, repeat. Every row is alike. Work 2 rows of cerise, 2 of black, 2 of cerise, 2 of maize, 2 of cerise, 2 of black, 2 of cerise, 2 of maize, 2 of cerise, 2 of black, and 2 of cerise; this completes the brace. The crochet should not be done too tightly, as a little elasticity is desirable. When finished, the lengths left at the end of the rows must be neatly run in, and some kid brace ends, that are kept ready for the purpose, stitched on. No lining is required, both sides of the work being exactly alike.

INSERTION.

HALF–FITTING PALETOT.

BY EMILY H. MAY.

WE give our readers, this month, a diagram for a Half-Fitting Paletot, feeling sure that it will be welcomed by them on account of its ex- and then simply to lay the paper pattern upon it, (after enlarging the diagram,) taking care that each section is straight, and that it is pin-

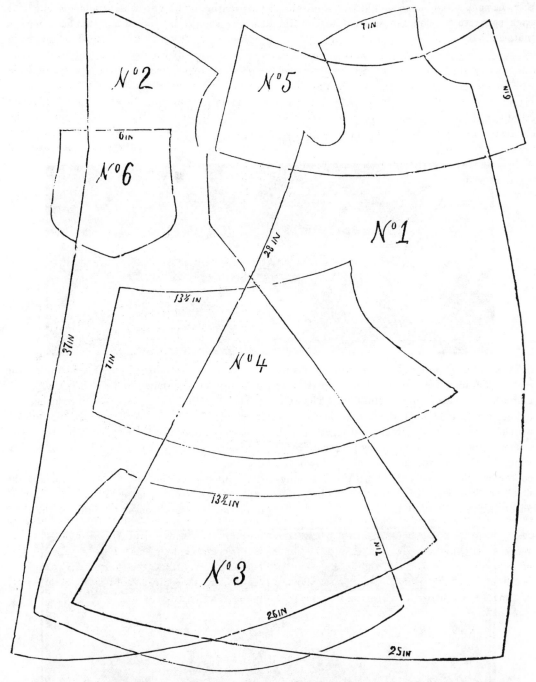

treme utility. The style of the garment will be seen at once, and no further trouble is required than to select the most appropriate material, ned down securely without any wrinkles either in the paper or material, before commencing to cut it out.

The present pattern will be found suitable for an ordinary-sized figure—one which measures twenty-four inches across the chest—and the length may be added to, or reduced, as desired, according to the height of the wearer. Turnings must be allowed for when cutting it out.

Our present pattern consists of six pieces, one front, half of back, upper and under part of sleeve, the *revers* for the bottom of sleeve, and the pocket; and care should be taken to cut each separate portion the straight way of the material.

As there is a joining down the center of the back, the most advantageous material will be a rich black silk, measuring twenty-four inches in width, and from five and a half to six yards, will be found requisite. The former measurement will be sufficient if the cutter-out is experienced. The Paletot should be fastened down the *inside* of the front with four hooks and eyes, and the trimming may be either gimp, braid, lace, flat chenille, etc., according to the taste of the wearer. The upper and under parts of the sleeves should be joined up the back with a piping.

TAPE–WORK EDGING.

BY MRS. JANE WEAVER.

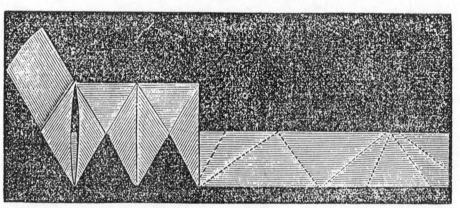

This Edging, which is very quickly made, will be found extremely durable for petticoats and other articles of under-clothing. The vandykes are formed by the peculiar manner in which the tape is folded, tacking it together with a needle and thread as the work proceeds; after which, a row of stitching is made down the center, which is easily done with any sewing-machine. The width of the edging can be varied according to the size of the tape.

MATERIALS.—Chinese tape, No. 4; and for the stitching, sewing-machine thread, No. 30.

The illustrated diagrams describe the manner in which the tape is folded, and in order quickly to learn it, it is advisable to mark the tape with a pencil, as shown in the dotted lines of the engraving.

Commence at the left corner by turning the tape over in front, pass it to the back, keeping it in the same position as the half of the third

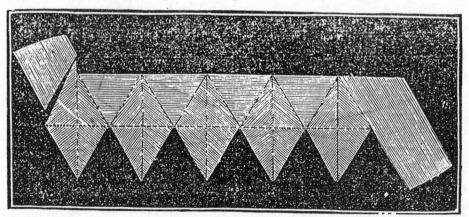

vandyke; then fold the tape over in front, at the angle described by the *second* line, then fold it over again at the first line, which forms the other half of the vandyke; then turn the tape down in front, in the same position as the right side of the engraving, and repeat from the commencement. When the required length is made, the row of stitching is to be worked along the center of the vandykes, as in the last engraving.

WAVED BRAID BORDER.

BY MRS. JANE WEAVER.

In the front of the number we give a pattern for this very useful and economical article; and shall now give directions for making it.

FOR ANTI-MACASSARS.—Dresden braid, crochet cotton No. 12, and uncotopic needle No. 2.

FOR PETTICOATS, DRAWERS, ETC.—Waved braid No. 2, cotton No. 18, needle No. 3½.

FOR FINE TRIMMINGS (the size of engraving.)—Waved braid No. 1, cotton No. 30, needle No. 4.

THE SCALLOPS.—Commence on the first wave of the braid, keeping the long piece to the left, work 4 chain, 1 plain on the same first wave as before, 8 chain, 1 plain on the next wave, 3 chain, 1 treble on the next wave, then 1 chain and 1 long on the four following waves; 1 chain, 1 treble on the 8th wave, 8 chain, join to the 3 chain before the first treble stitch, and in this 8 chain work 9 plain; then 3 chain, 1 plain on the 9th wave, 8 chain, 1 plain on the 10th wave. Repeat from the 4 chain at the commencement until the length required is made. Fasten off the thread and braid.

THE EDGE.—Work on the other side of the braid which forms the scallops, and commence on the wave between the two plain stitches on the other side, work 4 chain, 1 plain on the next wave, 5 chain, 1 plain on the next wave, * 6 chain, 1 plain on the same wave as the last plain, 5 chain, 1 plain on the next wave. Repeat from * 4 times more; then (1 chain and 1 treble on the next 2 waves), 1 chain, 1 plain on the next wave, 5 chain, join to the center of the 5 chain to the right, and in the last 5 chain work 5 plain, 2 chain, 1 plain on the next wave. Repeat from * at "6 chain" to the end.

THE HEADING.—Commence in the first 4 chain at the commencement of the scallops, and work 3 plain in it, 1 chain, take the piece of braid and join the first wave of it, then 2 chain, 2 plain in the 8 chain, 3 chain, join to the next wave of the braid, 2 chain, 2 treble in the center stitch of the 9 plain, 2 chain, join to the next wave; 2 chain, 2 treble in the same stitch of the 9 plain as the first 2 treble; then 2 chain, join to the next wave, 3 chain, 2 plain in the 8 chain; 2 chain, join to the next wave, 1 chain. Repeat from the 3 plain at the commencement of the heading to the end.

INSERTION AND EDGING.

CROCHET SILK BAG OVER RINGS.

BY MRS. JANE WEAVER.

MATERIALS.—2 skeins each of black, blue, rose, and drab coarse purse twist; 8 skeins of the spangled silk for the top part of the bag and strings; the tassel for the bottom is made of the silks that are left. Rings.—Work over a ring in double crochet, with black, 48 stitches and fasten off; this is for the center ring. Then with the rose-color take a ring and work 24 stitches in double crochet as before, take a second ring, and work 24 double crochet over it without cutting off the silk, work over 4 more rings in the same manner, then work on the other side of the rings to correspond, join the first and last ring together, and sew in the center ring; this completes the 1st circle. Work 12 more rounds in the same way, 3 rose-color, with drab center, 3 blue with black, 3 drab with rose center, 3 black with blue, join 6 circles of the alternate colors to the 1st circle, 1 to each ring, then sew the 2nd ring to the corresponding one of the next circle, till the 6 are united; join the other 6 circles in the following manner: join one ring to the second from the one that was sewed to the 1st circle, join the next ring to the corresponding one of the next circle (which will be the one opposite to the one sewed to the first circle), and repeat, joining the other 5 in the same way. For the small diamond, make a chain of 5 stitches and unite it, work 4 long stitches into the circle, make 2 chain, work 1 single stitch to the center of the ring missed in joining the last circle, make 2 chain, work 4 long into the circle. make 2 chain, and work a stitch of single crochet to the center of the next ring, make 2 chain, work 4 long into the same place, make 5 chain, work 4 long into the same place, make 2 chain, and work a stitch of single crochet to the next ring, make 2 chain, and join it to the first of the long stitches; this completes the diamonds; work 5 more, joining them in the same way, then work over 12 rings, and join one on each side of every diamond; this completes the lower part of the bag. For the top part of the bag work 3 stitches of double crochet to the center of each ring, make 5 chain, and repeat. 1st round: Work 1 long stitch, make 1 chain, miss 1 loop, and repeat. Work 12 more rounds in the same way, working the long stitch into the chain stitch of last row. Run some cord in the top of the bag to match one of the colors used, and make the tassel for the bottom from the silk that is remaining.

SHOE PIN-CUSHION.

BY MRS. JANE WEAVER.

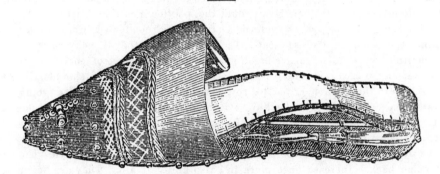

This Pin-Cushion serves also as a Needle-Book and Work-Case, and is useful for holding the thimble, bodkin, stiletto, etc. It is made with small pieces of different materials. The shoe is composed of two pieces—the upper part and the sole; the upper part is made of black and cherry-colored silk, the former being used for the point and the other for the border round it. This last piece is made with a straight strip, doubled, in the middle of which a fold is made the cross-way, to give it the shape of the top of the shoe. This strip of cherry-colored silk is edged, on each side, with a row of gold braid, divided by a double row of cross-stitch worked with bright blue silk. When the second row of gold braid is sewn on, fasten on the black silk, which is ornamented with gold beads and a row of cross-stitch in red silk. The sole, which forms a pin-cushion, consists of two pieces of card- board, between which a layer of wadding is placed. The under part of the sole is covered with white silk, and the upper part with red; these two pieces of silk are sewn together and bound with gold braid. To form a receptacle for the small implements of work, loops of silk are worked on the upper part of the sole, and each article is fixed to the sole by two loops, one at each end. Inside the upper part of the slipper, in the center, sew on a piece of ribbon in the shape of a thimble-case; then unite the upper part to the sole. Cut out two pieces of white flannel of the shape of the sole, edge them with button-hole stitch in red silk all round, and fasten them at one end to the point of the slipper, inside at the other to the point of the sole. Stick the needles on the flannel, and the pins place round the edge of the sole.

KNITTED JACKET FOR WEARING UNDER MANTLES OR DRESSES.

BY MRS. JANE WEAVER.

For the illustration for this Jacket see the front of the number.

MATERIALS.—12 oz. of single white, pink, or scarlet wool; thick steel knitting-needles. This bodice or jacket can be worn either over the stays or as an out-door wrap, and is very warm and elastic. It is begun at the waist. Cast on 108 stitches, and knit the two first rows plain, backward and forward. 3rd row: Slip the first stitch, * throw the wool forward, knit 2 together;

repeat from * to the end of the row. Coming back, knit one row plain, then knit 9 rows, working alternately one stitch plain and one purled, so as to form narrow ribs, work another plain row, then repeat the third row, and, coming back, knit one row plain. Over this waistband continue to knit in the following manner: Knit only the three first stitches of last row, increasing one stitch between the 2nd and 3rd, then in returning knit plain. Begin again and knit 5 stitches, increasing between the 4th and 5th, and return in plain knitting: in coming back knit 7 stitches, increasing between the 6th and 7th. Now begin the increasings for the chest by making 2 stitches in the 4th stitch; repeat this increasing in every fourth row, but one stitch further each time, so as to form a slanting line, the same as a dress-pleat. To prevent repetition, we shall no longer mention this increasing. In the next row knit 10 stitches, working the 10th in the 3rd hole of the 3rd row of the waistband; in the next row knit 12 stitches, the 12th in the same 3rd hole of the open row, and come back; in the next knit 15 stitches, the 15th in the 4th hole of the open row, and come back. Increase once more in the 4th hole of the open row, then work one row all round the waistband, and form a similar pointed piece or gore on the opposite side, coming as far as the 4th hole in the open row of the waistband. Go on with the jacket in plain knitting, always increasing slantways. After having thus knitted 4 plain rows, begin the increasings for the back. For this count 23 stitches on each side, beginning from the center, and increase on each side of these 46 stitches, in every 2nd row, placing the increasings each time two stitches further on each side. In the 56th row you will reach the armhole. To form this armhole count 47 stitches on each side for the fronts, and 74 in the middle for the back;

cast off the stitches between the back and fronts. First work the fronts, knitting 64 rows plain, then knit on the side of the shoulders the 2 stitches together before the last, in every 2nd row, at the same time, on the side near the neck; knit 7 times, once in every row, and afterward in every *second* row, the two stitches before the last together, until no stitches are left. At the shoulders, form a point, by increasing 15 stitches from the selvage; begin at the armhole with the two stitches of the selvage, just under the decreasings for the shoulders. Over these 15 stitches knit plain along the armhole, but knitting together the two stitches before the last at the other end of each row, until the pointed piece is finished. When the two fronts are completed, work 44 plain rows on the back, in the 32 next rows, decrease two stitches at the end of each row, then sew the pieces together at the shoulders. After this, beginning at the waist, and going up to the neck, along the front, work first one plain row, and then one row of open knitting (the same as that round the waist), then two more plain rows, and cast off the stitches. The sleeves are also knitted plain. They are begun at the top. Cast on 32 stitches, and increase in each row one stitch till you have 68 stitches. Knit 9 plain rows, in the 10th knit the two last together, and repeat this decreasing 9 times, knitting 9 plain rows between each decreasing. Then work 2 plain rows, then 9 rows, working alternately 2 plain stitches and 2 purled, so as to form ribs. Work one plain row, one row of open knitting, three more plain rows, and cast off the stitches. Sew up the sleeves and sew it into the armhole; finish the jacket by sewing on buttons and making loops. The difference in figures will render several changes necessary in the number of stitches, but these can very easily be made.

SCARF IN CROCHET.

BY MRS. JANE WEAVER.

In the front of the number we give a new and pretty pattern, printed in colors, of this Scarf.

MATERIALS.—One oz. of black split zephyr; half oz. of orange or salmon color.

With the black wool make a chain of seven inches long. Work in dc, making three stitches in a group. Repeat this every row until you have a piece worked twelve inches in length; then tie on the orange wool and work eight rows; then six rows black, eight rows orange. Repeat until the piece of work is three-quarters of a yard in length. This completes one half of the Scarf. Begin with the black, as at first, and work a second piece exactly the same as the first piece. Join at the back, and finish the ends with fringe alternate black and orange.

CHILDREN'S FASHIONS FOR AUGUST.

INITIALS.

WALKING DRESS.

INITIALS.

THE COAT BASQUE.

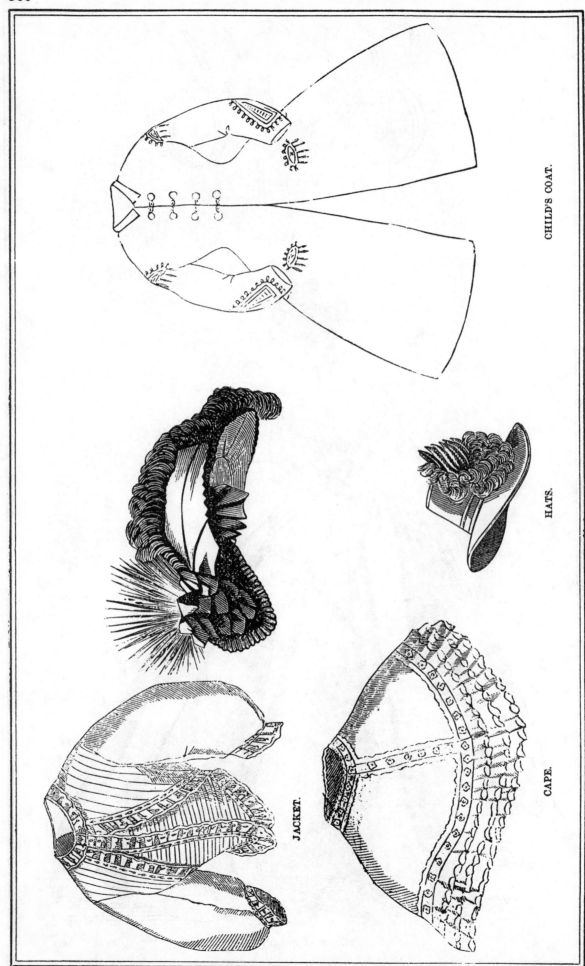

CHILD'S COAT.

HATS.

JACKET.

CAPE.

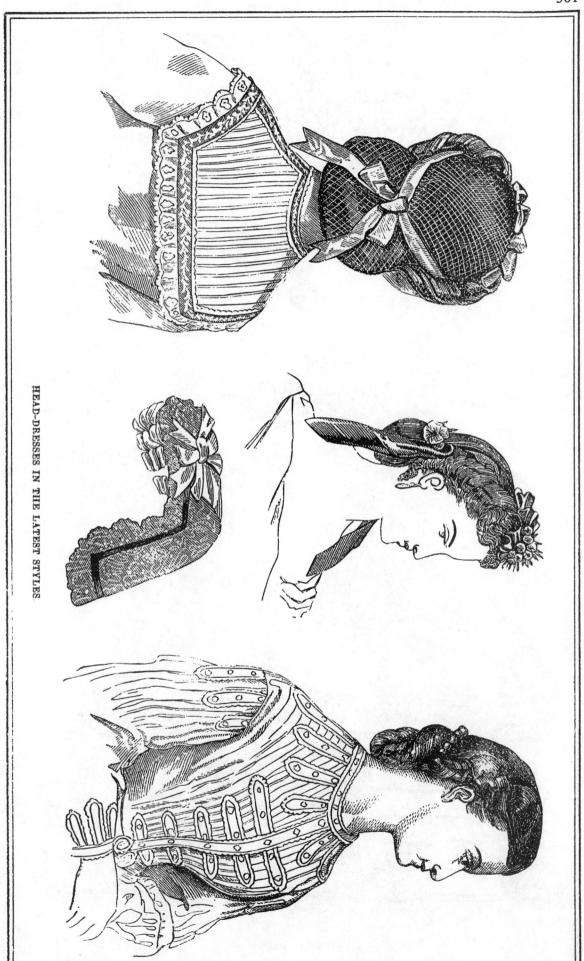

HEAD-DRESSES IN THE LATEST STYLES.

INITIALS.

EVENING DRESS.

INITIALS.

WALKING DRESS.

THE ADOLPHE COAT.

BY EMILY H. MAY.

Our illustration of this very novel and stylish garment so clearly depicts the arrangement of it, that an explanation is scarcely necessary. In Paris, for the last few weeks, both high and low coats have been much worn. Our pattern consists of seven pieces: The front; the back; the side-piece, that fits into the back; the sleeve; the revers for the front of bodice; the revers for the basque or tail behind; the collar. A row of tiny holes on the sleeve indicates the upper and under portion, the smallest piece being for the under part. The pattern is cut to fit a medium-sized figure, and it can easily be enlarged or diminished by cutting each piece a little larger or smaller, as may be required. For a very elegant garment, the revers should be in white silk, strapped with black velvet, but if required for a more useful style, silk, the same as the dress, or black silk, may be employed. The front of the coat is like a dress bodice, open a little in front, and ornamented with a revers which is carried round the arms and ends in the revers on the basque. A tiny collar finishes the top of the dress behind and just meets the revers in front. By consulting the diagram, our readers will experience no difficulty in putting the various pieces together. The back is shown with three stars, indicating the center. The side-piece is numbered 1, to correspond with fig. 1 on the back. The front is numbered 2 under the arm, and fits into the side-piece to the corresponding fig. 2. The revers for back is numbered 1, and must be placed exactly over the figures 1 of side-piece and back. The front revers joins at the two letters A to the back revers, and the collar meets the revers at B. From this diagram, giving the patterns on a small scale, cut full-sized paper patterns.

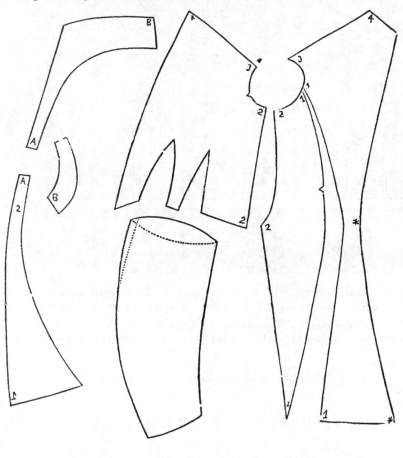

KNITTING-BOX IN WOOL AND PERFORATED CARD.

BY MRS. JANE WEAVER.

This pretty and useful adjunct of the Work-Table is composed of coarse perforated cardboard, graduated shades of German wool, from dark brown to very bright, light scarlet, and some white O. P. beads. Cut out four pieces of the cardboard ten inches long, and three inches wide; these are for the bottom, the two sides, and the lid, and must be all the same size; the two pieces which form the ends, are two squares three inches each way. A very regular and even margin must be left round each piece about half an inch wide. Commence with the dark brown wool, and work a row of squares the whole length of the box, leaving an alternate square uncovered the same size, upon which, after the wool-work is finished, the white O. P. bead is to be placed. Continue to work these squares of wool in as many shades as will fill up the cardboard; after which, on every alternate square, sew on, with a needle and strong white silk, the O. P. bead. After all the six pieces of cardboard are worked in this man-

ner, bind them all round neatly with a narrow ribbon, the same color as the light red wool, and sew them closely together. The handle is formed of a strip of cardboard worked in the same manner, and fastened on at each end with a bow of red ribbon. The lid is then sewn on the whole length of the back, and tied in the front with a bow of ribbon to match the handle.

FOR SILK EMBROIDERY.

BABY'S TIPPET IN TRICOT ECOSSAIS.

BY MRS. JANE WEAVER.

MATERIALS.—Half ounce of blue or Alpine pink, and half ounce of white, single Berlin wool; a tricot needle, the stem of which measures No. 9 Bell gauge; a piece of white sarcenet for the lining, and two buttons with an elastic loop for the fastening at the neck.

The whole of this Tippet is made in the ordinary tricot stitch; but the arrangement of the colors gives it an exceedingly pretty effect, the white wool having the appearance of being under the pink or blue loops.

THE RIGHT SIDE.—Commence with the pink wool and make a chain of 16 stitches, which is for the center of the back.

1st row—Keep the loop on the needle and put it into the last chain stitch but one, take the wool up on the hook, and bring it through the chain stitch, there will now be two loops on the needle; put the needle in the next chain stitch, and bring the wool through in a loop as before,

when there will be 3 loops on the needle; continue putting the needle into each chain stitch, and bringing the wool through until there are 16 loops on the needle; this is termed raising the loops or stitches. Join on the white wool. The wools are cut off every time, the joinings being kept on the wrong side, as they are covered with the linings.

To "work back."—Use the white wool and work from left to right thus—take up the wool on the hook and bring it through the two last pink loops, * take up the wool again and bring it through the white loop, and also through the next pink loop; repeat from * until there is only a pink and white one left on the needle. Join on the pink wool, and bring it through the remaining two loops to finish the row.

2nd row—Pink. Keep the pink loops on the needle and put it into the 2nd pink stitch, that is, the upright one to the left of the edge, take the wool on the hook and bring it through, so as to raise a stitch as before, then put the needle into the next pink upright loop and raise another stitch, and in the same manner raise a 4th and 5th pink stitch; leave the rest of the 1st row unworked. as the shaping for the back is now to be made. Join on the white wool, and

To "work back"—Take up the white wool and bring it through the last two pink loops on the needle, then take up the wool and bring it through a white and pink loop, take up the wool again, bring it through a white and pink loop; join on the pink, and bring it through the remaining two loops.

3rd row—Pink. Raise the four pink stitches of the last row, exclusive of the one on the needle, then on the first row raise two stitches; join on the white and "work back" as before, always joining on the pink wool to finish the last two loops.

4th row.—Pink. Raise the six stitches of the last row, then raise two more on the first row; join on the white and "work back" as before.

5th row—Pink. Raise the eight stitches of the last row, then two stitches on the first row; join on the white and "work back" as before.

6th row—Pink. Raise the ten stitches of the last row, then raise two more on the first row; join on the white and "work back."

7th row—Pink. Raise the twelve stitches of the last row; then raise three more on the first row; join on the white and "work back."

8th row—Pink. Raise all the stitches of the last row; join on the white, and "work back."

Work sixteen rows more the same as the last. This will make twenty-four rows, counting the short ones at the commencement. At the end of the last row, put the needle into a stitch at the side of the work, draw the pink wool through, and make eight chain stitches rather loosely. Cut off the wool, and draw it through to fasten it; these chain stitches will be used in the following rows; tie the white wool into the first of these chain stitches, and work back as usual.

25th row—Pink. Decrease at the beginning of this row, by putting the needle into the two first stitches of the row, and bringing the wool through as one stitch; raise the rest of the thirteen stitches as usual, then put the needle into the next chain stitch made in the last row, and raise a stitch, so that there will be still sixteen loops on the needle: join on the white, and "work back."

Work six rows more the same as the last.

Then work twenty-seven rows as the eighth row, that is, without shaping at the sides.

To form the Point at the end.—Work six rows more, decreasing at the beginning of each row, and at the end leaving one stitch unworked each time; this finishes one side.

THE LEFT SIDE.—1st row—This side is worked on the first row of the right side, and it will make the work neater if the foundation chain be unpicked, when the upright loops of the first row will be exactly the same as though just worked; however, the foundation may be left at the back, if preferred. In either case—commence with the pink wool at the right side of the first row, and raise the sixteen stitches of it, putting the needle into the upright loops as usual; at the end, the two last loops will be close together, being raised from the edge stitch. Join on the white, and to "work back"—(take up the wool, and bring it through two loops

three times); join on the pink and bring it through the white and pink loops; leave the rest of the stitches on the needle.

2nd row—Pink. Raise the four stitches to the left; join on the white, and to "work back"—(take up the wool and bring it through two loops five times); join on the pink and bring it through the white and pink loops.

3rd row—Pink. Raise the six stitches to the left; join on the white, and to "work back"—(take up the wool and bring it through two loops seven times); join on the pink and bring it through the white and pink loops.

4th row—Work as the last row, raising eight loops, and working back nine times instead of seven.

5th row—Work as the third row, raising ten loops, and working back eleven times.

6th row—Work as the third row, raising twelve loops, and working back to the end of the row.

Work seventeen rows without shaping it; and for the shoulder—

24th row—Pink. To increase a stitch, make one chain, put the needle into the edge stitch, and bring the wool through; then raise fourteen loops as usual, which will leave one stitch at the end of the row; join on the white, and work back.

Work six rows more as the last, then twenty-seven rows without shaping, and make the point the same as the other side.

THE EDGE.—1st round—White wool. Work a row of single crochet all round the Tippet, putting the needle sufficiently deep into the work to make it look neat.

2nd round—Make five chain, miss one, and work one single on the last round; repeat all round, and fasten off.

THE TASSELS.—Take a card about two inches wide, and wind the white wool twenty times round it; then with the pink make sixteen chain, pass it through the loops at one of the points of the Tippet; then place the ends by the side of the white folds, take them off the card and fasten them together so as to form the top of the tassel; making a few hem-stitches round it with the pink. Line it, and sew on the buttons.

QUILT FOR A BERCEAUNETTE.

BY MRS. JANE WEAVER.

PROCURE four pieces of stay-tape, or binding, the exact width of that represented at the end of this article; run the tape up and down in the same manner and number of times as indicated

by the lines, join together at the ends, and then draw the running tightly, and catch each point in the inside of the center with the needle and thread, and fasten off well, pull out the outer

points, and a well formed star will be completed. When several are made, sew together firmly in the manner shown in our engraving, and with the common looping-stitch make the crosses between. The quilt must be eighteen stars in breadth and twenty-four in length; line with blue silk, and trim round with six yards of cotton fringe.

INSERTION.

LADY'S KNITTED WAISTCOAT.

BY MRS. JANE WEAVER.

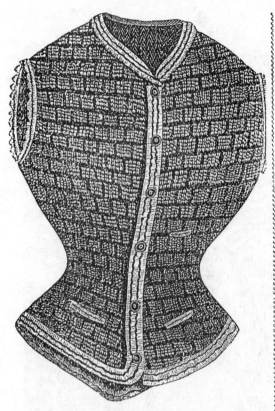

MATERIALS.—15 oz. of black Andalusian wool; 4 oz. of white; thick steel knitting-needles. The knitting for this jacket is done so tightly that ten rows of double knitting measure only two inches in width. The waistcoat may be done in purple, brown, or any other color; our pattern was black, with a white border, forming at the top a collar round the neck. The waistcoat has two pockets on one side, and one on the other. The work is begun at the bottom with white wool. Cast on 368 stitches, and work the double knitting in the following manner:—Bring the wool forward, slip 1, pass the wool back, knit 1, turning the wool twice round the needle; continue to the end of the row. Every row is alike: the stitch knitted in one row is the slip stitch in the next; it becomes one long loop, which is taken as one stitch on the needle. Knit 8 white rows and 2 black, 6 white and 2 more black. Before completing the border, begin to decrease in the center of the back and at the sides. Count the 7 stitches in the center of the row, and decrease once on each side of these 7 stitches in every second row, so that these 7 stitches may form a

marked stripe. On each side of these 7 stitches count 82 stitches, then 7, and decrease on each side of these last 7 stitches, which form a stripe on each side, the same as in the back. In every second row there will, therefore, be 6 decreasings. The stitches after the second decreasing, on each side, belong to the fronts of the waistcoat. To complete the border, work 6 more white rows, taking care to decrease as directed. Next take the black wool, and in the next row cast off the 4 first and the 4 last stitches. When you have worked 20 rows with decreasings, decrease in every third instead of in every second row nine times. The decreasings are then completed. In the 61st row form the slits for the pockets by casting off 30 stitches after the first 12 in the beginning of the row, and before the last 12 at the end; in the next row cast on the same number of stitches as you have cast off, and in the same places, and go on working as before. If you wish to form a third pocket, for a watch, make a slit 80 rows higher, by casting off 18 stitches in one row, and casting them on again in the next. In the 97th row begin to increase in the same place as you decreased before, but at first only on that side of the 7 stitches nearest the back; increase 2 stitches at that place in every 17th row. When you have done this regularly 3 times, increase 3 times (always 2 stitches at a time) on each side of the 7 stitches in every 19th row. Toward the back you have, therefore, increased 16 stitches, and 6 in each front, which makes in all 44 stitches. Go on working till you have in all 200 rows. The back is then divided from the front, to form the arm-hole. To do this, cast off 4 of the 7 stitches already mentioned, and go on for the fronts with 130 plain rows, and 120 for the back. Cast on 4 more stitches, to replace those that you cast off before to form the arm-hole. After this knit round the whole work, and begin the decreasings on the shoulders. These decreasings, the same as the former ones, are made on each side of the 7 stitches, of which the 4 you have just cast on must be the center ones. In the stripe toward the front decrease every third row, but toward the back only every fourth row; knit in this way 74 rows. After the 12th of these 74 rows, begin the decreasings for the neck. Cast off first 4 stitches (on each side, of course), knit 3 rows without casting off, and cast off 3 stitches in the 4th row; 3 more plain rows, cast off 3 stitches in the next, 3 more plain rows again, and cast off 3 stitches in the next; afterward cast off 2 stitches only in every fourth row, and lastly only 1. There must remain only 3 or 4 stitches in each front. When the 74 rows are completed, cast off all the stitches. To make the white border in front, a separate strip of knitting is worked. Cast on 158 stitches in white wool, and work, in the same way as round the bottom of the waistcoat, 8 white rows, 2 black, 6 white, 2 black, and 6 more white. Two borders of the same length are required, 1 for each front; in the 2nd the button holes are to be made by casting off 4 or 5 stitches at regular distances, and casting them on again in the next row. On the 1st border buttons are placed to correspond with the button-holes. The borders are then sewn down each front. A strip is next worked for the collar, in the same manner as the others, but, instead of the 6 last white rows, 16 are made. The last row is then cast off together with the castings on, so that the strip is doubled. Round the edge of the collar a row of crochet is worked, forming scallops. Each scallop is made thus:—1 stitch of double crochet, 2 treble crochet, and another double crochet. The collar is sewn on inside the neck, and turned back on the outside: it can also be fastened on by a row of crochet. The ends of the collar are fastened to those of the borders in front. Round the arm-holes work 2 white rows, 1 black, another white, and, for the edging, a row similar to that round the collar. Inside the slits, in front, place pockets of a convenient size, and bind the slits round with black sarcenet ribbon. It is also well to adapt a waistband inside the waistcoat, which, being fastened with hooks and eyes, would make the garment fit much better, and render it more durable.

PATTERNS FOR CROCHET LACES.

EDGING.

DINNER DRESS.

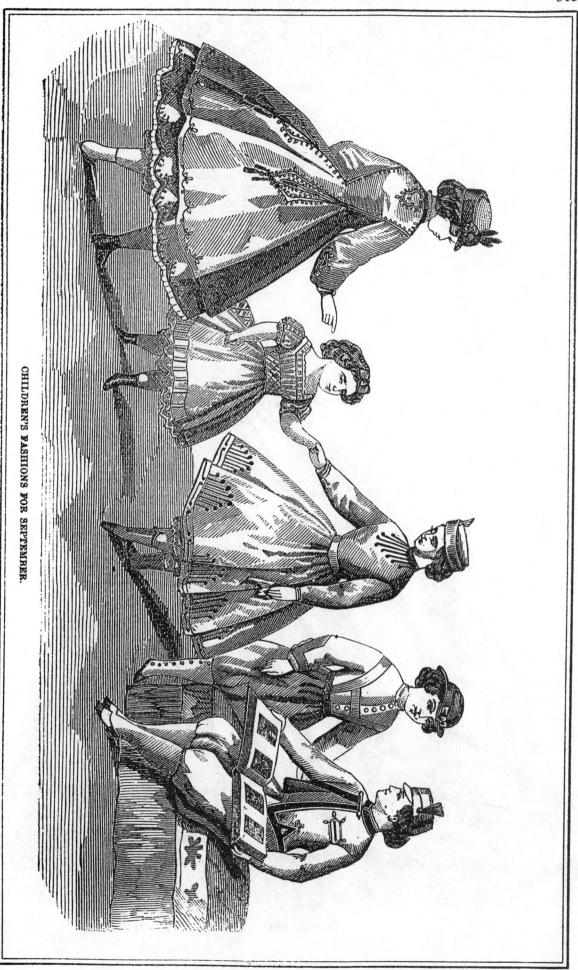

CHILDREN'S FASHIONS FOR SEPTEMBER.

EDGING.

WALKING DRESS.

BABY'S EMBROIDERED SHOE: SOLE, TOE, AND SIDE.

Charlotte

NAME FOR MARKING.

BALL DRESS.

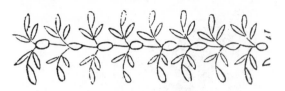

INSERTION.

WALKING DRESS.

FALL MANTILLA.

TASSEL PIN-CUSHION.

BY MRS. JANE WEAVER.

THIS novel Pin-Cushion is very easily made, and has a most elegant appearance. The foundation of the Tassel Pin-Cushion must be strong and firm. It can be made of cardboard; but in this case, extreme care must be used for the joints not to show, as that would much detract from the neatness, which is so requisite in every article of fancy work. The better way is to take some long strips of smooth cartridge paper, rather wider than the depth of the whole Pin-Cushion, and make a shape by winding them round and round a cylinder. A smooth jelly-jar makes a very good mould for this purpose. The strips of paper must be damped with a sponge, and then pasted on the other side, after which they are to be carefully passed round the jar. Of course, a length sufficient to enclose the mould must be left without paste, otherwise it will not separate from it when it is dry. In the process, the paper must be well rubbed down; and in taking a fresh strip, the edges must not overwrap each other, as the joint would then show. When completed, this moulded frame-work must be left until the next day, when the margins, both of the top and the bottom, being neatly cut, the work can be continued.

This frame is now to be covered with velvet, carefully and strongly stitched over its edges, both at the top and the bottom. An inner case for the cushion having been filled with wool, and covered with velvet sufficiently large for the surface to rise above the shape, also well stitched down all round, must be inserted in the inside of the frame, and in its turn carefully secured.

The decoration now remains, of which our illustration will furnish a clear idea. The diamond-work round the top is done by threading first a row of loops at the given distances, and then forming the diamond by successive loops, continued by taking up the central bead of the first; and so repeating. The roll of beads at the top and bottom of the cushion are then to be added. These may be done in different ways, according to taste; a roll or a plait of beads look equally well. The roll is easily done, by taking a few strings of beads and sewing them on, the silk of each encircling-stitch being also covered with beads; but always remembering to take the same number on the needle.

The tassels are best made by threading a long string, dividing it into the proper lengths, fastening it in the middle with a needleful of silk, threading both ends into a strong needle, passing it through the large beads which forms its head, and, with the same silk, fastening it on to the shape; these tassels being too heavy to be left suspended from the diamond bead-work.

The beads for this Pin-Cushion should be about equal quantities of chalk-white and transparent-white, relieved by a smaller portion of steel. In threading for the tassels, a certain length should be allowed for the chalk-white loops; and the same length for the transparent-white. Five loops of each of these, with three or four of the steel, make a pretty tassel.

Ruby-colored velvet forms an excellent contrast with these white beads; but there are other colors which are very handsome also in their effect, so that the choice is open as a matter of taste.

THE NEW STYLES FOR FALL BONNETS.

INITIAL LETTERS FOR MARKING.

BY MRS. JANE WEAVER.

In the front of this number we give an alphabet, printed in colors. It is for marking towels, etc., etc., and is to be done in black silk and colored working cotton. The black is to be done in fine chain-stitch, and the letter filled in with the cotton. For colored bordered towels, the letters should be filled in with cotton, the same color as border; but red washes best.

POSTILLION BODY.

BY EMILY H. MAY.

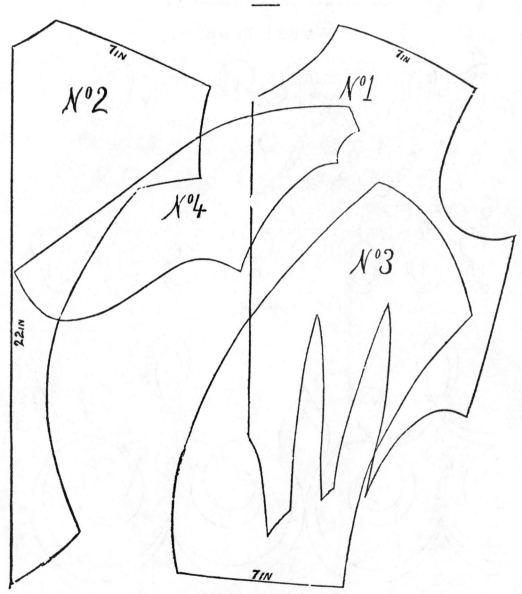

Our diagram, this month, is that of one of the Postillion Bodies, now so fashionable. This diagram is drawn for a lady of good figure and medium height, and consists of back, side-piece, front, and sleeve. It is, of course, to be made of the same material as the dress, and may be trimmed in various ways, according to taste.

We take this opportunity of reminding our readers, that in cutting out from our patterns nothing should be allowed for seams, as all the necessary allowances have been already made. The sizes of the different parts of the pattern are given in inches, so that a full-sized paper pattern can be cut from this diagram.

BABY'S EMBROIDERED SHOE.

BY MRS. JANE WEAVER.

In the front of the number we give patterns for a baby's embroidered shoe: the sole, the toe, and the side. These are all given of the natural size, so that any of our fair readers can make up one, if she wishes to offer an acceptable gift to a friend.

VARIETIES.

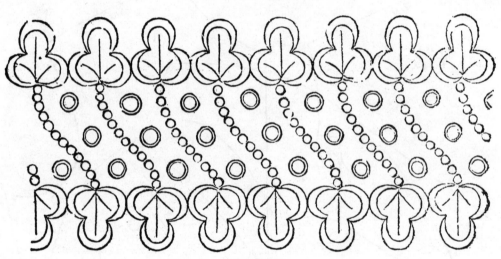

INSERTION.

EMBROIDERY FOR FLANNEL.

BAG IN BERLIN WOOL AND BEADS.

BY MRS. JANE WEAVER.

Our design representing a succession of stripes, it allows the wallet to be made of any size. One twelve inches in width would be quite suitable for most purposes; and for this it will be necessary to purchase a quarter and a half of Penelope canvas of medium fineness. This is to be folded in the middle, and must be about twenty-two inches wide. As the wallet is to be ten inches deep, the extra quantity is left for turnings-in. The size being thus determined, the canvas must be well overcast all round.

The wool is to be double Berlin. The colors used for the stripes are shaded down from yellow to brown, as thus: light yellow, darker yellow, orange brown. The stitch is done as follows:—It is simply the herring-bone stitch, taking two threads upon the needle, leaving two between each time, top and bottom, passing over four threads, which makes the width of the row. This will leave two threads between each stitch uncovered, on which the beads are to be inserted with a needle and thread after the wool-work is done. Four rows being thus worked in—namely: the four shades, light yellow, dark yellow, orange and brown, forming one stripe—six threads are to be left clear between that and the next stripe, which is to be worked in the same way.

When all the stripes of wool-work have been done, and the beads put in (steel beads look the best, but chalk white are very pretty,) rows of ribbon velvet are to be inserted. Care must be taken that this velvet is exactly of the width which will accurately cover the six threads of canvas left between the stripes of wool-work.

The velvet is put on with blue *chenille* in a wool needle, the stitches being six threads apart, which leaves a slanting line on the velvet like a spiral twist.

The fancy work being now completed, it only remains for the wallet to be made up, which is done by folding it in the center, fastening it up at each side, and covering the same with a twisted cord. A lining of twilled calico, or silk of any dark color, answers very well, with a strip of whalebone on each side of the opening. The handles are of twisted cord of the same kind as that carried up the sides, and the tassels of variegated wool or silk.

BEAD AND LACE BUTTERFLIES.

BY MRS. JANE WEAVER.

THIS Butterfly is meant for an ornament in dress, and can be placed in the center of a rosette of ribbon or lace, or of a bunch of flowers. To make it, begin by cutting out the shape represented at the lower corner of the opposite engraving. Cut it out in cardboard, and cover it entirely with black silk; then pass a piece of black silk through the whole length of the body. One end of this silk is used to thread the beads, the other to fasten them on. First arrange one row of beads round the edge of the body, then thread as many beads as will cover the width of it, and fasten them on by inserting the needle through one of the beads at the edge. Repeat the same process for the opposite side, and continue in the same way until the body is completely covered. If you wish the Butterfly's back to be rounded a little, you have only to fasten a few ends of wool along the top before putting on the beads. The long feelers are imitated by two bits of wire with a bead at the top; the short ones by three beads, threaded on wire; the eyes by larger beads. A long piece of wire forms the stem of the winged flower. The wings are very easy to make from the annexed cut. The beads are

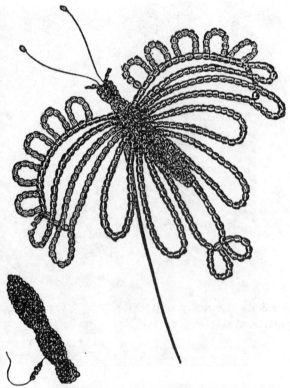

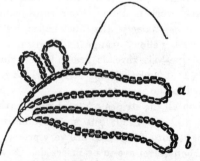

threaded on very fine wire. When the two large loops *a* and *b* are finished, the smaller ones are begun over the first. This loop *a* is joined on to the other at the point by a bead, and two more small loops are then added. All the ends of wire must be joined on to the principal stem. After the wings are joined on to the body, five more loops should be made and fastened on through a bead; the middle one has two smaller loops formed at the point. The wire stem is wrapped over with a very narrow piece of silk cut the cross way. The color of the beads can be chosen according to taste.

Our next engraving represents a lace Butterfly. The body of this Butterfly is made in exactly the same manner as the preceding, but in white beads. The wings should be cut out in lace or blonde, and edged on the wrong side with wire: the ends of the wire serve to fasten them on. The Butterfly can also be made in steel or coral beads. The wings are ornamented with beads, or small patterns cut out in paper.

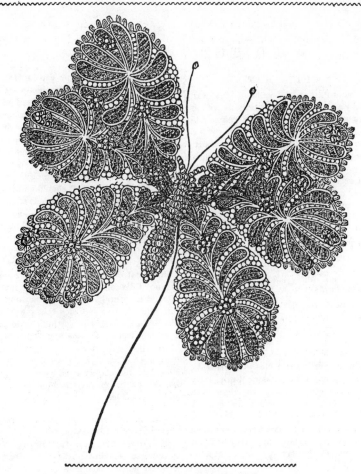

ANDALUSIAN JACKET.

BY EMILY H. MAY.

AMONG the many new patterns of Spanish *Andalusian*, is one of the most stylish. These jackets, that which we give below, called *The* jackets continue as fashionable as ever.

EDITOR'S TABLE.

EDITORIAL CHIT-CHAT.

DRESSING AT WATERING-PLACES.—In spite of the war, ladies dress elaborately at watering-places here, as well as abroad. In the days when Marie Antoinette reigned in France, people were accustomed to blame her for the extravagance which she introduced into the French court; and censure was heard on all sides on account of the foolish, senseless expenditure which the ladies in personal attendance upon the queen were forced to incur. But how paltry such expenditure now appears when we compare it with what is being daily carried on at the present time. In those days the queen and her attendants were, in summer time, dressed, throughout the day, simply in white cambric, and straw hats with long veils. It was only in ceremonious toilets that the queen introduced and carried out her fantastic ideas. But the grumblers of a hundred years ago, what would they say now? Many ladies of the present day would be truly thankful if they had only to think about ceremonious toilets, and be permitted to wear cambric dresses all the day through during the summer season; and the worst feature about the matter is, that one handsome dress daily is not now considered sufficient; there are many ladies who change their toilets four and even five times every day! Fifteen years ago, ladies at the seaside, even in Europe, met each other on the shore, in the early part of the day, dressed in morning-gowns, with light cloth mantles over their shoulders, and coarse straw bonnets upon their heads. This was laughingly called their *chenille* (caterpillar) costume, but it was a very pictorial expression, for three hours afterward the caterpillar was a brilliant butterfly, fluttering about in the gayest attire. But now-a-days ladies dress before their bath, then they dress to take their bath—that is to say, their bathing-dress is a fanciful costume, made of white or colored flannel, braided or embroidered in a most elegant design; then, for breakfast, there is another dress, for the promenade still another, for dinner there is a change for the fifth time, and for the ball a sixth change. And as it would not be thought proper to appear in each dress more than four times, continued variety is wanted, and so much novelty is consequently sought after that both dress-makers and their employers scarcely know where to turn for change of color and style of make.

CHILDREN'S DRESS.—The dress of their children is a very important consideration for mothers. It is natural for all women to desire that their children should look becomingly dressed: but for this purpose health is often sacrificed. In selecting clothing for children, the age of the child must be taken into account, so that the organs of the body, which are in greatest activity, should not be checked in their action by cold or undue pressure. In the very young child, the domestic organs are most actively at work, to supply the necessary nourishment for the rapidly developing body, but as the child gets older, the lungs and heart increase in activity, and require great protection. To guard against cold, the child should wear flannel, of varying thickness, according to the season of the year, next to the body, and fitting tolerably close, for, without this protection, the present style of dress, causing the clothes to project away, leaves the body exposed to sudden chills. Under ordinary circumstances, the clothing should cover the whole chest up to the collar-bones. The head should be lightly covered, so as to protect it from the sun, or sudden change of temperature; but it should never be covered with thick or heavy material. Anything causing fullness or congestion about the head will very commonly act by sympathy, as it is called, on the stomach, and cause obstinate and violent vomiting. Again, the body or the extremities being chilled, will often produce congestion of the brain, headache, and convulsions; and this congestion, reacting on the stomach, will cause sickness. A great improvement has latterly been made in the dress of children by clothing the lower extremities, and thus diminishing the chances of cold. In the clothing of a child, it should be borne in mind whether the child has ever had any serious affection of any particular organ, as, if so, greater care should be given for its proper protection. No part of a child's dress should fit so tightly as to hinder the free use of the limbs and respiration. Anything that hinders the free use of the muscles, hinders growth, and promotes deformity. Stays or tight bands about the ribs compress them readily, as these bones are not fully formed, hence readily cause deformities, and alter the natural and healthy position and action of the lungs, heart, liver, and stomach, and produce a tendency to disease in these organs. A pin should never be used about a child's clothes at any age; buttons or strings should always be the modes of fastening, both for neatness of appearance and comfort of the child. All clothes of children should be thoroughly aired before using; and if they have got wet by any means, should be taken off and changed as soon as possible.

THE HAIR.—Perfect cleanliness is indispensable for the preservation of the health, beauty, and color of the hair, as well as its duration; this is attained by frequently washing it in tepid soft water, using those soaps which have the smallest portion of alkali in their composition, as this substance renders the hair too dry, and by depriving it of its moist coloring matter, impairs at once its strength and beauty. After washing, the hair should be immediately dried; and when the towel has ceased to imbibe moisture, brushed constantly in the sun or before the fire until its lightness and elasticity are fully restored; and in dressing it, a little marrow pomatum, bears'-grease, or fragrant oil should be used. The belief that washing the head induces catarrh, or headache, or injures the hair, is erroneous; as the application of water to the skin is the most natural and effectual method of cleansing it, and keeping open the pores, through which the perspiration must pass, in order to ensure its healthy condition: besides, scales naturally form around the roots of the hair of the most cleanly person; and these can be only completely detached by the use of soap. The constant and preserving use of the brush is a great means of beautifying the hair, rendering it glossy and elastic, and encouraging a disposition to curl. The brush produces further advantages, in propelling and calling into action the contents of the numerous vessels and pores which are interspersed over the whole surface of the head, and furnish vigor and nourishment to the hair; five minutes, at least, every morning and evening, should be devoted to this purpose. If these rules be abided by, there will be no scurf in the hair. The only true mode of managing the hair is to dress it in a style consistent with the character of the face. Young ladies ought never to wear many flowers in their hair, or many leaves, or whatever be the fashion. If a bud, it should just peep out, now and then, while the lovely wearer, with a light laugh, sweetly waves her ringlets to some pleasant whisper; if a full-blown rose, let it—as ye hope to be happily married—be a white one; white for the hair, a "blush" for the blossom.

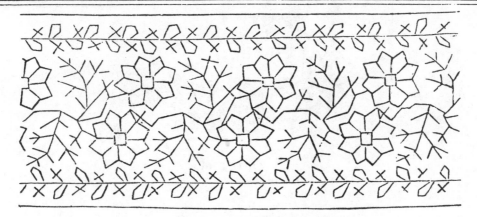

BORDER IN RUSSIAN EMBROIDERY.

YOUNG MISSES' AND CHILDREN'S FASHIONS.

WHITE BODY.

COAT DRESS.

COLLAR AND SLEEVE.

LOUIS XV. PALETOT AND WAISTCOAT.

330

EDGING.

DINNER DRESS.

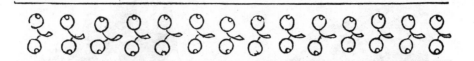

INSERTION.

WALKING DRESS.

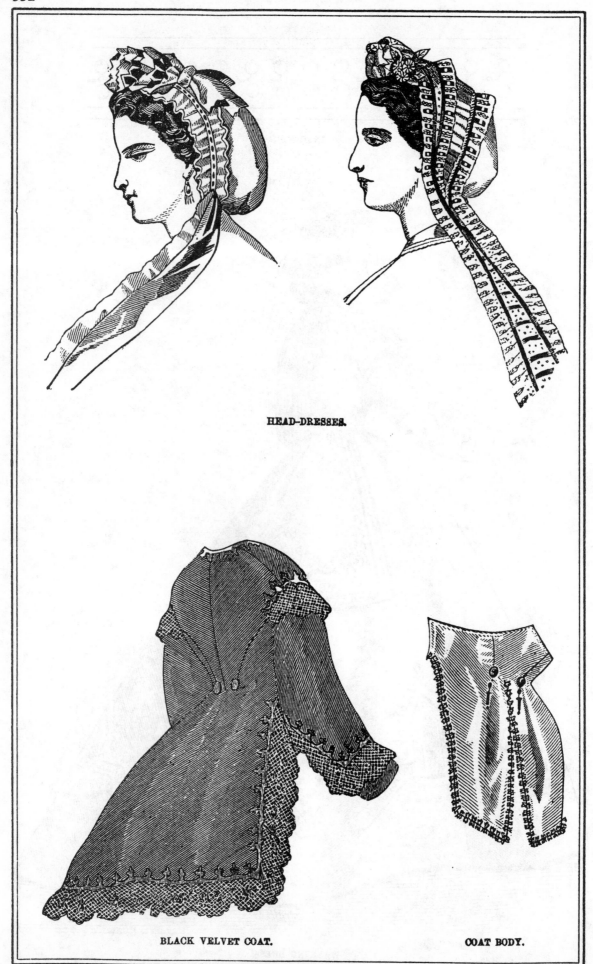

HEAD-DRESSES.

BLACK VELVET COAT.

COAT BODY.

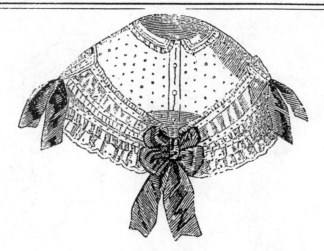

LACE CAPE.

MUSLIN AND LACE BODY.

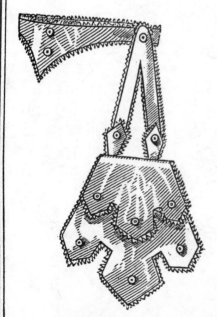

WAISTBAND AND BAG.

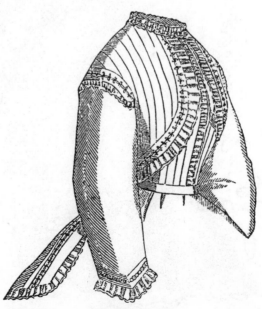

COAT BODY.

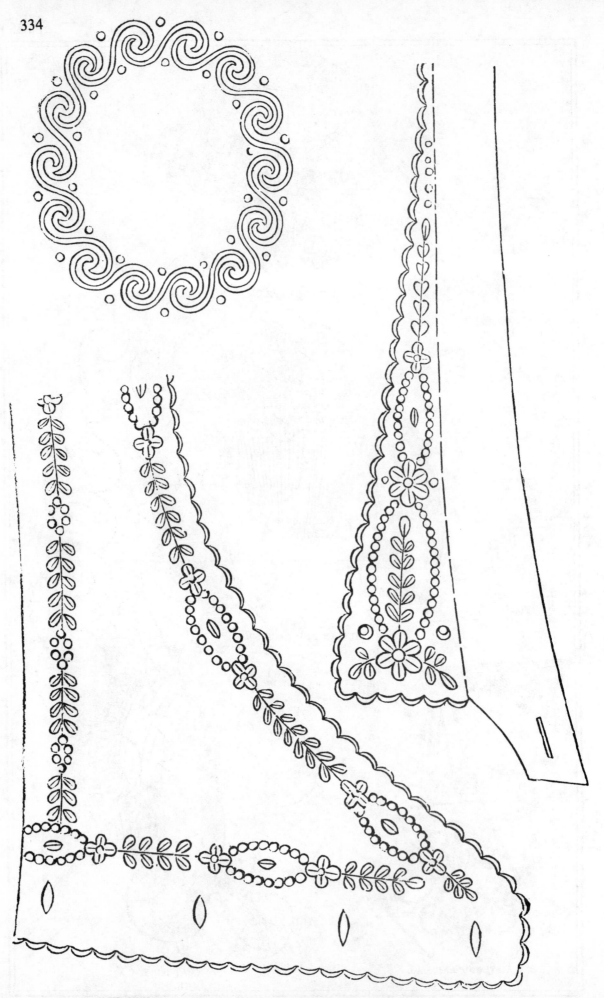

NEW STYLE COLLAR AND CUFF: HANDKERCHIEF CORNER IN CHAIN-STITCH.

SILK EMBROIDERY ON FLANNEL

BUTTERFLY IN EMBROIDERY.

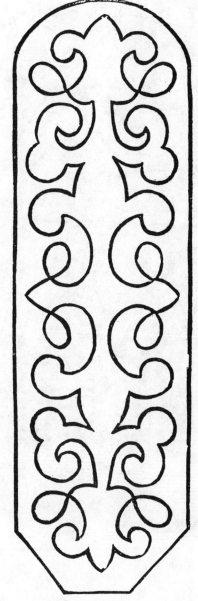

SPECTACLE-CASE.

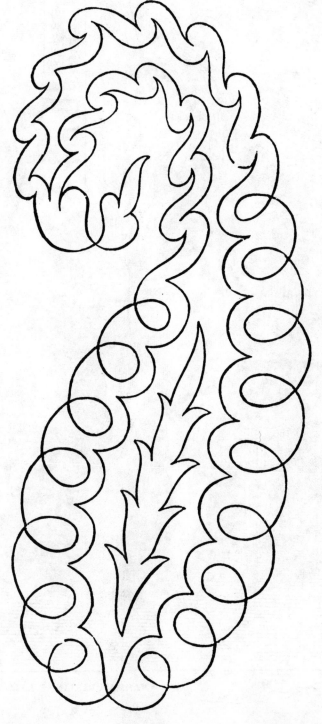

BRAIDING.

"MAMMA'S DARLING:" LATEST FASHIONS.

VARIETIES FOR THE MONTH

BY EMILY H. MAY

accordingly we have had several of the newest patterns engraved, and give them here. The first is a dress and paletot of dark-blue merino,

THE preparations for winter are very elegant. This is, especially, the case with wraps, and

trimmed with bias bands of gay plaid silk. This paletot is thickly wadded and quilted, and is very suitable for a young lady. The second is

a cloak of black velvet, trimmed with heavy chenille fringe and lined with white silk. The third is a dress of gray poplin and paletot of heavy cloth of the color of the dress. Both dress and paletot are trimmed with gimp and fringe.

We also give a very beautiful walking dress: that is the hat and bodice, the skirt being merely a plain, full one: it is singularly stylish.

In the front of the number we give various patterns for the new style coat bodies, muslin bodies, capes, etc., etc. We add here a low body, and give, at the end of this article, a white body, both very new and elegant.

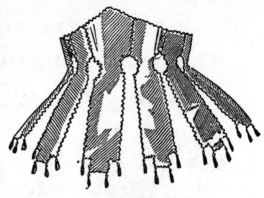

LOW BODY.

WHITE BODY.

VARIETIES IN MARKING.

LOUIS XV. PALETOT AND WAISTCOAT.

BY EMILY H. MAY.

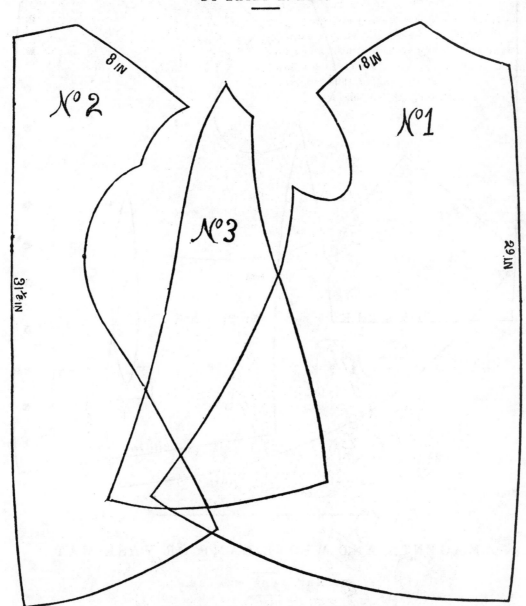

In the front of the number we give a full-length engraving of the *Louis XV. Paletot and Waistcoat,* one of the most fashionable (perhaps the most fashionable) out-of-door costumes for this winter. We now give here two diagrams, for cutting out the Paletot and Waistcoat: one on this page and one on the next.

No. 1. FRONT OF PALETOT.

No. 2. BACK OF PALETOT.

No. 3. SIDE-PIECE OF BACK OF PALETOT.

At the bottom of these three portions of the pattern four inches must be added to obtain the proper dimensions.

No. 4. SLEEVE OF PALETOT.

No. 5. FRONT OF WAISTCOAT.

No. 6. BACK OF WAISTCOAT, drawn at the waist behind, and composed simply of silk lining. This back must not come so low down on the hips as the front part; the sides end nearly at the waist.

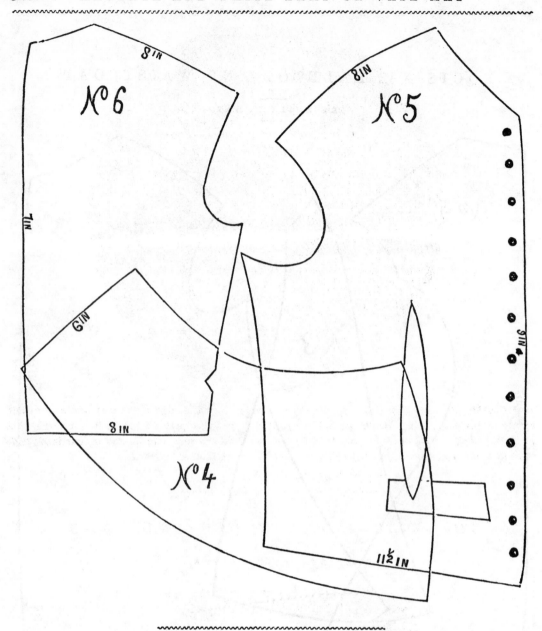

MAGENTA AND WHITE LAMP OR VASE MAT.

BY MRS. JANE WEAVER.

MATERIALS.—A round wooden frame with pegs; one ounce of 4-thread Berlin wool of the brightest possible shade of magenta; half-ounce of white wool the same thickness; a netting-needle. Procure the wool in half-ounce skeins, as thereby much joining is saved, and wind it round the pegs of the frame in the same manner as shown in our sketch—namely: two rows of magenta, and one of white alternately. Cross these in the same manner, so that the white comes to the white, and allow for each winding eight double or sixteen single rows of wool.

When the wool is wound, unite it in squares by making a strong knotted cross-stitch with single white wool, this wool being carried on the wrong side from one stitch to the other, and the long netting-needle being used for the purpose of holding sufficient wool to complete the mat. Take the mat off the frame, and add the fringe, which is sewn just over the loops made in the foundation of the mat. We will endeavor to explain how this fringe is made. Double a piece of wool four yards long, loop this into four sets of loops (it can be done very easily

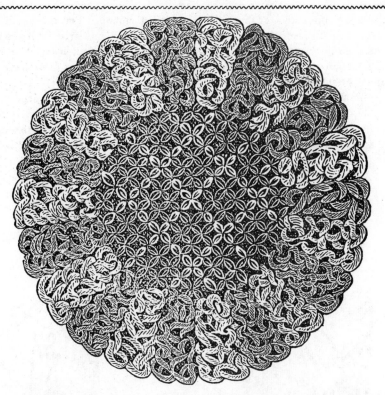

over the fingers,) and sew the looped wool securely to the mat, using strong thread for the purpose. The last or smallest set of loops are then threaded and drawn across the other loops which hide the edge of the mat, and at the same time make a pretty finish to it. A single trial will, we are sure, enable any of our intelligent workers to accomplish this.

TOILET-BOX FOR BRUSH AND COMB.

BY MRS. JANE WEAVER.

THIS very useful and pretty ornament for the toilet-table is easily made, and capable of many variations, both in material and color. Some are quite expensive, being made of silk quilted in diamond in contrasting colors, and elaborately trimmed with lace and ribbon. We have seen one for a bridal gift made of white silk, quilted with blue and trimmed with Maline lace. To make the box: First procure one of the common basket-knife trays, take out the division in the center, cover the basket neatly with a piece of white muslin (inside and outside,) over this sew the covering of quilted silk, which should have a half-sheet of wadding quilted in it, as it improves the appearance of the quilting. Gather the lace and dispose of it around the upper edge as seen in the design. Quill a one and a half-inch ribbon and place above the frill, laying flat upon the upper edge.

For the top: Take a piece of the stiffest paste-board that can be procured, cut exactly the shape of the bottom of the tray, cover on both sides with the quilted silk, and trim with the quilled ribbon. For the handles: Cover some wire ribbon, and trim with the ribbon same as above—in the center fasten a pretty group of artificial flowers or a bow of ribbon. To make a cheaper and more useful box: Cover first with pink or blue muslin, and over that dotted Swiss or lace, and use a worked muslin frill; trim with ribbon or a little Swiss ruffle, gathered in the center, in place of the ribbon.

LADY'S VELVET SLIPPER.

BY MRS. JANE WEAVER.

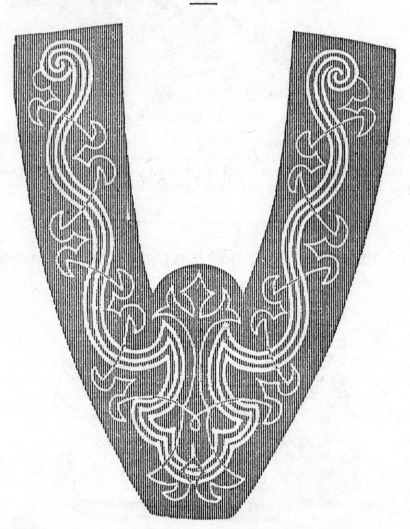

THE Velvet Slipper is, perhaps, the most elegant and luxurious of all the various sorts now in fashion. The one which we are describing is in violet velvet, ornamented with a mixture of maize-color braid, and a pattern in chain-stitch executed in maize-color crochet silk. The serpentine lines are in the braid, being also continued in a changed form, so as to vary the design on the front of the slipper. The ends of the braid must be passed through the velvet and secured on the under side. The lighter pattern is worked in the chain-stitch, using maize-color crochet silk. This Slipper would make a pretty Christmas gift.

ALGERIAN EMBROIDERY.

BY MRS. JANE WEAVER.

As this style of work is now becoming very fashionable, and will be extensively used for ornamenting winter robes, shawls, and circular capes, we give a pattern suitable for border for a jacket or tunic.

Cashmere, Llama, or alpaca, are the materials on which the embroidery is executed, and part of the pattern may be worked with a sewing-machine, if preferred. The colors are generally very bright and effective; if the material be black, the whole of the pattern, with the exception of the pines, should be worked with crimson and gold silk; or, if the dress is composed of magenta, then black and gold silk should be substituted.

Before working, the cashmere must be lined with stiff muslin to keep it firm, and, when finished, this lining may be cut away, leaving it only under the part embroidered.

The slanting lines of the lattice-pattern are formed of coarse crimson Maltese silk, carried from one edge to the other, using Walker's Elliptic-eyed needles No. 4; these lines are attached to the cashmere by a small stitch worked at each crossing with gold or black silk, and over this two longer stitches are made to form the small cross.

The *Fleur-de-lis* edge is composed of two rows of chain-stitch, worked with gold-color silk of a finer quality than the cross lines; between these two rows French knots are worked with crimson silk, also of a finer quality. The rounds between the *fleur-de-lis* are of crimson. The edge at the lower part is worked to correspond.

THE PINES.—The whole of the black outline should be in chain-stitch, worked with gold-color or black silk, and each part divided by these lines is filled with long-stitch embroidery, using a different color for each space. Two shades of green, blue, claret, and white fine Maltese silk may be used.

IMPERIAL LOUNGING-CAP.

BY MRS. JANE WEAVER.

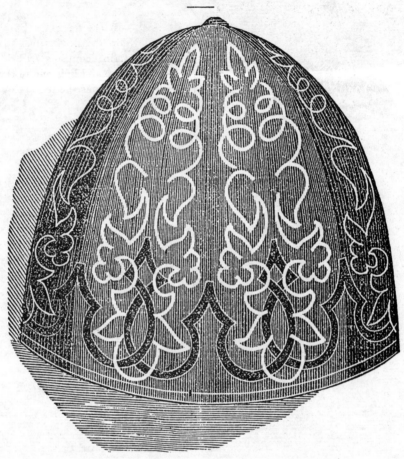

THE Imperial Lounging-Cap possesses a very Oriental appearance when seen complete. It is composed of six portions of velvet in two alternate colors, a rich violet and dark crimson. The scroll, which appears black in the illustration, is formed of narrow black ribbon velvet, with a gold thread at each edge. The design may be braided in narrow gold braid, or two silk braids of different colors. A violet braid on the crimson velvet, and a crimson braid on the violet velvet, has a very rich effect. A long silk tassel made of the two colors, interspersed with gold, is fastened at the top, and hangs down the side of the cap. This would make a very pretty Christmas, New-Year's, or birthday gift for a gentleman.

INITIALS.

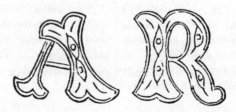

GENTLEMAN'S NECK-TYE IN BRIOCHE KNITTING.

BY MRS. JANE WEAVER.

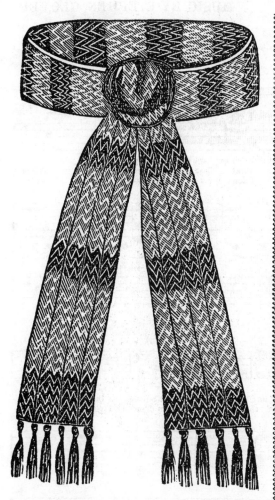

MATERIALS.—Two skeins of black; three skeins of brown and white partridge, and three

skeins of magenta, mauve or claret, double Berlin wool; a pair of knitting-needles No. 3.

Commence with the black wool, cast on twenty-six stitches.

1st Row.—Black, bring the wool in front of the needle, slip the first stitch, then knit the next stitch plain; continue to bring the wool forward, slip one and knit one to the end of the row. This row forms the foundation and is not to be repeated.

2nd Row.—Bring the wool in front, slip one, then knit the two stitches which cross together; repeat to the end. All the rows are now the same.

Work three rows more as the second row, still using the black wool; join on the partridge wool. Every two rows form one link or chain in depth.

Work four rows with the partridge wool, then ten rows the same, using the magenta or mauve wool. Work four rows with the partridge wool. These four stripes form one pattern.

Commence again with the black, work six rows as before, and then repeat the partridge and magenta stripes until the required length is made. Cast off.

THE FRINGE.—Cut the magenta and partridge wools in lengths of eight inches, take three of these pieces, and with a crochet needle loop them into a link of the knitting, bringing the ends through the loop and then drawing them tight. Continue the same along both ends.

We recommend this for a present for the holidays.

SPECTACLE-CASE.

BY MRS. JANE WEAVER.

IN the front of the number we give a design for a Spectacle-Case, which would make a good Christmas gift to an old person. The materials for this Spectacle-Case may be of rich purple velvet, braided with gold on both sides, made up over thin cardboard, lined with purple silk, and finished off with a gold cord—not braid—sewn round the edge. Only the angular end should be left open. Three yards of gold braid will be required for this design, and half a yard of gold cord, rather fine. The outline in the engraving marks the exact size of the Spectacle-Case when made. To work gold braiding perfectly, every stitch should be a fine back stitch, and number about eight stitches to an inch.

The Good-by at the Door.

WORDS BY J. E. CARPENTER.

MUSIC BY STEPHEN GLOVER.

1. Of all the mem'ries of the past, That come like sum-mer dreams, Whose
2. But time and place have quite estranged Each ear - ly friend we knew, How

rain - bow hues still round us cast, Their bright, their bright but fleeting beams, The
few remain, how many changed, Of those, of those we deemed so true. Those

dear - est, sweetest that can be, Of days gone long be-
hap - py hours a-gain to me, But mem' - ry can re-

BEAD WATCH-POCKET.

BY MRS. JANE WEAVER.

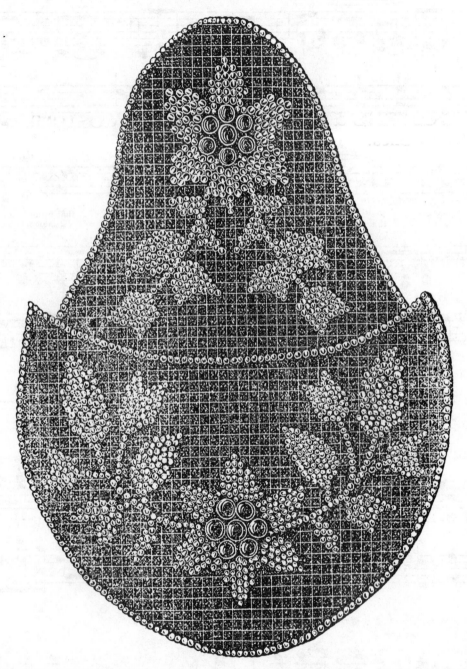

MATERIALS.—A quarter of a yard of canvas, No. 40; half a row of the large pearl-beads; half an ounce of chalk-beads; 1 oz. of crystal ditto; 1 oz. of large-sized crystal for the edge; 1 skein of azuline blue filoselle; three-quarters of a bunch of steel beads, No. 7; a small piece of blue silk for lining; and cardboard. These watch-pockets may be worked in two ways, either on canvas or velvet; the latter being by far the most elegant and effective mode of making them. A piece of canvas must be cut the size of our entire illustration, and a piece the size of the little pocket. These must be worked with the beads, the pocket lined with silk, and the back with cardboard and silk. The two pieces must be sewn together, and the whole of the pocket edged round with the larger-sized crystal-beads.

Titles published by R.L. Shep

ART OF CUTTING & HISTORY OF ENGLISH COSTUME (1887)
by Edward Giles.

THE BOOK OF COSTUME: or Annals of Fashion (1846)
by The Countess of Wilton. Annotated Edition.

CIVIL WAR ERA ETIQUETTE: Martine's Handbook & Vulgarisms
in Conversation.

CIVIL WAR LADIES: Fashions and Needle-Arts of the Early 1860's
from *Peterson's Magazine 1861 and 1864*; and additional hair styles
and hair jewelry from Campbell's *Self-Instructor in the Art of Hair
Work 1867*.

DRESS & CLOAK CUTTER: Women's Costumes 1877-1882
by Charles Hecklinger. Rev. & Enlarged Edition.

THE HANDBOOK OF PRACTICAL CUTTING on the Centre Point
System (1866) by Louis Devere.

THE LADIES' GUIDE TO NEEDLE WORK (1877) by S. Annie Frost.

THE LADIES' SELF INSTRUCTOR in Millinery & Mantua Making,
Embroidery & Applique (1853).

For more information and prices, write to:

R.L. Shep, Box 668, Mendocino, CA 95460 USA